Brenda O'Neill

Civic Education
Participation

CIVIC AND POLITICAL EDUCATION

Series Editor:
Murray Print, *University of Sydney, Australia*

This series of publications addresses a wide range of key issues in the increasingly important area of civic and political education. Fundamentally the series is concerned with the preparation of future citizens but that in itself raises issues. What role should civic education play in developing future citizens? What forms of civic and political education are needed to prepare citizens for the future? What curriculum is appropriate? What role does the informal curriculum play? How can civic and political education be assessed? There are cognate questions as well. What do young people understand as democracy? What interest do they have in politics? And are they concerned with civic participation?

In this series the key topic of civic and political education will be written from multidisciplinary perspectives by groups of international scholars, representing a range of disciplines from political science, to education, to sociology and youth studies. The publications will present new evidence as well as reflect and argue previous international research on civic and political education. They will present best practices and innovations that can inform nations as they consider how they educate their next generations of young citizens.

The publications will be of value to academics, researchers, students as well as policy makers and practitioners such as those engaged with electoral and intergovernmental agencies.

Civic Education and Youth Political Participation

Murray Print
University of Sydney, Australia

Henry Milner
University of Montreal, Canada

SENSE PUBLISHERS
ROTTERDAM/BOSTON/TAIPEI

A C.I.P. record for this book is available from the Library of Congress.

ISBN 978-94-6091-023-4 (paperback)
ISBN 978-94-6091-024-1 (hardback)
ISBN 978-94-6091-025-8 (e-book)

Published by: Sense Publishers,
P.O. Box 21858, 3001 AW
Rotterdam, The Netherlands
http://www.sensepublishers.com

Printed on acid-free paper

All Rights Reserved © 2009 Sense Publishers

No part of this work may be reproduced, stored in a retrieval system, or transmitted in any form or by any means, electronic, mechanical, photocopying, microfilming, recording or otherwise, without written permission from the Publisher, with the exception of any material supplied specifically for the purpose of being entered and executed on a computer system, for exclusive use by the purchaser of the work.

TABLE OF CONTENTS

Acknowledgement vii

Introduction ix
    Murray Print, Henry Milner and Chi Nguyen

Part I: Youth Political Participation and Civic Education

1. Democracy, Models of Citizenship and Civic Education 3
    Brenda O'Neill

2. Is Civic Education the Answer? The Futile Search for Policy Solutions
    to Youth Political Apathy in Canada 23
    J.P. Lewis

3. Voting Assistance Applications as Tools to Increase Political
    Participation and Improve Civic Education 43
    Andreas Ladner, Jan Fivaz and Giorgio Nadig

4. Attitudes toward Citizenship and Political Participation underlying
    Approaches to Civic Education: A Comparative Analysis 61
    Vincent Tournier

5. Citizenship Education and Political Interest: Is there a Connection? 85
    Ellen Claes and Marc Hooghe

Part II: Civic Education Applications and Programs

6. A World Pattern for Civic Education: From the IEA Civic Education
    Study to the IDEA CIVICED Database Project 103
    Henry Milner, Chi Nguyen and Frances Boylston

7. Connecting Youth Political Participation and Civic Education in Schools 123
    Murray Print

8. Children's Understandings of Democratic Participation Lessons
    for Civic Education 143
    Alan Sears

TABLE OF CONTENTS

9. Developing Citizens: The Impact of Civic Learning Opportunities on Students' Commitment to Civic Participation 159
   Joe Kahne and Susan Sporte

10. Does Civic Education Boost Turnout? A Natural Experiment........................187
    Henry Milner

Short Bibliographical Note on Authors 197

ACKNOWLEDGEMENT

The editors wish to acknowledge the significant contribution made by the authors, first to contributing to a workshop organized by the Chair in Electoral Studies, at the University of Montreal and then reworking their papers to become chapters in this book.

We also wish to acknowledge the support from the Social Sciences and Humanities Research Council of Canada for its assistance with this project.

The project received support from the International Institute for Democracy and Electoral Assistance in Stockholm for the creation of an international database on civic education practice.

Finally we wish to thank Chi Nguyen for her contribution to developing the IDEA CIVICED database and to assisting with this publication.

Murray Print
University of Sydney

Henry Milner
Université de Montréal, Canada

MURRAY PRINT, HENRY MILNER AND CHI NGUYEN

INTRODUCTION

Democracy depends on all of us: the price of liberty is not just 'eternal vigilance', as Abraham Lincoln said, but eternal activity.

Sir Bernard Crick (2008)

In the late twentieth century interest in the condition of democracy was becoming of increasing concern to many political scientists, international organizations, political commentators, political parties and governments. In addition to declining support for political processes by the public one more potentially significant issue had been identified – Why does it appear that many young people are disengaging from democracy and political participation?

This question raised many issues concerning the nature of disengagement, how it might be measured and what impact it is having upon political participation and democracy. Many of these issues are raised in the chapters within this book.

Nevertheless there remains a widespread interest in how young people may become more engaged in politics and democracy. Civic education has reemerged as a possible answer to this question, though not necessarily in the form in which it may be currently known. Civic education has a long history in many democracies where in some, such as the US, it was generally believed to be effective in building political engagement. These days we'd be more circumspect. Although the evidence from Niemi and Junn (1998) is comforting (that civic education makes a difference) and Putnam's conclusion that education also makes a difference to social capital, there are multiple issues at play that require investigation. One of the strangest is that, as Putnam (2000) noted, as education has increased in the United States over the past three decades, so political participation has generally declined.

What can be done? An increasing body of research evidence indicates that providing specific civic education opportunities can produce more politically engaged young citizens with more active civic participation. Some of that research is presented in the chapters of this book.

This volume comprises a collection of essays on the topic of civic education, written from multidisciplinary perspectives by a group of international scholars, representing a range of disciplines from political science, to education, to sociology. The group came together in Montreal in June, 2008 as a result of efforts by Henry Milner to chart the scope of civic education internationally. The presentations made were on aspects of research undertaken in civic education by the participants to complement the earlier national data on civic education and were subsequently debated and refined.

Civic education is predicated on the notion that individuals in a democracy do not automatically become politically responsible, participating citizens, but rather must be educated for citizenship. It is the primary means by which citizens acquire the knowledge and skills necessary to participate in their democracies in an informed and engaged fashion. Incorporated into the public education curriculum, its primary object is to teach civic literacy, which can be defined as a knowledge and understanding of the basic principles of government, as well as a basic familiarity with dominant social values and norms within a country. In addition, civic education aims to improve citizens' knowledge and understanding of fundamental rights and responsibilities. In short, civic education aspires to cultivate the virtues, knowledge, and skills necessary for meaningful citizen participation in public life.

The need to address issues of declining political participation was the task presented to a working group first established in 2002 at the European Consortium on Political Research conference in Turin. The ECPR joint workshop on political knowledge and political participation included 23 papers, drawing on individual-level data from more than a dozen countries. These assembled data confirmed that, regardless of the specific content of the questions, more knowledgeable citizens are significantly more likely to vote, even when controlling for variables such as education, age, political interest, associational participation, and trust. In the following years, further data confirmed that turnout decline was in large part a generational phenomenon coinciding with a decline in levels of political knowledge; perhaps most notably, the IEA Civics Study (Torney-Purta et al., 2001) drew wide attention to the relationship between civic education and voter turnout.

A common obstacle for scholars in the field was the dearth of multidisciplinary and comparative data available to those researching political knowledge and civic education. The consensus among the participants of the ECPR joint workshop was that it would be a significant improvement to the field if such multi-disciplinary material was widely available and out of this, the concept of the IDEA civic education database was born. Scholars concluded that data regarding different national approaches to civic education needed to be collected and compiled in a comprehensive, accessible format. The resultant project, the IDEA database, was first presented at the ECPR conference in Pisa, Italy in 2007. The next year Henry, with Murray's support, applied for a grant from the Social Sciences and Humanities Research Council of Canada to bring together a group of recognized scholars in the field to extend the research discussions raised earlier through an invited workshop in Montreal. The result, after debate and review, is this book.

The book has been divided into two sections: the first contains an overview of significant issues addressing youth participation in politics. The second section includes several approaches civic education from an education perspective.

Part I begins with Brenda O'Neill's chapter on assessing the education in civic education which poses the question: What kind(s) of engagement, if any, should be encouraged in a democracy? O'Neill appeals to democratic theory in formulating a response to this question. She also assesses the citizen's role within the democratic context and suggests that instead of attempting to provide cohesiveness of vision and 'right' answers in an attempt to create 'model citizens', civic education could

INTRODUCTION

instead embrace the range of contradiction inherent to the conception of citizenship, and teach students to be think critically about politics. Ultimately, O'Neill contends that "while politics might be 'messy', its avoidance is impossible".

Lewis contributes an argument, in the context of Canada, against civic education as a policy solution to political apathy. He contends that, in light of its fluctuating goals and relative unimportance to the state, civic education in Canada has become an increasingly esoteric field, generally ignored in the public political sphere. Lewis goes on to recommend a greater degree of cooperation between provinces, as well as more coordination between private actors and government agencies. Ultimately, however, Lewis argues for the necessity of an accepted Canadian civic education narrative and the adoption of a common national civic education curriculum. Such a narrative, he contends, would be free of the constraints imposed by shifting government interests and regional disagreements.

Andreas Ladner, with Jan Fivaz and Giorgo Nadig offers a detailed report on the use of e-tools for civic education in Switzerland. More specifically, Ladner et al. focus on the use of the "Parteienkompass" and "myVote" tools in the lead-up to the Swiss parliamentary election of 2007. The authors also discuss the use of similar e-tools in other Western European countries, and evaluate the efficacy of such methods, and their potential to improve voter engagement in Switzerland and internationally.

In his chapter on attitudes toward citizenship, political participation, and civic education, Vincent Tournier examines citizenship traditions and their influence on civic education. He describes in some detail three types of citizenship – political, social, and civil – identified by the 2004 ISSP citizenship survey and puts forth for consideration the notion that there is a link between the differing types of citizenship and political participation and engagement. Tournier contends that there is an increased likelihood of developing civic education in cases where political citizenship is strong and civic citizenship is weaker.

Marc Hooghe and Ellen Claes from the University of Leuven, Belgium have used data from the McGill Youth Survey (2006) to produce an in-depth analysis of the relationships between political interest and political knowledge, and political interest and civic education experiences. Claes and Hooghe examine the nature and significance of the impact of civic education on political interest, and contend that this impact, both direct and indirect, is significant.

Part II addresses different programs in civic education in a variety of contexts but set within the confines of examining the impact of such programs on political and democratic participation. In chapter six, Henry Milner, Chi Nguyen & Frances Boylston describe the IDEA database project and assess its potential for becoming an important resource for researchers, policy makers, educators and academics worldwide who attempt to address questions of citizenship and civic participation. They examine the IDEA CIVICED database for scholars who have been attempting to document and analyze the nature, effects, and value of civic education, particularly as it pertains to youth political behaviour and attitudes.

Murray Print of the University of Sydney presents a compelling argument in support of civic education in public schools as key in facilitating youth participation in democracy. He discusses the Australian Youth Electoral Study, an investigation into declining youth political participation and civic education in schools and argues that the viability and efficacy of civic education in schools could be improved through better teacher preparation, a greater focus on participatory approaches, and the inclusion of critical discussion with non-partisan teachers.

The University of New Brunswick's Alan Sears is strongly in favour of a constructivist approach to civic education. He advocates more inclusion of education practitioners in the process of curriculum design, and stresses the importance of the civic education community incorporating complementary research done in the fields of pedagogy and cognition. Sears calls for civic education researchers to question entrenched assumptions and preconceptions, and to take into account the sophistication and complexity of children's cognitive processes as well as the contribution of teachers themselves.

Joe Kahne and Susan Sporte report on a research study which examined developing citizens in terms of the impact of civic learning opportunities on student commitment to future civic participation. In a rigorous quantitative study they found that specific kinds of civic learning opportunities fostered improvements in student commitment to civic participation. In particular a set of classroom civic learning opportunities were able to meaningfully develop student commitment to civic participation in urban public schools. As with Print's Youth Electoral Study the researchers found that a significant factor in engaging youth was discussing civic and political issues with parents.

To conclude the book Henry Milner reflects on an effort to increase political participation in Ontario through posing the question – does civic education boost turnout? In the context of Canadian turnout, and the extremely low levels of youth voting, he reviews the 'experiment' of Ontario where civic education was introduced as service learning it appears to have made negligible impact on young people's political participation. This, Milner concludes, is due, in part, to a civic education program that placed great emphasis on service learning and insufficient on political dimensions both inside and outside the classroom.

Ultimately, this volume presents new evidence and collectively argues for the need for civic education throughout the globe. These comparative reflections demonstrate that there are best practices and innovations that can inform nations as they consider how they educate their next generations of young citizens.

REFERENCES

Crick, B. (2008). Democracy. In J. Arthur, I. Davies, & C. Hahn (Eds.), *The SAGE handbook of education for citizenship and democracy*. London: Sage Publications.

PART I: YOUTH POLITICAL PARTICIPATION AND CIVIC EDUCATION

BRENDA O'NEILL

1. DEMOCRACY, MODELS OF CITIZENSHIP AND CIVIC EDUCATION

INTRODUCTION

The decline in turnout in a number of advanced Western democracies has led to significant attention being devoted to trends in political participation. For some, the changing nature of participation patterns signals fundamental changes in civil society that portend badly for the future of democratic states (Putnam, 2000). Not all are convinced, however, that the evidence points to a crisis in advanced democracies. Where some see the relative withdrawal from electoral politics as a test of the legitimacy of a democratic system, others argue that the decline in electoral politics signals a shift in political participation patterns towards non-electoral forms of participation (Norris, 2002). Others challenge the conclusion that turnout has declined to dramatically low levels, at least in the United States (McDonald & Popkin, 2001). Like the reading of tea leaves, drawing conclusions from the evidence is less than straightforward.

The political participation of young citizens has attracted significant research attention given evidence that changing participation patterns appear to be concentrated among this generational cohort. In Canada, for example, voter turnout and membership in political parties and interest groups is lower among younger than among older Canadians, gaps that appear to have widened in recent years (Gidengil et al., 2004; O'Neill, 2007). Additionally, younger Canadians are less knowledgeable about and less interested in politics, and pay less regular attention to the news than older Canadians. On the other hand, their rates of participation in non-traditional political acts such as signing a petition, demonstrating, and political consumerism are closer to, and in some cases, higher than older Canadians. They are also more likely to volunteer than other Canadians although this may be linked to an increased trend toward mandatory volunteering in high schools (Stolle & Cruz, 2005). Beyond high school, this increased tendency to volunteer is unlikely to "stick" (Ibid.). Conventional wisdom notwithstanding, the decline in electoral turnout among young Canadians has not been paralleled by an increase in political cynicism; rather the evidence suggests that they are less rather than more politically cynical than other Canadians (Gidengil et al., 2003). They do however reveal weaker levels of political efficacy overall (Archer & Wesley, 2006). Some of these differences are due to the life cycle; as young Canadians age and assume an increased set of responsibilities and stake in the political system, their political participation and engagement are likely to increase. Others, the decline in turnout especially, appear to be the result of more permanent generational changes, and as a result are unlikely to diminish in the near future (e.g. Norris, 2002).

The increased attention to political participation among younger citizens has renewed interest in political socialization. The relative absence of contemporary political science research examining education's role in shaping democratic impulses springs from research in the 1970s that found little evidence of its impact on the political attitudes and knowledge levels of the young (Jennings & Niemi, 1974; Langton & Jennings, 1968). The perception of an existing 'democratic crisis' by some, however, has provided an important spur for re-examining early political socialization processes and the teaching of citizenship and democratic values.

The importance of citizenship education for stemming the tide of disengagement has been reinforced by contemporary research that provides for optimism, such as Niemi and Junn's finding that civics or citizenship education is strongly and positively correlated with political engagement (Niemi & Junn, 1998). Citizenship education or civic education is the "preparation of young people so that they possess the knowledge, skills, and values necessary for active participation in society" (Ross, 2004: 249). There are a number of important questions to ask regarding the inclusion of a civics component to the education of young citizens. One particularly important question is what the civics education curriculum ought to include in its attempt to prepare the young to be 'good' citizens. Democracy is a rather loaded and normative term without a single commonly accepted definition beyond perhaps 'the rule of the many.' To the extent that civic education has as one of its goals to impart a set of values and skills to young people that will equip them to become effective citizens, how one defines democracy and, indeed, how one defines a successful and well-performing democracy, have implications for what one includes in the curriculum, and by extension, for what students will come to see as 'good' citizenship.

The question of how a civic education curriculum frames norms and expectations follows directly from a set of questions raised in a number of papers included in the April 2004 issue of PS: Political Science and Politics on the "Politics of Civic Education." In one of these articles, Westheimer and Kahne (2004) argued that the broad consensus in the US regarding the importance of developing student capacities and commitments to democracy largely disappeared when the discussion turned towards what democracy requires and how it ought to be taught. As they noted,

> For some, a commitment to democracy is a promise to protect liberal notions of freedom, while for others democracy is primarily about equality or equality of opportunity. For some, civil society is the key, while for others, free markets are the great hope for a democratic society. For some, good citizens in a democracy volunteer, while for others they take active parts in political processes by voting, protesting, and working on political campaigns (241).

This paper addresses the politics of civic education, that is, the assumptions regarding democracy that are brought to bear on models of citizenship in civics education. In order to do so, I review the dominant conceptions of democracy and variation in prescriptions for civics education that stem from them. My goal is neither to assess which conception is more appropriate nor to render a judgment on how best to teach civics to young citizens. Instead, I hope simply to encourage increased reflection on the norms and assumptions that inform civics education programs. I extend the investigation to include a review of how to reconcile these prescriptions with the realities of civics education. I agree with Galston when he argues that "it is reasonably clear that good citizens are made, not born" (2001: 217). Citizen education instills a set of skills and a knowledge base which reduces participation barriers. Moreover, it can prescribe a model of values, such as tolerance and openness to new ideas, on which democracy rests. In short, citizen education increases the *effectiveness* of political participation (Milligan, Moretti & Oreopoulos, 2004). By the same token, there are real constraints on the teaching of civics in contemporary classrooms which ought to be considered prior to a review of the models of citizenship.

CIVIC EDUCATION

Formal education has long been understood to play an important role in encouraging political engagement, for its capacity to increase both participatory abilities and motivation (Dalton, 2006; Gidengil et al., 2004). The development of general knowledge and skills that accrue broadly from education, in such areas as mathematics, science, reading and writing, increase citizen capacity, perceived efficacy and willingness to engage in political processes. Civic education, on the other hand, provides a more pointed curriculum designed with the objective of developing knowledge about, skills for and a commitment to citizenship in democracies. Evidence suggests that where levels of formal education have increased over time, civic knowledge has largely stalled.

According to Galston (2004), this seeming puzzle is explained in the United States by a lack of congruence in a professed commitment to the goal of civic education and a less structured commitment to its implementation in the classroom, the limited civics training provided to history and social studies teachers, the minimal time devoted to civics curricula in an average school day, and to a tendency to approach "politics as a distant subject-matter, often with little explicit discussion of citizens' rights and responsibilities" (2004: 264). Similarly, Hughes and Sears (2006) find that while Canadian governments profess a commitment to such practices, their implementation has received decidedly less support. A lack of discussion on and setting of goals for citizenship education, little development and distribution of supportive teaching and learning materials, little development of teacher capacity in and the lack of establishment of a research base for civics education have combine to effectively stall the practice of citizenship education across the country. Government investment in curriculum resources and teacher training does occur, such as the Discovering Democracy programme in Australia, but even there results indicate that such commitments are necessary but not sufficient for enhanced civic learning to place (Print, 2007).

According to Hughes and Sears, best practice in citizenship education must "engage students in meaningful activities designed to help them make sense of, and develop competence with, civic ideas and practices" (2006: 7). This requires a commitment to both its formal and informal elements. The formal aspect of learning requires the acquisition of knowledge, skills and a set of values that facilitate and encourage participatory culture among youth within the classroom through curriculum and activities. The informal element takes place outside the curriculum and includes such things as a school culture that reinforces democratic values and which provides hands-on opportunities for developing democratic skills and experience, such as student government (Print, 2007). The classroom context – the degree to which open discussion and the expression of opinions in class are encouraged – and the school context – the degree to which students are encouraged to voice opinions regarding school policies or to play a more formal role in shaping them – have been found to play a key role in reinforcing the democratic curriculum encountered in the classroom (Sears & Perry, 2000). Participation in activities that exposes youth to conflict allows them to appreciate its role in democratic governance and its inevitability (Hibbing & Theiss-Morse, 1996). A classroom that fosters "a free, open and respectful exchange of ideas is positively related to young people's level of knowledge about democratic processes," to their appreciation of conflict and to their expectation of voting in the future (Campbell, 2008: 450).

It is, then, clear that what happens in the classroom and in the school, especially that beyond learning how governments work and "how bills become law", can have important consequences for how and whether youth participate in the democratic processes. The success of civic education programs requires a government commitment that extends beyond the symbolic, schools that devote significant time to civic education within the curriculum, and teaching staff that are provided with skills development, materials and a school environment genuinely committed to supporting real, effective engagement both in and out of the classroom. Yet what often happens in the classroom is citizenship education designed to "teach about democracy, not practice it" which risks increasing political alienation among the young rather than instilling a habit of participation (Sears & Perry, 2000: 28). Difficulty in putting a democratic curriculum into practice may stem in part from a desire to avoid any form of conflict; it may also stem from a lack of consensus on what democratic citizenship entails.

WHAT IS DEMOCRACY?

According to David Held, "Democracy, as an idea and as a political reality, is fundamentally contested" (1996: xi). One can nevertheless identify general agreement on the basic elements that are considered necessary for the existence of democratic government. At the outset, it ought to be emphasized that the term democracy has become synonymous with representative democracy; although elements of direct democracy have been advocated by many, their use is encouraged within the framework of representative democracy rather than as a stand-alone political system. Bearing this in mind, Diamond and Morlino (2004: 21) provide an overview of the essential elements of contemporary democracies. At a minimum, they suggest that democracy requires universal adult suffrage; recurring, free, competitive and fair elections; more than one serious party; and alternative sources of information. Additionally, they outline the goals of a democracy as being political and civil freedom, popular sovereignty and political equality, and ultimately good governance (which includes transparency, legality and responsible rule). The former are mechanical requirements that relate to the selection of representatives designed to ensure that the results of elections are legitimate. The goals of democracy, on the other hand, are ideals that are often harder to meet but no less important to the quality of democracy. Freedom of expression and association, respect for the rule of law, accountability of government and the equality of citizens in political decision-making are but a few of the essential qualities that democracies hold as standards. Importantly, Diamond and Morlino note that these various elements of democracy overlap and sometimes work in tandem. Achieving success on one goal can indirectly improve results on another. Yet at the same time, "there can be trade-offs between the different dimensions of democratic quality, and it is impossible to maximize them all at once. In this sense at least, every democratic country must make an inherently value-laden choice about what *kind* of democracy it wishes to be" (2004: 21, italics in original).

One of the major and longstanding divisions in contemporary theories of democracy rests on the level of participation that is required of citizens. The pluralist or participatory democracy form of democracy accords a high degree of engagement from the population. In such a system, direct participation of citizens is encouraged in as many arenas as possible and explicit goals in this theory of democracy include "foster[ing] a sense of political efficacy, nurture[ing] a concern for collective problems and contribut[ing] to the formation of a knowledgeable citizenry capable of taking a sustained interest in the governing process" (Held, 1996: 271). John Stuart Mill, for example, argued that citizen participation in representative democracies provides the best mechanism for the articulation of interests but also serves as an end in itself for its educative role among citizens (Ibid.: 100). Contemporary arguments for increased citizen engagement are not hard to find. A Standing Committee of the American Political Science Association charged with investigating the perceived decline in civic engagement developed a number of arguments for the value of robust citizen engagement in the American (and presumably any Western) democracy (Macedo et al., 2005: 4-5). These included: providing a direct mechanism for the voicing of interests; the legitimacy of democratic government requires increased citizen engagement in that governments are likely to be more responsive to citizens as greater numbers of them participate; citizens' skills and knowledge are developed with political participation; and civic engagement provides a mechanism for the provision of a number goods and services that might not otherwise be provided leading to improved lives and stronger communities.

Diamond and Morlino argue that the right and the ability to participate for all adult citizens are essential in democracies in that they provide the mechanism by which citizens influence decision-makers (2004: 23). The responsiveness of governments, they argue, is directly linked to the level of citizen participation. Moreover, they suggest that the quality of democracy is greater when citizen participation is extensive in "the life of political parties and civil society organizations, in the discussion of public policy issues, in communicating with and demanding accountability from elected representatives, in monitoring official conduct, and in direct engagement with public issues at the local level" (Ibid: 23-24). Political participation, voter interest, and turnout are all crucial to ensuring vertical accountability (25). Vertical accountability involves the obligation of elected officials to account for their political decisions to those who elected them. It is vertical in that the obligation runs from the government to the citizenry, and the ability to act on this information with either punishment or rewards rests in the hands of the citizenry.

Not all are equally convinced, however, that high levels of political engagement ought to be encouraged within democracies. Schumpeter, for instance, argued that the political engagement of citizens in a democracy ought to be restricted to voting in general elections for the selection of political representatives and for ensuring government accountability (Held, 1996: 179). Political elites, he argued, possessed the skills and knowledge necessary for other types of decision-making. Writings in this vein often focus on providing a version of democracy that is realistic in light of the perceived limitations exhibited by a majority of citizens in democracies (see Saward, 2003, esp. Chapter 2). In light of their findings indicating that Americans failed to meet expectations regarding skills and knowledge for a successful democracy, Berelson, Lazarsfeld and McPhee (1954) provide an explanation for why the American democratic system nevertheless appeared to work successfully. They argue that successful democracies require a balance of various types of citizens in the aggregate: a balance of politically interested and uninterested citizens, of politically engaged and disengaged, and so on. Too much of any one property can lead, for example, to various forms of extremism which tend to decrease the stores of much needed tolerance. Almond and Verba (1963) develop a similar argument for limited political engagement by pointing out that the ability of governments to be responsive to citizen demands requires that those demands be relatively limited in number. For them, "the ordinary citizen ought to be relatively passive, uninvolved, and deferential to elites" (343). The key is achieving a balance of political types to avoid government overload. The legal democracy model links to this argument in suggesting that the market provides the best mechanism for collective choice; majority rule and the rule of law ensure that democratic impulses and coercive power are constrained (Held, 1996: Chapter 7). A minimal role for the state, particularly, in civil society, limits the necessity for citizen engagement within the political sphere. Pluralists such as Robert Dahl (1961) and David B. Truman (1951), on the other hand, emphasize the important role played by interest groups in voicing interests, and in ensuring government responsiveness and accountability. Others argue that the reality is such that most citizens hope to avoid the conflict inherent in politics; even if provided with greater opportunities for engagement, it is argued, citizens would not likely take advantage of them (Hibbing & Theiss-Morse, 2002).

DEMOCRACY, MODELS OF CITIZENSHIP AND CIVIC EDUCATION

CIVIC EDUCATION AND THE ROLE OF THE CITIZEN

Thus, we have two very different accounts of the role and abilities of citizens in democracies: the participatory democracy model that advocates a strong citizen participatory dimension and the pluralist/elitist/legal democracy models that advocate a much more limited role for citizens. Given the lack of consensus on the roles of citizens in democracies, there is a concomitant lack of simple answers to questions that one might ask when thinking about the framing of civics courses. Among these many questions are the following:
- What are the responsibilities of democratic citizens?
- What kinds of engagement ought to be encouraged?
- What of protest and other forms of non-traditional political behaviour? Are they in the best interest of a successful democracy? Ought they to be encouraged?

The first question addresses the obligations that citizens have to others and to ensuring the success of the system. Citizenship norms are a "shared set of expectations about the citizen's role in politics" (Dalton, 2008: 78). Expectations directly shape behaviour. As such, civics education shapes citizen behaviour in part by establishing the norms and expectations of citizenship.

The two models outlined above provide largely different responses to this question. For one, the responsiveness, accountability and overall quality of democracy rests squarely on the existence of a citizenry that is active, knowledgeable, interested and engaged in both the civil and political arenas. In the other, the role of citizens is more constrained, either due to limitations on the part of citizens, to an inability of government to respond to excessive demands, to the existence of a division of labour where interest groups perform the role of voicing interests and assisting in government responsiveness, the balancing of roles across publics, or to the realistic understanding that the majority of citizens do not wish to be highly engaged. An appeal to democratic theory provides multiple and competing responses to this question.

With a direct focus on this question, Dalton (2008) outlines the four broad principles that he argues can be found within the theoretical literature on democratic citizenship. First, a key principle of citizenship is political participation. Citizen participation in the selection of representatives, in influencing government decisions, and sometimes in the direct selection of policy choices is essential to the legitimacy of a democratic state and for meeting the goals of responsiveness and accountability. Democracy ought to reflect citizen values and demands. Second, individual autonomy is identified as an essential element to 'good' citizenship. Autonomy implies the ability to act on one's own and in the case of citizenship it requires possession of information about government that allows one to effectively participate in politics. Thus knowledge of government and politics is essential for citizens' ability to participate effectively. For Diamond and Morlino, "a modicum of knowledge about government and public affairs" is required for widespread participation (2004: 24).

Good citizenship additionally requires "a commitment to social order and the acceptance of state authority" (Dalton, 2008: 79). Accepting the process of government and the rule of law are key components of democratic citizenship.

A final component to good citizenship addresses responsibilities to other citizens. According to Dalton, this element of citizenship stems from the expansion of the welfare state and the creation of a welfare 'safety net' designed to ensure that few, if any, citizens fall below a minimum level of service provision. Described as social citizenship by T.H. Marshall (1950, cited in Dalton, 2008: 23), it involves the ethical and moral duty that citizens have to others. Thus this theory of citizenship incorporates knowledge, participation, agency and social citizenship.

What citizenship entails in theory, however, need not necessarily correspond with its practice, understanding or teaching. An additional contribution to the discussion regarding the norms of citizenship lies in Dalton's mapping of the perceptions of Americans regarding good citizenship through the use of survey data (Ibid.). He identifies two overlapping and yet somewhat distinct frameworks: duty-based versus engaged citizenship. As shown in Table 1, a factor analysis of several citizenship norms included in the General Social Survey[1] identifies two models, the first emphasizing doing one's duty with only limited political participation and, the second, a more engaged model of citizenship that emphasizes collective activity and concern and tolerance for others. These two conceptions of citizenship reflect the different citizen roles emphasized in the two models of democracy outlined earlier. And while they include many of the elements found in the theory of citizenship, each distinct model includes only a more limited set of these requirements.

Table 1. Dalton's Dimensions of Democratic Citizenship Based of 2004 GSS Data

	Citizen Duty	Engaged Citizen
Vote in elections	.65	.17
Never evade taxes	.65	-.01
Serve in Military	.54	.07
Obey the law	.51	.10
Keep watch on government	.51	.40
Active in association	.39	.54
Understand others	.28	.59
Choose products	.22	.59
Help worse off in the world	-.12	.77
Help worse off in America	.02	.77
Eigenvalue	1.95	2.37
Percent Variance	19.5	23.7

Source: Dalton (2008:27).

Thus where theory sees a set of elements that are essential for citizenship, the public breaks the set down into two more manageable sets of requirements. Some see citizenship as involving a set of duties that from a political decision-making perspective includes voting and a duty to 'keep a watch on government.' This model includes little in the way of personal responsibility to bring about change. Others see citizenship as a more personally and individually driven set of requirements to act driven it appears by the demands of social citizenship. This latter conception includes little in the way of involvement with government decision-making. Together they provide for all the elements of citizenship outlined by Dalton; individually they fall short.

Using a very different approach, Westheimer and Kahne (2004) also attempt to model conceptions of citizenship but their approach looks at citizen education programs rather than survey data. Evaluating a selection of programs teaching democratic citizenship in the Surdna Foundations Democratic Values Initiative, they find three distinct models of citizenship: personally responsible, participatory, and justice-oriented (See Table 2). As such they reflect the assumptions that civics programs bring to bear in their teaching of 'good citizenship.' Each of the three models focuses on a different set of teachings: the first on character and personal responsibility; the second on knowledge of the mechanics of government and other public institutions, and planning and organizing community efforts to bring about social change; and the third, the least common of the three, on critically evaluating social, political and economic structures with the goal to eliminating existing shortcomings in each. The first two models parallel somewhat the citizen-duty and engaged citizen models of citizenship identified by Dalton (2008). The third, focused on critically evaluating social problems, is relatively distinct from the models examined to date.

Like the models identified in opinion surveys, these models of citizenship are more limited in scope than that suggested as necessary by either democratic theory or citizenship theory. The personally responsible citizen is 'good' in the sense of being law abiding and responsible, engaged during times of crises and exhibits elements of social citizenship in providing food for food banks and donating blood. Notably absent in this model, however, is any link between citizenship and governance, either in the form of interest articulation or government accountability. The second model provides a far more demanding vision of citizenship that requires active engagement in communities to achieve social and economic goals but here too the emphasis is on citizen-directed action with government and politics limited to only a secondary role (Westheimer & Kahne, 2004). In this model citizens identify problems and collectively organize to solve them. The final model emphasizes a role for citizens that focussed largely on the development of a critical lens that is more likely to advocate system change rather than modification at the margins. As in the previous two models, government and politics play a minor role and, moreover, are framed as a root cause of the problem rather than as an agent of change.

Table 2. Westheimer and Kahne's Typology of Citizenship in U.S. Civic Education Programs

	Personally Responsible Citizen	**Participatory Citizen**	**Justice-oriented Citizen**
Description	Acts responsibly in his/her community Works and pays taxes Obeys laws Recycles, gives blood Volunteers to lend a hand in times of crisis	Active member of community organizations Organizes community efforts to care for those in need, promote economic development, or clean up environment Knows how government agencies work Knows strategies for accomplishing collective tasks	Critically assesses social, political and economic structures to see beyond surface structures Seeks out and addresses areas of injustice Knows about social movements and how to effect systemic change
Sample action	Contributes food to a food drive	Helps organize a food drive	Explores why people are hungry to solve root causes
Core assumptions	To solve social problems and improve society, citizens must have good character; they must be honest, responsible, and law abiding members of the community	To solve social problems and improve society, citizens must actively participate and take leadership positions within established systems and community structures	To solve social problems and improve society, citizens must question and change established systems and structures when they reproduce patterns of injustice over time

Source: Westheimer and Kahne (2004: 242).

The IDEA Civic Education Database provides another avenue for assessing the content of civics education programs (Milner et al., 2008). Collecting information from 40 programs in various countries around the world on the various components of their civics education programs provides the means of assessing the relative importance placed on varying elements of the curriculum. The data is still largely in the development stage but in a preliminary review Milner et al. (2008) note a distinction between programs that focus on institutional knowledge versus those that emphasize values, including democratic values, 'good' citizenship, and civic values. Unfortunately the data set does not provide definition for what is meant by each of these particular sets of values or for the 'good' citizen. A second distinction that they note is between countries that emphasize community involvement over voting procedures. Although how these two dimensions relate to one another is not yet known, this preliminary evidence seems to confirm a similar trend to that noted above, namely the distinction made between traditional forms of participation (voting) and more contemporary forms of participation commonly referred to as civic/community engagement. Without further information on how these various programs define 'good' citizenship, democratic values and civic values, it is difficult to speak confidently about how this second dimension relates to those identified above. But one could make an initial claim that the emphasis appears to be on either the obligations of citizenship (both duties and values) or the knowledge requirement.

At the risk of generalizing on the basis of a small sample, there exist two dominant models of citizenship in popular thinking and in civics curriculum: the individually responsible citizen and the collectively responsible citizen. A third model, the critical citizen, also exists but is less common and so will be given less attention here. Returning to the questions posed above, one can reflect on the prescriptions made in each.

The individually responsible citizen model emphasizes the personal character of the citizen, to be honest and law-abiding. Political engagement is limited to voting, in that it is required for the selection of government representatives and leaders and for maintaining government accountability. Civic engagement is encouraged but limited to donating and volunteering. Non-traditional political behaviour is notably absent in this model; citizens, to the extent that they are allowed to register unhappiness or disagreement, are limited to the use of the ballot. Good citizens are virtuous, honest and decent. They vote and obey the law. They donate to charities. One can speculate that this is a model that could easily form the basis of a civics curriculum in that it requires relatively little in the way of knowledge of governmental structures and processes, and adopts a model of behaviour that is likely to produce little controversy, in part by avoiding any mention of dissent as a politically acceptable form of engagement.

The collectively responsible citizen, on the other hand, emphasizes the responsibilities of citizens to the larger society. In this model, the expectation is that citizens will engage but the emphasis is on civil society rather than the political arena. By joining together with others, citizens can organize collectively to provide needed services and goods and/or to pressure governments to act in areas of perceived need. Non-traditional avenues of participation, protest, organizing petitions and boycotting, are seemingly potential forms of engagement but they are not to be encouraged as avenues of first resort. An understanding of how government works should allow the collectively responsible citizen to avoid such forms of engagement. In the end, good citizens get things done. As a normative model within a civics curriculum, it would present somewhat of a greater challenge than the individually responsible citizen in that it requires the development of an understanding of governmental structures and processes, the instilling of a commitment to active and effective engagement, and a willingness to engage in an evaluation of the relative weight that ought to be accorded to competing societal demands and needs. Yet this model is also unlikely to generate much controversy since it fails to encourage the development of citizens that are critical of government or of societal structures and processes; instead, it encourages citizens to step in themselves to fill apparent needs.

THEORY AND PRACTICE

In much the same manner, the theory of citizenship and its modelling in the public and in civics education programs fail to identify a single normative prescription for the ideal citizen. Bearing in mind those differences identified in theory, we can assess the implications of the teaching of two models outlined above in practice for contemporary democracies.

The individually responsible citizen model fits in well with models of democracy that emphasize its representative over its participatory dimension. Citizens in this model are encouraged to vote, which emphasizes their role in selecting political representatives and in holding governments to account, and to be personally responsible. Beyond this, however, their political and civic roles are largely nonexistent reflecting Almond and Verba's description of the model ordinary citizen as "relatively passive, uninvolved, and deferential to elites" (1963: 23-24). Conflict and deliberation are remarkably absent. Citizens are encouraged to influence decision-makers rather than to participate in decision-making, and to accept and monitor political authority rather than to challenge it outright. Responsibility involves abiding by the law rather than in actively participating in its drafting, passage or critique. Engagement is limited to one aspect of the political arena, elections, and to minimal participation in the civic arena, limited to donating and volunteering. The model corresponds with democracy theory that suggest too much participation can lead to government overload, that citizen abilities limit the participatory demands that should be made of them, that a limited state supplanted by market forces is ideal, and the citizens generally seek to avoid conflict.

The collectively responsible citizen model fits more comfortably with models of democracy that emphasize engagement, although with significant limits. Participatory models of democracy emphasize the importance of participation for the legitimacy of governments, holdings governments to account, the effective representation of interests, the development of knowledge, skills and capacity within the citizenry, and the provision of goods and services. The collectively responsible model emphasizes citizen participation but within the civic rather than political arena. The citizen in this model arguably never bowls alone *a la Putnam* but rather is active in a number of civically-oriented organizations and groups, has a well-developed social network and a high level of trust (Putnam, 2000). While participation in the civic arena has been argued to hold the potential for encouraging participation in the political arena, the two are nonetheless distinct:

> [A]lthough equally important, activities directed at the formal political arena are not the same as those directed at the civic community either for the

reasons that lie behind that involvement or for the expectations tied to that participation (O'Neill, 2006: 4).

Citizens in this model are encouraged to engage in decision-making that will involve some conflict and deliberation but this is directed at the provision of goods and services not provided by the state rather than more collective decisions regarding state provision of goods and services. Citizens ought to possess a knowledge and understanding of government processes and structures but largely in order to be more effective and efficient themselves in the provision of goods and services in the civic arena rather than to critique and/or challenge the state for the choices it makes. And citizens ought to understand that the choices that they make as consumers in the marketplace have an impact on citizens around the world but they are not expected to challenge laws, regulations and trade agreements that are arguably far more important to such outcomes. This model of the citizen, while successful in encouraging a citizen that acts responsibly vis-à vis other citizens, fails in the development of citizens that are sensitive to the fact that governments, in where and how they choose to act and, importantly, in where they choose not to act, actively shape the welfare state.

Importantly for civic education, the two models offer a fairly restricted and incomplete view of government as an organization that exists beyond and outside of citizens, that can be appealed to when needed to assist groups with their work in the volunteer sector, and that requires monitoring. In these models government appears at worst to be something that exists outside of and thus largely unconnected to citizenship, and at best a decision-making body that citizens must continually check. Government is not taught to constitute an integral element of citizenship. The model citizen does not, it appear, aspire to work *inside government* itself to help solve problems or to participate in any meaningful way in *politics*, which can be understood to consist of the "authoritative allocation of values" (Easton, 1957). Conflict and deliberation are largely limited to the work that goes on within civic organizations, ones one might underline are normally established on the basis of a common set of values and goals. To the extent that such models provide an avenue for developing a competence in 'civic ideas and practices' within civics education curriculum, these are largely limited to voting and volunteering.

Politics also fails to appear in the models in that the only organizations that appear are focussed on volunteer activities. Despite the key role that political parties and advocacy groups play in democracies, the model citizen is not expected to participate in them. Their function in articulating and aggregating interests, as instruments of mobilization, in candidate recruitment and selection, and in policy development notwithstanding, political parties and interest groups are largely invisible and outside of the realm of citizenship.

Additionally, the models offer little in the way of explicit discussion of non-traditional forms of participation, actions that have as their goal to pressure governments to affect a desired change, and which include legal and illegal demonstrations and protest and the development and signing of petitions. The one exception is found in the focus on consumer-driven forms of engagement (boycotting and buycotting) within the collectively responsible citizen model.

Political consumerism, the selection of specific consumer goods and services and avoidance of others, is, however, more focussed on corporate entities than it is on governments and as such, reinforces a consumer model of citizenship where purchasing power equals strength. The citizen who seeks action though more visible, collective, and controversial forms presumably hinders rather than helps in the goal of achieving a successful democracy. According to Westheimer, a review of the cases of American educators arrested for various anti-war acts in the classroom revealed that "dissent, rather than being an essential component of democratic deliberation, [was] seen as a threat to patriotism" (2004: 232). As an element of citizenship, freedom of expression must include the right to express both support *and opposition to the state*. Given that "protest is the domain of the young" (Dalton, 2006: 71), civic education programs that fail to include content on legitimate forms of opposition outside of elections for keeping governments to account fail in their duty to teach about all legitimate forms of engagement.

Existing norms and teachings of citizenship identify a more limited set of requirements for citizenship than that found in theory, either in emphasizing duties and obligations or individual responsibilities to civil society, but not both. The ideal citizen identified in participatory democratic theory, while important for modelling all of the elements that would seem to be required of citizens, may well impose an unrealistic set of requirements on citizens. As such, a balance of citizen types may well meet the needs of representative democracies; so long as sufficient numbers of each 'type' of citizen exist, democracies may be able to perform effectively. To this end, allowing for variation in curriculum content within a country would be advisable if content unnecessarily limits the type of citizenship that is advocated and if greater freedom to set content actually does result in variation in the form of citizenship that is advocated. But the models provide a relatively limited set of citizen models, too few to adequately address the range of actions, organizations and strategies required of citizens in modern democracies.

GENERATIONS AND CITIZENSHIP

Do we need to take into account "increasing education levels, political sophistication, and participation norms among younger generations" (Dalton, 2006: 71) when considering the content of civic education? Inglehart (1990) was one of the first to identify the link between increased education levels and shifts in the patterns of values identified in recent generations, what he termed the 'post-material' generation. A number of authors have taken up this line of argument and added that these shifts include a participatory component: younger citizens are moving away from voting towards more individualized and direct forms of participation (Dalton, 2007; Marsh, O'Toole & Jones, 2007; Norris, 2002). Importantly, not everyone agrees that this shift is away from traditional forms of participation towards more individualized forms. Gidengil et al. (2003), for example, argue that young Canadians have been tuning out rather than turning towards more participatory forms of engagement.

Dalton, however, provides convincing evidence that the two models of perceived norms of citizenship he outlines have a distinct generational component to them: older generations tend to emphasize the duty-based form of citizenship while more recent generations emphasize the engaged form (Dalton, 2007, 2008). Further, he argues that there are important positive implications to the shift towards more engaged forms of participation among youth. The more engaged form of citizenship provides greater political influence, allows individuals to select the issues over which they wish to involve themselves and allows them to decide when and how they will participate (2007). It reflects, then, greater individual agency. Additionally, he finds that these norms matter for the type of political participation engaged in by citizens. Norms of civic duty appear to encourage electoral participation but not other forms of participation and they discourage protest behaviour. Norms of engagement, on the other hand, encourage all forms of participation except voting (Dalton, 2008). These effects are large, and in some cases, outperform the impact of education on participation.

The norm of citizenship emphasized in civic education can, then, come up against a very different set of norms among the youth in these courses. The adoption of a duty-based model of citizenship is likely to clash with the norms and expectations of many of the students in those classes. The adoption of the engaged model of citizenship, while more in line with the norms of recent generations, risks overlooking important elements of the traditional political system and encouraging a form of engagement devoid of conflict and deliberation. There are consequences to teaching a model of citizenship that downplays voting as an important element of citizenship. Democratic government must be responsive to citizen demands and interests, and elections provide an important mechanism for responsiveness and vertical accountability. The legitimacy of the democratic state is diminished if increasingly fewer people feel it is a duty to render a retrospective judgment on the current government and a prospective evaluation on a future one.

A model of citizenship that emphasizes volunteering and community efforts presents a too-limited and somewhat distorted view of politics. Volunteering has direct and immediate consequences; politics is slow and often unsuccessful. Volunteers choose the organization and cause that is important to them; politics and governing involves decision-making in multiple policy arenas, not all of which are equally interesting to all those involved. Volunteering is praised; politics is denigrated. Volunteering involves little in the way of conflict. Politics is messy and there are both winners and losers. Instilling in youth an understanding that politics "involves the collective imposition of decisions, demands a complex communication process and generally produces messy compromises" is crucial to their willingness to engage in it (Stoker, 2006: 68) for "[d]emocracy is about competition and choice, and losers are bound to be dissatisfied, at least temporarily" (Diamond & Morlino, 2004: 30). Conflict and deliberation cannot be avoided. Tolerance, in this sense, ought not to be confused with an inability to challenge the opinions and views of others; instead, tolerance requires that such challenges occur within a climate of respect. And a model of citizenship that is silent on the importance of protest and dissent (beyond boycotting and buycotting) risks creating citizens that see themselves as service providers rather than as government monitors, and importantly, as *potential governors*.

CONCLUSION

A review of the role of the citizen in democratic theory, in public understanding and within civic education programs raises several points. First, there is no single agreed upon model of the 'good citizen.' Theories of democracy that argue for less than the full participation of a majority of citizens raise that possibility that rather than requiring a single type of citizen, successful democracies may result from the proper mix of types of citizens. Moreover, a focus on a single model citizen risks placing too heavy a burden on young citizens who fail to meet this ideal, resulting in a potential withdrawal from political and civic engagement altogether.

Second, public and civic education programs elevate one dimension of citizen above others, creating one-dimensional citizens. The individually responsible citizen model risks the development of democracies where government accountability atrophies. By focussing on a version of citizenship that reinforces duty, citizens are unnecessarily limited in the degree to which they are required to hold and in the mechanisms available to them for holding governments accountable. The focus on voting to the neglect of other forms of participation limits their monitoring role as citizens. For Diamond and Morlino, "participatory citizens, voting at the polls and *acting in various organized ways in civil society*, are the last line of defense against potential executive efforts to subvert rule-of-law and good-governance institutions" (2004: 29 emphasis added).

The collectively responsible model, on the other hand, risks the development of creating democracies with parallel sets of institutions for dealing with social and economic concerns: the civic and the political. Creating a model of citizenship that focuses exclusively on volunteering and community problem-solving risks a downgrading of the importance of government structures as mechanisms for problem solving. Governments are not perfect solutions for collective decision-making but to divert attention and effort away from them risks increasing rather than decreasing their limitations. As Westeheimer and Kahne (2004) argue, many civic education programs in the U.S. embrace a model of citizenship that is devoid of politics, fostering a commitment to service rather than democratic deliberation and decision-making. The focus is on being a 'good' person as much as it is on being a good citizen. This goal leads to a privileging of individual over collective action, and provides a rationale for avoiding politics by emphasizing volunteering.

Third, models of citizenship are surprisingly devoid of government and politics. The role of discussion and debate, of political parties, of protest and demonstration, and of political ideologies do not appear to form a central component of citizenship. Democracy is a system designed to allow for collective-decision making within a set of constraints. Collective-decision making in these citizenship models is often limited to voting, to a rather limited set of citizens deciding amongst themselves on how to meets the needs of the community. While these are all in themselves worthy, they do little to reinforce the difficulty of attempting to reach decisions within the reality of competing interests, values and demands. Citizenship ought to include simple elements such as joining a party, attending debates, contacting officials and reading the newspaper. But it ought also to include running for office. To exclude the latter risks perpetuate the myth that politics and government is something for people other than responsible and 'good' citizens.

Fourth, the absence of politics from the models reinforces the perception that dissent and opposition are for those who are not 'good' citizens. Civic education should not devolve into state endorsed and sanctioned 'participatory engineering' designed to artificially inflate acceptable forms of participation and consensus beyond their 'natural' levels. Engagement requires more than simply support for the system to include close and careful monitoring of government and the voicing of opposition. It also requires more than engagement in civil society given that the formal political system is where collective decision-making power and legitimate authority lie. Citizenship ought to include an understanding that while politics might be 'messy,' its avoidance is impossible.

Fifth, the most successful civic education programs are those that foster an open climate, where opinions are freely expressed and deliberation practiced and encouraged. Such programs encourage the practice of democracy rather than simply learning about it in the abstract. The model of citizenship adopted within a civics programme is likely to shape the degree to which this occurs. The individually responsible citizen model discourages dissent, prioritizes obeying laws, encourages assuming responsibilities, and limits participation to voting, a relatively passive, individual and conflict-free act. The collectively responsible citizen model encourages civic action, collectively with like-minded others or individually through consumer action. Neither model adequately addresses nor encourages citizenship that includes openly and visibly challenging and critiquing governments. As such, such activity is unlikely to be encouraged or promoted in the classroom or school. If this is the case, young citizens will be neither prepared to voice dissent nor to work with those who do.

Finally, it is unlikely that the correspondence in the models of citizenship outlined by the public and those found to dominate in civics education programs is coincidental. Any number of possibilities exists for explaining it. One such possibility is that educators hope to avoid conflict by adopting programs that will be acceptable to the public. As public organizations, schools are ultimately accountable to the public that they serve. It is completely understandable that the programs they adopt are in line with public thinking. The irony is, however, that such a possibility only serves to underline the strength in the desire to avoid conflict and thus reinforces the importance of programs in schools designed to develop an appreciation for its role in politics.

NOTES

[1] It ought to be noted that the results are to some extent shaped by the set of norms and expectations included in the survey. A set of questions tapping a wider set may have resulted in somewhat different results.

REFERENCES

Almond, G., & Verba, S. (1963). *The civic culture.* Princeton, NJ: Princeton University Press.

Archer, K., & Wesley, J. (2006). *And I don't do dishes either! Disengagement from civic and personal duty.* Delivered at the annual meeting of the Canadian Political Science Association. Toronto, ON: York University.

Berelson, B. R., Lazarsfeld, P., & McPhee, W. N. (1954). *Voting: A study of opinion formation in a presidential campaign.* Chicago: University of Chicago Press.

Campbell, D. E. (2008). Voice in the classroom: How an open classroom climate fosters political engagement among adolescents. *Political Behavior, 30*(4), 437–454.

Dahl, R. (1961). *Who governs? Democracy and power in an American city.* New Haven, CT: Yale University Press.

Dalton, R. (2006). *Citizen politics: Public opinion and political parties in advanced industrial democracies* (4th ed.). Washington, DC: CQ Press.

Dalton, R. (2007). *The good citizen: How the young are transforming American politics.* Washington, DC: CQ Press.

Dalton, R. (2008). Citizenship norms and the expansion of political participation. *Political Studies, 56,* 76–98.

Diamond, L., & Morlino, L. (2004). An overview. *Journal of Democracy, 15*(4), 20–31.

Galston, W. A. (2001). Political knowledge, political engagement and civic education. *Annual Review of Political Science, 4,* 217–234.

Galston, W. A. (2004). Civic education and political participation. *PS: Political Science & Politics, 37*(2), 263–266.

Gidengil, E., Blais, A., Nevitte, N., & Nadeau, R. (2003). Turned off or tuned out? Youth participation in politics. *Electoral Insight, 5*(2).

Gidengil, E., Blais, A., Nevitte, N., & Nadeau, R. (2004). *Citizens.* Vancouver, BC: UBC Press.

Held, D. (1996). *Models of democracy* (2nd ed.). Stanford, CA: Stanford University Press.

Hibbing, J., & Theiss-Morse, E. (2002). *Stealth democracy: Americans' beliefs about how democracy should work.* Cambridge, UK: Cambridge University Press.

Hughes, A. S., & Sears, A. (2006). Citizenship education: Canada dabbles while the world plays on. *Education Canada, 46*(4), 6–9.

Inglehart, R. (1990). *Culture shift in advanced industrial society.* Princeton, NJ: Princeton University Press.

Jennings, M. K., & Niemi, R. N. (1974). *The political character of adolescence: The influence of family and schools.* Princeton, NJ: Princeton University Press.

Langton, K. P., & Jennings, M. K. (1968). Political socialization and the high school civics curriculum in the United States. *American Political Science Review, 62*(3), 852–867.

McDonald, M. P., & Popkin, S. (2001). The myth of the vanishing voter. *American Political Science Review, 95*(4), 963–974.

Macedo, S., et al. (2005). *Democracy at risk: How political choices undermine citizen participation and what we can do about it.* Washington, DC: Brooking Institution Press.

Marsh, D., O'Toole, T., & Jones, S. (2007). *Young people and politics in the UK: Apathy or alienation?* New York: Palgrave.

Milligan, K., Moretti, E., & Oreopoulos, P. (2004). Does education improve citizenship? Evidence from the United States and the United Kingdom. *Journal of Public Economics, 88,* 1667–1695.

Milner, H., with Nguyen, C., & Boylston, F. (2008). *Variations in civic education: The IDEA Civic Education Database.* Paper prepared for the Civic Education and Political Participation Workshop, Université de Montréal, June 17–19, 2008.

Niemi, R. J., & Junn, J. (1998). *Civic education: What makes students learn.* New Haven, CT: Yale University Press.

Norris, P. (2002). *Democratic phoenix: Reinventing political activism.* Cambridge, UK: Cambridge University Press.

O'Neill, B. (2006). *Human capital, civic engagement and political participation: Turning skills and knowledge into engagement and action.* CPRN's Skills and Knowledge for Canada's Future: Seven Perspectives—Towards an Integrated Approach to Human Capital Development. Ottawa, ON: CPRN.

O'Neill, B. (2007). *Indifferent or just different? The political and civic engagement of young people in Canada*. CPRN Democratic Renewal Series: Charting the Course for Youth Democratic and Political Participation. Ottawa, ON: CPRN and Elections Canada.

Print, M. (2007). Citizenship education and youth participation in democracy. *British Journal of Educational Studies, 55*(3), 325–345.

Putnam, R. D. (2000). *Bowling alone: The collapse and revival of American community*. New York: Touchstone.

Ross, E. W. (2004). Negotiating the politics of citizenship education. *PS: Political Science and Politics, 37*(2), 249–251.

Saward, M. (2003). *Democracy*. Cambridge, UK: Polity Press.

Sears, A., & Perry, M. (2000). Beyond civics: Paying attention to the context of citizenship education. *Education Canada, 40*(3), 28.

Stoker, G. (2006). *Why politics matters: Making democracy work*. New York: Palgrave.

Stolle, D., & Cruz, C. (2005). *Youth civic engagement in Canada: Implications for public policy*. Social Capital in Action: Thematic Policy Studies. Ottawa, ON: Policy Research Initiative.

Truman, D. B. (1951). *The governmental process*. New York: Knopf.

Westheimer, J. (2004). Introduction – The politics of civic education. *PS: Political Science and Politics, 37*(2), 231–235.

Westheimer, J., & Kahne, J. (2004). Education the 'good' citizen: Political choices and pedagogical goals. *PS: Political Science and Politics, 37*(2), 241–247.

J.P. LEWIS

2. IS CIVIC EDUCATION THE ANSWER?

The Futile Search for Policy Solutions to Youth Political Apathy in Canada

INTRODUCTION

In recent years there have been three occasions for mainstream media to sound the alarm on the civic illiteracy of young Canadians: Canada Day, Remembrance Day and any major election. On both national holidays, non-governmental organizations and history lobby groups such as the Dominion Institute, regularly release survey and poll results demonstrating how little young Canadians know about their country. Respondents normally cannot correctly answer when Canadian Confederation occurred or name the capitals of the ten provinces. The result of all the attention is a growing consensus on the existence of a political knowledge deficit. A related consensus has developed over the "democratic deficit" in political skills and actions, or more explicitly voting. During election campaigns, Elections Canada and non-governmental groups such as Student Vote and Apathy is Boring prod Canadians, especially young Canadians, to vote and in the aftermath of low turnout numbers, lament the perceived decline of the Canadian democracy.

Concern does not just rest with lobby groups and election administrators. Experts echo Richard Johnston's blunt 2001 statement that "Electoral democracy in Canada is sick." Johnston's dramatic observation was not an exaggeration; the recent voting figures are discouraging. According to Elections Canada, the turnout for those between 18 and 24 years old in the 2004 election was 37 percent and 41 percent in 2006. Civic education advocate and Dominion Institute co-founder Rudyard Griffiths warns that Canada is becoming a nation of civic slackers whose focus is on consumption opposed to responsibility (Campbell, 2007). While the blame can shift from individual decision-making to the failure of government delivery of public education, whether approaching the issue from a conservative and knowledge-based frame or a progressive and participation-based lens, civic advocacy actors in Canada agree that young Canadians must become more politically engaged.

The dominant discourse has centred on the concept of "civic literacy". Henry Milner (2002) has termed "civic literacy" as "the knowledge and ability of citizens to make sense of their political world." Knowledge and skills are two parts of the pedagogical triangular model accepted by a majority of those involved in the study and delivery of education. The third tenet is attitudes. Regardless of knowledge levels (understanding of political systems and institutions) or skill levels (comprehension and means of participation), attitudes may be the final and most challenging obstacle to recruiting young Canadians to participate in the political sphere. This paper stresses the effect of attitudes rather than knowledge or skills as the main obstacle preventing a significant increase in young Canadian civic engagement despite numerous policy attempts and government activity. Attitudes can be the most difficult to change. The current Canadian civic education regime does not appear to be adequately impacting the attitudes of young Canadians to boost the level of engagement. As the American-based Center for Civic Education puts it, the aim of civic education is "not just any kind of participation by any kinds of citizen; it is the participation of informed and responsible citizens, skilled in the arts of effective deliberation and action" (Keller, 1996). In this chapter I argue that we cannot assume civic education, though it has a legitimate place in the public school curriculum, to be a means of attaining such participation and overcoming youth political apathy. In attempting to make this argument I will cite historical and contemporary curriculum documents, previous political participation research and information acquired from interviews completed on the state of civic education in Canada.

THE NOTION OF CIVIC EDUCATION

Classic political theory is filled with references to, and notions of, the connection between education and a democratically healthy polity. Alexis de Tocqueville mused that if schools had existed in America before courts, social problems would have ended up in the public school rather than the courtroom (Postman, 1995). Due to its theoretical and normative nature, civic education is a highly fluid pedagogical product. Niemi and Junn (1998) contend, "Civics by its very nature is a controversial subject, and there is imperfect agreement on both its meaning and how to test whether students are well informed about it." Difficulty arises with not only the competition for narrative within education but also the contestation of meaning over citizenship. Canada as a federated and conceptually contested state is particularly susceptible to questions of identity and citizenship. Since Confederation, the evolving narrative of imperial ties to the United Kingdom and economic links to the United States has been a trend mirrored in the history, civics and social studies curriculum. The question "What is Canada?" exists alongside the question "How do citizens act in Canada?"

While contemporary interest may suggest novel policy directions, civic education in Canada is not an incarnation of the 21st century. Provinces have a long tradition of including explicit civics courses or implicit moral education in their pedagogical delivery. While language and religion concerns in state schools have been at the peak of the politicization in the Canadian education regime, the meaning of civic education has become the fodder of academics and education experts more than the public or elected politicians. In this context we briefly revisit the policy discourse and curriculum narrative informing the civic education story in Canada since Confederation.

A CHANGING TRADITION OF CIVICS

In the early stages of Canadian public education development, Province of Canada-era educators supported the worth of schools as a catalyst for creating citizens even though Canadians officially remained British subjects until 1947. Egerton Ryerson (1847), Superintendent of Education from 1846 to 1876, argued education would help prepare individuals for "life as Christians, as persons of business and members of the civic community." Following Confederation, Prime Minister John A. Macdonald emphasized education's "potential to build support for the new political community" (McDonald, 1982). In the relatively young country, a program of civic education could aid in reconciling differences in language, religion and race. The early curriculum writers and education leaders stayed on a conservative course, framing citizenship in a colonial and Christian lens. In 1878, Manitoba Superintendent of Education Tasse argued,

> Moral instruction forms the Christian, the devoted citizen, the steady soul, the grateful child, the good father; – almost the whole of man. It is in this direction that the teacher should bend the weight of his efforts. The religious sentiment is the foundation of all society; and the teacher should cultivate it in the hearts of his pupils with assiduous constancy (Gregor & Wilson, 1984).

The lessons taught in social studies and history textbooks such as the 1880s-era Gage's Fourth Reader were dominated by colonial and British sentiments. The book argued for only one acceptable option for the new Canadian dominion, "to seek, in the consolidation of the empire, a common imperial citizenship, with common responsibilities and a common heritage" (Stanley, 1995). While contemporary civic textbooks and curricula attempt to empower the individual citizen, early Canadian civics stressed allegiance and identity built on the appreciation of certain historical and "heroic" figures. In 1884, Ontario's Education Minister, George Ross stated,

> The history of the community and nation to which we belong…shows the young the springs of public honour and dishonour; sets before them the national feelings, weaknesses and sins; warns them against future dangers by exhibiting the losses and suffering of the past; enshrines in their hearts the national heroes; and strengthens in them the precious love of country (Conley, 1989).

According to the Saskatchewan Annual Report of the Department of Education in 1901, the lives of great historical figures were studied "to form moral notions in children" and "to teach patriotism and civic duty" (McDonald, 1982). The early pedagogical efforts attempted to combine knowledge and skills but tended to stress political and civic responsibilities rather than political and civic involvement when discussing participation.

After the First World War, with increased attention on nation-building and sovereignty for Canada, civic education gradually emerged as more "Canadian". In 1920, Manitoba's Minister of Education, R.S. Thornton stated: "A teacher should be a teacher, not for one province but for all Canada. Our schools should not be Manitoba schools, but Canadian schools located in Manitoba" (Tomkins, 1986).

Slowly, the modern Canadian civic education narrative was emerging, as Ontario's 1937 curriculum contended

> The social virtues of the good citizen are not things merely to learn about. They are to be achieved by practicing them. The development of qualities of cooperation, respect for the rights and feelings of others, willingness to accept responsibility, and other attributes of the good citizen can be developed only by exercising them in situations that demand their practice. They are to be accepted willingly as desirable forms of conduct; they cannot be developed by coercion. The school must, therefore, be so organized as to permit of their growth and exercise in situations that require their practice.

As the country gradually became more concerned with questions of national identity and statehood, Canadian education as a whole was placed under greater scrutiny by a flurry of royal commissions on education in the provinces. The initial calls for reform primarily addressed organizational, administrative and financial questions but starting with Quebec's Parent Commission in the early 1960s, the curriculum content, including civic education, came under focus. A relevant example is found in the 1967 report of the Newfoundland Royal Commission on Education which noted,

> There are some who contend that no part of the curriculum has greater potential or importance than social studies. Social studies can help students understand the present through a study of the past, give them some understanding of the influence of the physical environment on human progress, and provide insights into the social, economic, and governmental systems now in operation. The overall objective is to promote good citizenship.

The 1970s Canadian social studies and civics policy scene was affected by a number of converging trends. The scrutiny to which the history curriculum was subjected by such critics as A.B. Hodgetts and a new philosophical approach that placed the student at the centre of the education system encouraged new directions for Canadian civics teaching. The national mood was one of collective naval-gazing around patriotic events such as the Centennial celebrations and the youth-enthused "Trudeaumania". In conjunction with other factors, this context influenced the development of a new social science discipline termed "Canadian Studies", and a more progressive and pluralist educational approach. The budding pluralist theme is found in Ontario's 1973 History for the Intermediate Division: "Through study of the human experience in the Canadian setting both through time and in a global context, it is hoped that the student, as a citizen, will be able to understand the complexities of the nation of which he is a part and to develop some perception of the wider world, the community of nations of which he is also a part."

The 1970s eventually gave way to a new education movement in the 1980s, responding to neo-conservative political trends and souring economic times, with calls for a return to the basic skills in education. However an approach focusing on civics gradually began a comeback. In the late 1980s, Canadian political scientists made one of their first comprehensive contributions to the field of citizenship education with a collection of conference papers titled *Political Education in Canada*. In the past, Canadian political scientists had investigated political socialization, but did not take an active interest in political or citizenship education. Ronald Landes noted in 1988 that "it is still true to say that no full-length analysis of political learning in Canada has ever appeared in the pre-eminent journal of Canadian political scientists ... of the five research notes which did appear, four were contributed by researchers at American universities."

Empirical research in political participation and knowledge, and thus on civic education in the United States was stimulated in the 1960s at the intersection of new methodological enthusiasm for quantitative survey research and the subfield of political socialization, though that interest faded in the next two decades. By the 1990s, the field was revived as civics became a popular policy option for major Anglo-liberal democracies such as the United States, the United Kingdom and Australia. In 1991, the American government introduced a new framework for civic education called CIVITAS, followed in 1994 by the National Curriculum Standards for Civics and Government (Cogan, 1996). In the United Kingdom, compulsory citizenship education for students aged eleven to sixteen has been a part of the national curriculum since August 2002 (Davies, 2003), on the impetus of the 1999 British Crick Report, which sought "no less than a change in the political culture of this country both nationally and locally: for people to think of themselves as active citizens, willing, able and equipped to have an influence in public life and with the critical capacities to weigh evidence before speaking and acting" (Osler & Starkey, 2004). In Australia, civic education became a policy priority in 1993 under Prime Minister Paul Keating, who reasoned that a better-informed populace would lead to a more independent and unified national identity (Kennedy & Howard, 2004).

Thus a wealth of experience exists for Canadian education policy makers to consult. There has not, however, as we see from the divergent policy paths followed by Canada's three largest English provinces, been any single influential model. It is worth briefly noting the differences between the three civic education approaches. British Columbia introduced a Grade Eleven civics course in 2005 that is not mandatory but can replace social studies or native studies as the student's grade eleven social studies credit. In 2007, Alberta began phasing in a three-year mandatory social studies/civic education component into the high school curriculum with each year (grade ten through twelve) focusing on a grand societal and political theme. In 2000, Ontario introduced a mandatory half-year civics course for grade ten students. The students would complete the other half of their grade ten-year with a mandatory course in career planning.

Although each path represents a brand of civic education that differs greatly from the early narrow, colonial and Christian programs from decades earlier, each represents varying levels of acceptance and commitment to civic education. Moreover, the organization and administrative intent of the courses demonstrate inconsistent governmental and political commitments to the pursuit of improved civic literacy and enhanced political participation. The following section looks at why a clear civic education policy has been so difficult to formulate.

FORMULATING A PUBLIC PROBLEM

Though election turnout rates and survey findings regularly portray a youth more concerned with consumer and material items than active and engaging citizenship, the issue does not have the visual impact of health care, the environment or national security. While most politicians express support for civic education, this support runs shallow. In interviews with four former Ontario education ministers questioned about the 2000 Grade Ten civics course, each showed little knowledge of its development, implementation, content or success, but nonetheless supported the notion of expanding civic education objectives in public schools.[1]

A major challenge for civic education actors has been the continuously contested notion of citizenship. As Langton and Jennings (1968) argued, "While most educators can agree that the development of good citizenship is important, the 'good citizen' is something of an ideal type whose attitudes and behaviour vary with the values of those defining the construct." Voting is frequently identified as a quality of good citizenship; its absence as the most unequivocal evidence of declining engagement.

In addition, the school is accepted as an agent of change for the politically apathetic and uninterested, yet until the 1990s, most research suggested there was little correlation between the completion of a high school level civics course and political involvement. Langton and Jennings' 1968 finding that high school social studies classes had little impact on the political participation of students was challenged by new findings including Niemi and Junn's 1998 *Civic Education: What Makes Students Learn*, which suggested social studies classes did influence high school students. Overall, the research claims are contradictory.

The case for constructing youth engagement as a policy problem is fostered by contemporary non-governmental organizations involved in civic promotion. Conservative, more conventional groups, such as the Dominion Institute or Historica, frame the problem as a civic knowledge deficit. Surveys and polls are presented as empirical evidence that young Canadians are ignorant towards their country. Young, more progressive groups such as Apathy is Boring or Student Vote Canada construct their concern around a lack or under usage of civic skills. The Dominion Institute's use of poor historical test survey results and the election agencies emphasis on the low turnout numbers both portray a deliberate attempt to gain support for their lobby industry.[2]

Therefore we can ask if governments' pursuit of civic education programs is due more to policy path dependency than proven practical results. We know that the presence of federalism in Canada benefits education through the existence of pedagogical laboratories. Conversely, in the case of civic education more provincial policy options may work against the original intent of the programs by diluting national citizenship ideals. Each province is able to be the central arbiter in education policy formulation. Canadian elites have long been wary of the arrangement as Canada's first Prime Minister, John A. Macdonald once admitted that having the federal government withdraw from control and supervision of education was "unwisely" (Johnson, 1968).

As mentioned earlier, Ontario and Alberta formulated different approaches to civic education policy. Ontario's civic education curriculum stresses aspects of participation and activity while Alberta's curriculum is framed around questions of identity and belonging. In Alberta, civic education is delivered through three years of mandatory courses based on ideological themes while in Ontario the course is packaged in a half-year program focusing on participatory ideals. Both Ontario and Alberta policy makers recognize the existence of civic apathy but have designed solutions that are much different. The recommendations for mandatory civics and career development in Ontario came from the Royal Commission in 1994, rather than in response to public pressure. Interviews with Alberta officials indicate that the policy process was much more organic in their province. Pedagogical interest in identity and citizenship had increased in 21st century Alberta.[3] Development of citizenship-based education in Alberta was based more on identity and culture in relation to Aboriginal, immigrant and francophone perspectives than concerns with general youth political apathy.

As noted earlier in the chapter, issues of civic concern benefit from their general acceptability across ideological and political lines. Many agree with C.B. Macpherson's (1977)notion, "Low participation and social inequality are so bound up with each other that a more equitable and humane society requires a more participatory political system." Civics benefits from relative consensual acceptance. This type of status allows civic education to be viewed as a so-called "valence issue". Valence issues are defined as "those in which only one side of the debate is legitimate", for example there is little debate over whether drug use is bad or good (Baumgartner & Jones, 1993). Partisanship or ideology can have little influence over the support civic education enjoys. Nevertheless, the support for civics tends to be shallow. This situation results, on occasion, in a tendency to oversimplify problems and solutions concerning education (Sears & Hughes, 2005).

Possibly the most important call for greater citizenship education in Canada was A.B. Hodgetts' 1968 publication *What Culture? What Heritage? A Study of Civic Education in Canada*. Three years prior, a $150,000 National History Project was initiated by the Board of Governors of Trinity College School. Out of this project arose the Canada Studies Foundation in 1970 and the publication of Hodgetts book in 1968 (Tomkins, 1977). The study was based on an examination of 951 classes in 247 schools across Canada (Bowd, 1978). Hodgetts (1968) complained "we are teaching a bland, unrealistic consensus version of our past: a dry-as-dust chronological story of uninterrupted political and economic progress told without the controversy that is an inherent part of history." Ten years after the highly influential *What Culture? What Heritage?*, Hodgetts collaborated with Paul Gallagher on *Teaching Canada for the 80s*. While *What Culture?* evaluated the past, *Teaching Canada* (1978) looked to the future, calling for a different civic education, one unlike the old 'civics' courses, which dealt almost exclusively with a description, frequently an unrealistic one, of the structure of government. In the last decade many more have followed in Hodgetts and Gallagher's footsteps but for different reasons. Today's civic alarmist is more concerned with the output, the level of political participation, than the input, the content of the policy or in this case curriculum. It is now time for academics to return to the potential solution, civic education policy, and whether or not the search for one is worthy at all.

FINDING A POLICY SOLUTION

Schools have been involved in citizenship education ever since it was accepted that the school could play a role not just in preparation for vocation but also for preparation of life within a democracy. Gradually, civic education received separate billing as an individual course and would gain the attention of academics as a solution to the policy problem of teaching deference and civic compliance. By 1915, 'civics' referred to the teaching of citizenship and politics in American high schools (Langton & Jennings, 1968). The term "social studies" was first used in Canadian curriculum documents in western Canada in the 1920s and Ontario in 1937 (Clark, 2004). During this time, American academics began to take note of the new connections forming between the school and the state. Charles Merriam published the influential *Making of Citizens* (1931) and *Civic Education in the United States* (1934) and the Civic Training series that would inspire Gabriel Almond and Sidney Verba's *The Civic Culture* (1963) (Bennett, 1999). M. Kent Jennings was responsible for a decades-long study of a 1965 high school class and the connection between civic education and political socialization which produced such important books as *The Political Character of Adolescence* (1974) and *Generations and Politics* (1981). In 1965, Jennings and Niemi surveyed 1,669 senior students in 97 American secondary schools in the United States and found little support for the notion that the civics curriculum was a source of political socialization. The Torney et al. 1975 study, *Civic Education in Ten Countries*, based on research dating back to 1967 with survey data from more than 30,000 students and teachers from Germany, Finland, Iran, Ireland, Israel, Italy, the Netherlands, New Zealand, Sweden and the United States. While a lull in the civic education literature followed, momentum for further research returned by the mid-1990s.

In the last decade, each Canadian province has experienced civic education curriculum reform, with new curricula in Newfoundland (1998), Nova Scotia (2002), Prince Edward Island (2007), New Brunswick (2006), Quebec (1998), Ontario (2000), Manitoba (2007), Saskatchewan (1999), Alberta (2007) and British Columbia (2005). A growing trend for education policy makers in the 2000s was to expand citizenship beyond traditional civics classes with programs promoting character and volunteerism. With the acceptance of pluralism in Canadian education, the "citizen" becomes a much more complex concept than that of the good Christian British subject idealized in early versions of Canadian civics courses. The following table presents a current snapshot of civic education in Canada identifying when recent reforms were made and how provinces have configured the delivery of civic education. While almost all courses are compulsory or may serve as compulsory courses, the units and themes differ from a focus on strands of citizenship (Ontario) to contemporary political eras (Quebec) to variations on the role of Canada (Prince Edward Island).

Table 1. *"Civic" Education Across Canada – Knowledge, Skills and Values Delivery (as of 2008)*

Province	Year	Course Title	Units/Themes	Status
Nfld.	1998	Canadian Issues (Grade 10)	1. Cultural and Social Issues 2. Political and Legal Issues 3. Economic and Environmental Concerns 4. Global Concerns	One of three options for compulsory social studies credit with: Canadian History Canadian Geography
NS	2002	Canadian History (Grade 11)	1. Globalization 2. Development 3. Governance 4. Sovereignty 5. Justice	One of three options for compulsory social studies credit with: Mik Maq Studies African Canadian Studies
PEI	2007	Canadian Studies (Grade 10)	1. Canada's Place in the World 2. Canada's Voices of the Past 3. Canada as a Democracy 4. Canada's Work and Worth 5. Canada's Global Connections 6. Canada's Cultural Mosaic	One of four options for two compulsory social studies credit: History Geography Social Studies
NB	2006	Canadian Identity (Grade 9)	1. Exploring Canadian Identity 2. Geographic Influences 3. Decades of Change 4. Citizenship 5. Challenges and Opportunities 6. Reflections on Canadian Identity	Compulsory
Quebec	1998	History of Quebec and Canada (Grade 10)	Economic, Social and Political Domains for following Eras: 1. 1960 – 1970 2. 1971 – 1980 3. 1981 to present	Compulsory
Ontario	2000	Civics (Grade 10)	(Strands – Informed, Purposeful and Active Citizenship) 1. Democracy – Issues and Ideas 2. Democracy – The Canadian Context 3. Democracy – Global Perspectives	Compulsory

Province	Year	Course Title	Units/Themes	Status
Manitoba	2007	Social Studies (Grade 9)	1. Active Democratic Citizenship in Canada 2. Canadian Citizenship for the Future 3. Citizenship in the Global Context 4. Environmental Citizenship	Compulsory
Sask.	1999	Social Studies (Grade 9)	1. Time 2. Change 3. Causality 4. Culture: First Nations Roots	Compulsory
Alberta	2007	Social Studies (Grade 10 to Grade 12)	Grade 10 – Perspectives on Globalization – Living in a Globalizing World Grade 11 – Perspectives on Nationalism – Understanding of Nationalism Grade 12 – Perspectives on Ideology – Understandings of Ideologies	Compulsory
BC	2005	Civics (Grade 11)	1. Skills and Processes of Civics Studies 2. Informed Citizenship 3. Civic Deliberation 4. Civic Action	One of three options for compulsory social studies credit with: Social Studies 11 Native Studies 11

My research has focused on British Columbia and, especially, Ontario. The British Columbia experience has been quite bleak. Out of the roughly 50,000 Grade 11 course students in British Columbia, only 645 students were enrolled in Civics grade 11 in 2005-2006 and 669 students in 2006-2007.[4] With such a low number of students enrolled and completing the Civics 11 course it is difficult to describe the policy effort in any manner other than incomplete. Compared to the civics course in Ontario where all students are required to complete the course, in British Columbia barely 1 percent of eligible students are participating in the new course. Those involved in the course have suggested that the concept was not well received by social studies teachers across the province because the ministry decided Civics 11 could take the place of the traditional and popular Social Studies 11 course in the students' diploma requirements.

The development of the Ontario Grade 10 Civics course dates back to early 1990s. The recommendations for mandatory civics and career development came in 1994 from the Royal Commission. Commission member Avis Glaze recalls, "I don't remember many people coming up with it, it is safe to say the commission recommended it...we wanted to focus on citizenship...we talked about creating communities of concern."[5] Former New Democratic Minister of Education David Cooke (1993-1995) remembers there being some talk of civic education but "in terms of real specifics or it being a top notch... (Civics) was overtaken by other priorities." Between 1995 and 1996, during the eight or nine rounds needed to develop the new common curriculum, Grade 10 Civics was an early addition. Former Progressive Conservative Minister of Education John Snobelen (1995-1997) notes, "had there been another government committed to changing government, they probably would have pulled civics out of history as well." The ministry's backgrounder on the changes to civics stated, "For the first time under the new high school program, students will take Civics as a separate, compulsory course, rather than as only a unit of the Canadian History course" (Government of Ontario, 1999). Problems appeared in the early stages of policy implementation. When the course was introduced one teacher observed,

> No advance preparation for the civics course...they just arrived on our doorstep...the documents came out the fall the course was introduced...no supporting resources...there was really nothing for them (the teachers) in 1999...the first time I taught the course I tried to work within the profile of the civics course but it wasn't very good so I went back to old civics lessons from the law and government course ("Canadian History course").

The Ontario Civics course was reviewed in 2003-04 as part of an ongoing curriculum review. When the civics course profile was reformed in 2004 the expectations were greatly reduced. One former civics teacher and member of the curriculum writing team was still very critical after the reforms had been completed,

> Most kids really dread it (Civics)... The first few years were okay if you were experienced but the problem was they put any Tom, Dick or Harry in the classroom because of the scheduling...not only could you be a new teacher but you could also be a new phys ed teacher...that's why it became a mess around the province, it depends on the school...Sometimes because it is a half course principals don't take consideration into staffing...You could be a corpse and pass it, it's not hard.

The sample of twenty teachers that I interviewed came from all around Ontario with a variety of experience, from second year-teachers to twenty-year veterans. The teachers also varied in their experience teaching the Grade 10 Civics course with some having taught the course only a few times and others having taught the course thirty or forty times since its implementation. Regrettably this could not be a representative sample since many boards denied approval for their employees to be interviewed, and among those where such permission was granted, a certain self-selectivity of keen teachers was unavoidable. As one respondent noted: "How can you have a student buy into what you are talking about if you aren't passionate about it yourself?" Not surprisingly, then, the teachers interviewed generally supported the course's existence, most believing it was having an impact, and that students demonstrate increased levels of civic knowledge at the end of the course than the beginning. Yet even the most ambitious teachers noted that at the beginning of the course many students were negatively predisposed with low to no civic knowledge; they were unfamiliar with current events and lacked any desire to participate politically. The students of one teacher had great difficulty identifying the prime minister.[6] Another routinely started the semester with a simple political quiz that the classes regularly failed. A third teacher stated that most have no idea what civics is, while another estimated that one percent of the students at the beginning of the course show any interest at all in political involvement.

By placing mandatory status on the course Ontario's Ministry of Education has symbolically stressed its importance without providing resources proper and conditions for success. Teaching ability was repeatedly raised in the interviews as the key to the success of the course:

> So much hinges on the ability of the teacher that teaches the course. If they are interested in the course and are enthused about it then it can definitely do a good job of promoting civic knowledge. Often this course is one that gets dumped into a teacher's lap that has no interest in the course. When that happens the students tune out and walk away from the course with distain and disinterest.

Overall, the interview responses present a number of concerns with Ontario's Grade 10 Civics course. Most of the teacher critiques were related to the administration and organization of the course. Teachers expressed concern over the length of the course (too short), the age of the students (too young) and the composition of the classes ('open' to all levels of learning). The minor but multitude of problems reveals an ambiguous attitude from Ontario policy leaders. It does not appear the government actions have been malicious or deliberate but rather reflect the relative unimportance of civic education to the government. According to interview responses, principals administer civics as a timetable "dumping ground", while assigning the course to new and unqualified (lacking social studies or history training) teachers. Secondly, there is little uniformity in curriculum delivery, as some teachers continue to stress institutions and others rarely mention the traditional lessons and focus on contemporary events and concerns. While the broad flexibility of curriculum interpretation allows the teachers choice over content, which can be useful in the hands of experienced teachers, in other cases, which seem more typical in Ontario, it leads to courses that may fail to integrate political institutions with current events and community level participation.

Despite their disappointment with the curriculum and textbooks, most teachers believed they could reach the students through engaging activities such as mock trials, parliaments and elections, as well as participation in their own community. Many agree with the observation of a veteran of thirty-five years of teaching who has taught the course more than a dozen times that "at the end of the course the students that do well in civics know more about their society than most of their parents." This matters because, as a fifteen-year veteran of teaching asserted: "It reaches kids who come from non-voting families."

The Ontario, British Columbia and Alberta cases all present considerably different approaches to civic education in Canada. All are education policies adopted in the post-material and post-Meech Lake and Charlottetown age of Canadian politics. Canadians are more educated and less engaged, enjoy more affluence and participate less. Civic apathy in Canada should be a puzzling problem. On the surface the Ontario, British Columbia and Alberta programs all appear to exist as policy solutions to the public problem of civic apathy. With a closer analysis it is suggested here that Alberta's three-year program has been more based in identity politics, British Columbia's pilot grade eleven course has been close to irrelevant and the Ontario Grade 10 course is a seemingly empty vessel always in need of keen pilots (effective teachers).

CONCLUSION

This chapter has not attempted to answer the question the title poses but rather present the rationale for asking the question. The historical record and recent political realities are clear. Civic education in Canada has gone through many variations over time and currently exists in many forms across the country. The current generation of young Canadians is recording historic lows in voting and participation. The inconsistency between policy inputs (more concentration on civic education) and outputs (less civic engagement) should create cause for more scrutiny not merely on the public problem but the proposed solutions. Moreover, there are a number of actors that may propel Canadian civic education to a more effective future. First, more cooperation between provinces may lead to better testing of course effectiveness. Curriculum collaboration has occurred in both Western and Atlantic provinces on subjects from math to science to social studies. In 1993, the Atlantic Provinces agreed on the development of a regional curriculum and four western provinces and the two territories endorsed the Western Canadian Protocol for Collaboration in Basic Education (Dunning, 1997). The formation of the Western Canadian Protocol Common Curriculum Framework for Social Studies in 2002 was the first inter-provincial/territorial curriculum endeavour to include both Aboriginal and francophone representatives in course development (Manitoba, 2007).

With the major advancements in information technology it would seem only appropriate for provinces to naturally drift towards a more collaborative spirit; yet still most claim the forces or programs uniting civic educators across the country are private initiatives. More coordination is needed between private actors such as the Dominion Institute and Historica and government agencies such as Elections Canada and the federal department of Canadian Heritage. These groups along with less permanent bodies such as Student Vote and Apathy is Boring need to pool resources to present a consistent message around civic participation. Finally and possibly most unlikely, civic educators across Canada need to work toward an accepted and authentic civic education narrative. While all provinces have accepted a modern version of Canadian citizenship that is inclusive, pluralist provincial jurisdiction over education produces ten distinct approaches to civic education. This sentiment, while long accepted, may need to be reconsidered.

Unless governments seek new policy paths that are committed to successful and realistic models of civic education, Canadian civic education will remain compromised of arbitrary planning and ambiguous objectives. By adopting a common national civic education curriculum, provinces could pool resources for nation-wide implementation. Such a program could encourage more cooperation between non-governmental organizations, various levels of government and election administration agencies. Considering the major differences in civic education delivery between Canada's three largest provinces, British Columbia, Alberta and Ontario, it would take an ambitious and historical policy effort to accept a national civics curriculum. If this cannot be achieved, more cooperation, coordination and consensus of pedagogical aims would at least begin to build a new policy path that is not dominated by fluctuating government and public interest and diverging educational goals. Without a cohesive plan, Canadians may have to look forward to more annual reminders on Canada and Remembrance Day of their declining civic knowledge and on Election Day of their decreasing civic participation.

NOTES

[1] Interviews completed for dissertation research. January – March 2008.

[2] Some even within the political science profession are sceptical about civic education efforts. In response to the American Political Science Association's 1998 Task Force on Civic Education in the Next Century, Stephen Leonard wrote, "I think most political scientists may be sympathetic to the ideal of civic education and thus with TFCE's efforts... but sympathy and well-crafted plans will not carry the day in the absence of compelling reasons for acting on these sentiments and implementing these plans.... unfortunately, the TFCE (does not) provide compelling reasons for action, mainly because they do not have a suitably robust account of why similar efforts have failed in the past, and why they are likely to fail today." Stephen T. Leonard. " 'Pure Futility and Waste': Academic Political Science and Civic Education" *PS: Political Science and Politics*. Vol. 32. No. 4. December 1999. Pg. 749.

[3] A spokesperson for the Ministry of Education of Alberta in a phone interview, on March 4 2008 noted: "September 11th and a huge influx of immigrants coming into Alberta, not just into the cities but the small towns to work in the oil fields... A huge culture clash... Suddenly farm communities were dealing with Somalians and they didn't know what to do." In terms of curriculum development, the ministry official said, "A lot of tears shed and a lot of people have left these projects... when Aboriginal people tell you their stories it is heartbreaking."

[4] British Columbia Ministry of Education Official. Email Interview. 24 April 2008

[5] Along with interviewing teachers, interviews were also completed with former bureaucrats and politicians including four former ministers of education (David Cooke, John Snobelen, Janet Ecker, Elizabeth Witmer)

[6] All interviews were anonymous and conducted over the phone between November 2007 and March 2008. Boards and schools also remain anonymous in the research, the intent of the interviews was to emulate Hodgetts "fly-on-the-wall" type observations without actually setting foot in the classroom.

REFERENCES

Aristotle. (1948). *Politics*. Oxford, UK: Clarendon Press.
Baumgartner, F. R., & Jones, B. D. (1993). *Agendas and instability in American politics*. Chicago: University of Chicago Press.
Bell, D. V. J. (1988). Political education and political culture. In J. Pammett & J-L. Pepin (Eds.), *Political education in Canada*. Halifax, UK: Institute for Research on Public Policy.
Bennett, S. E. (1999, December). The past need not be prologue: Why pessimism about civic education is premature. *PS: Political Science and Politics, 32*(4).
Bruno-Jofre, R. (2002). Citizenship and schooling in manitoba between the end of the first world war and the end of the second world war. In Y. Hebert (Ed.), *Citizenship in transformation in Canada*. Toronto, ON: University of Toronto Press.
Bowd, A. D. (1978). Political knowledge of Canadian and Australian high school Students. *Canadian Journal of Education, 3*(3).
Cairns, A. C. (1993). The fragmentation of Canadian Citizenship. In W. Kaplan (Ed.), *Belonging: The meaning and future of Canadian citizenship*. Montreal, QC: McGill-Queen's University Press.
Campbell, M. (2007, June 29). Canadians' self-knowledge dismal, poll shows. *The Globe and Mail*.
Clark, P. (2004). The historical context of social studies in English Canada. In A. Sears & I. Wright (Ed.), *Challenges and prospects for Canadian social studies*. Vancouver, BC: Pacific Educational Press.
Cogan, J. J. (1996, December). Civic education in the United States. *Canadian and International Education, 25*(2).
Conley, M. W. (1989). Theories and attitudes towards political education. In K. A. McLeod (Ed.), *Canada and citizenship education*. Toronto, ON: Canadian Education Association.
Davies, I. (2003). Citizen education in England. *Orbit, 33*(2).
Dunning, P. (1997). *Education in Canada: An overview*. Toronto, ON: Canadian Education Association.
Evans, M. (2003). Educating for citizenship in schools in Canada. *Orbit, 33*(2).
Evans, R. W. (1992, Spring). Is social studies dying? Reflections on educational reform. *International Journal of Social Education, 7*(1).
Gidengil, E., Nevette, N., Blais, A., & Nadeau, R. (2003, July). Turned off or tuned out? youth participation in politics. *Electoral Insight, 5*(2).
Government of Manitoba. (2007). *Ministry of Education. Education, Citizenship and Youth*. Grade 9 Social Studies Canada in the Contemporary World: A Foundation for Implementation.
Government of Newfoundland and Labrador. (1967). Report of the royal commission on education and youth.
Government of Ontario. (1973). *Ministry of Education. History. Intermediate Division*.
Government of Ontario. (1937). *Ministry of Education*. Programme of Studies for Grades I to VI of the Public and Separate Schools.
Government of Ontario. (1999, March 4). *Ministry of Education*. Backgrounder: Highlights of the New High School Program.
Gregor, A., & Wilson, K. (1984). *The development of education in manitoba*. Dubuque, IA: Kendall Hunt.
Guess, G. M., & Farnham, P. G. (2000). *Cases in public policy analysis*. (2nd ed.). Washington, DC: Georgetown University Press.
Hodgetts, A. B. (1968). *What culture? What heritage? A study of civic education in Canada*. Toronto, ON: OISE Press.
Hodgetts, A. B., & Gallagher, P. (1978). *Teaching Canada for the '80s*. Toronto, ON: Ontario Institute for Studies in Education.
Jenson, J. (1997, December). Fated to live in interesting times: Canada's changing citizenship regimes. *Canadian Journal of Political Science, 30*(4).
Johnson, F. H. (1968). *A brief history of Canadian education*. Toronto, ON: McGraw-Hill Company of Canada Limited.
Johnston, R. (2001). Canadian elections at the millennium. *Choices, 6*(6).
Keller, S. J. (1996, October 27). Bringing up Citizens. *New York Times*.
Kennedy, K. J., & Howard, C. (2004). Elite constructions of civic education in Australia. In J. Demaine (Ed.), *Citizenship and political today*. New York: Palgrave Macmillan.

Kymlicka, W. (2001). *Politics in the Vernacular: Nationalism, Multiculturalism and Citizenship.* Oxford, UK: Oxford University Press.

Landes, R. G. (1988). Political education and political socialization. In J. Pammett & J-L. Pepin (Eds.), *Political education in Canada.* Halifax, UK: Institute for Research on Public Policy.

Langton, K. P., & Jennings, M. K. (1968, September). Political socialization and the high school civics curriculum in the United States. *American Political Science Review, 62*(3).

Leonard, S. T. (1999, December). 'Pure Futility and Waste': Academic political science and civic education. *PS: Political Science and Politics, 32*(4).

Lewington, J., & Orpwood, G. (1993). *Overdue assignment: Taking responsibility for Canada's schools.* Toronto, UK: John Wiley and Songs.

Lindblom, C. E. (1959, Spring). The science of 'muddling through. *Public Administration Review, 19*(2).

MacKinnon, M. P., Pitre, S., & Watling, J. (2007, October). Lost in translation: (Mis) understanding youth engagement: Synthesis report: Charting the course for youth civic and political participation. *CPRN Research Report.*

Macpherson, C. B. (1977). *The life and times of liberal democracy.* Oxford, UK: Oxford University Press.

McDonald, N. (1982). Canadianization and the curriculum: Setting the stage, 1867–1890. In E. B. Titley & P. J. Miller (Eds.), *Education in Canada: An interpretation.* Calgary, AB: Detselig Enterprises Limited.

McDonald, N. (1982). Canadian Nationalism and North-West Schools, 1884–1905. In E. B. Titley & P. J. Miller (Eds.), *Education in Canada: An interpretation.* Calgary, AB: Detselig Enterprises Limited.

Milburn, G. (1972). *Teaching history in Canada.* Toronto, ON: McGraw-Hill-Ryerson.

Milner, H. (2002). *Civic literacy: How informed citizens make democracy work.* Hanover, NH: University Press of New England.

Munger, M. C. (2000). *Analyzing policy: Choices, conflicts and practices.* New York: W.W. Norton and Company.

Niemi, R. G., & Junn, J. (1998). *Civic education: what makes students learn.* New Haven, CT: Yale University Press, 1998.

Niemi, R. G., & Smith, J. (2001). Enrollments in high schools Government classes: Are we short-changing both citizenship and political science training? *PS: Political Science and Politics. 34*(2) June.

Osborne, K. (1982). *The teaching of politics: Some suggestions for teachers.* Toronto, ON: Canada Studies Foundation.

Osler, A., & Starkey, H. (2004). Citizenship education and cultural diversity in France and England. In J. Demaine (Ed.), *Citizenship and political today.* New York: Palgrave Macmillan.

Pierson, P. (2000, June). Increasing returns, path dependence and the study of politics. *American Political Science Review, 94*(2).

Postman, N. (1995). *The end of education: redefining the value of school.* New York: Alfred A. Knopf.

Ryerson, E. (1847). *Report on a system of public elementary instruction for upper Canada.* Montreal, QC: Lovell and Gibson.

Sears, A., & Hughes, A. S. (2005, July). Learning from each other: Toward a democratic approach to international collaboration in civic education. *International Journal of Citizenship and Teacher Evaluation, 1*(1).

Stamp, R. M. (1982). *The schools of Ontario, 1876–1976.* Toronto, ON: University of Toronto.

Stanley, T. J. (1995). White supremacy and the rhetoric of educational indoctrination: A Canadian case study. In J. Barman, N. Sutherland, & J. D. Wilson. *Children, teachers and schools in the history of British Columbia.* Calgary, AB: Detselig Enterprises Ltd.

Stevenson, H. A. (1973). Ten years to know-where. In D. Myers (Ed.), *The failure of educational reform in Canada.* Toronto, ON: McClelland and Stewart Limited.

Stone, D. A. (1989). Causal stories and formation of policy agendas. *Political Science Quarterly, 104*(2).

Tomkins, G. (1986). *A common countenance: Stability and change in the Canadian curriculum.* Toronto, ON: Prentice-Hall.

Tomkins, G. (1977). The Canada studies foundation: A Canadian approach to curriculum intervention. *Canadian Journal of Education, 2*(1).

Torney, J. V., Oppenheim, A. N., & Farnen, R. F. (1975). *Civic education in ten countries: An empirical study.* New York: John Wiley and Sons.

Van Brummelen, H. (1986). Shifting perspectives: Early British Columbia textbooks from 1872 to 1925. In N. M. Sheehan, J. D. Wilson, & D. C. Jones (Eds.), *Schools in the west: Essays in Canadian educational history.* Calgary, AB: Detselig Enterprises Limited.

Whitman Hertzberg, H. (1982). Social studies reform: The lessons of history. In I. Morrissett (Ed.), *Social studies in the 1980s: A report of project span.* Alexandria: Association for Supervision and Curriculum Development.

APPENDIX – CIVIC EDUCATION IN CANADA THROUGH THE YEARS

Ontario Grade 10 Canadian History and Citizenship Aims – 1938

1. To give an understanding of the importance of Canada's past in relation to her present position and to study the progress made;
2. To show how Canada's history is linked with that of the Empire and related to that of other parts of the world;
3. To promote tolerance, respect and goodwill towards other races and classes;
4. To foster a spirit of unity among the provinces of Canada;
5. To train the pupil to collect, organize, and use information for the purpose of thinking critically and forming conclusions;
6. To show the pupil that institutions are subject to change; that in seeking to effect changes methods of discussion and persuasion should be preferred to methods of force;
7. To lead the pupil to see that he has duties and responsibilities towards his family, his school, his community, his province, the Dominion of Canada and the British Empire.

Source: Government of Ontario. Department of Education. Courses of Study. Grade X. Social Studies. Canadian History and Citizenship. 1938. Pg. 3

Ontario History Intermediate Division Aims – 1977

1. To develop an understanding of the Canadian identity and societal goals;
2. To develop an understanding of the roots of Canada's cultural heritage;
3. To develop a reasoned pride in Canada;
4. To develop an understanding of civic responsibility;
5. To develop an understanding of fundamental concepts central to the human experience, such as justice, change, diversity, order, individualism, the common good, worth of the individual, concern for others, dignity of labour, tradition, culture;
6. To develop the ability to imaginatively recreate the past;
7. To develop an awareness of the contributions of both women and men of all ages and groups to the development of our country.

Source: Government of Ontario. Ministry of Education. History. Intermediate Division. 1977. Pg. 6

Ontario Grade 9 or Grade 10 Contemporary Canada: Life in the Twentieth Century Aims – 1987

1. Develop an understanding of the Canadian political and legal systems;
2. Develop an appreciation of their rights and responsibilities as Canadian citizens;
3. Develop the ability to analyze, in historical perspective and in terms of future implications, contemporary issues of concern to Canadians as citizens of Canada and members of the world community;
4. Extend the cognitive skills needed to process and communicate information in a variety of contexts.

Source: Government of Ontario. Ministry of Education. History and Contemporary Studies. Intermediate Division. 1987. Pg. 47

Three Strands of Ontario Grade 10 Civics Course

Informed Citizenship	Purposeful Citizenship	Active Citizenship
An understanding of key civics questions, concepts, structures, and processes is fundamental to informed citizenship. In a diverse and rapidly changing society that invites political participation, the informed citizen should be able to demonstrate an understanding of contrasting views of citizenship within personal, community, national and global citizens. As well, they will learn the principles and practices of decision making.	It is important that students understand the role of the citizen, and the personal values and perspectives that guide citizen thinking and actions. Students need to reflect upon their personal sense of civic identity, moral purpose and legal responsibility – and to compare their views with those of others. They should examine important civic questions and consider the challenges of governing communities in which contrasting values, multiple perspectives, and differing purposes coexist.	Students need to learn basic civic literacy skills and have opportunities to apply those skills meaningfully by participating actively in the civic affairs of their community. Civic literacy skills include skills in the areas of research and inquiry, critical and creative thinking, decision-making, conflict resolution, and collaboration. Full participatory citizenship requires an understanding of practices used in civic affairs to influence public decision making.

Source: Government of Ontario. Ministry of Education. The Ontario Curriculum Grades 9 and 10. Canadian and World Studies. 2005. Pg. 63.

ANDREAS LADNER, JAN FIVAZ AND GIORGIO NADIG

3. VOTING ASSISTANCE APPLICATIONS AS TOOLS TO INCREASE POLITICAL PARTICIPATION AND IMPROVE CIVIC EDUCATION

In Switzerland, like in many other countries, low voting participation and a lack of political interest and knowledge have been a major concern for quite some time. Starting with some facts about the actual situation this article will present a promising way to enhance political interest, political knowledge and voting participation especially among younger people. At the core of these endeavours is a voting assistance application called *smartvote*.

POLITICAL PARTICIPATION IN SWITZERLAND

At the last Swiss parliamentary elections in October 2007 only slightly more than 48% of the Swiss citizens went to the polls (see Lutz 2008). Low voter turnout is, of course, not only a Swiss problem, but compared with other advanced democracies voter turnout in Switzerland is particularly low. According to the IDEA database on voter turnout since 1945, Switzerland ranks 138th of 172 countries.

As far as socio-demographic characteristics and attitudes of voters and non-voters are concerned, Switzerland shows a pattern which is well known to electoral researchers (see e.g. Bühlmann et al., 2003): voter turnout is lower among younger voters and higher among male voters, better educated voters and voters with higher income. Further it seems that citizens with a clear political orientation to the left or to the right are also more likely to participate in elections (see Table 1).

Switzerland is not only low in voter turnout but is also often regarded as low in political knowledge (see Linder, 1999: 272-275 and Kriesi, 1995: 111). Like low voter turnout – insufficient political knowledge is not exclusively a problem of younger citizens, but it is concentrated among them, an IEA study of political knowledge, political participation, politics and democracy among students ranked Switzerland near the bottom of the 27 countries included in the study (see Oser/Biedermann, 2003).

One reason that the situation in Switzerland is not very encouraging is that civic education is not very well developed. In several cantons it is not even mentioned in the curriculum, and in others there are no specific civic education classes. Instead, it is expected that civic education is taught in history or geography classes. And textbooks and other teaching materials for civic education are often inadequate.

Table 1. *Voter Turnout by Specific Groups at Elections in Switzerland, 1995-2007 (in percent)*

	1995	1999	2003	2007
Overall voter turnout	42	44	45	48
Gender				
Men	46	51	52	55
Women	39	37	40	43
Age				
18-24 years old	21	28	33	35
25-34 years old	30	29	31	34
35-44 years old	43	40	37	39
45-54 years old	51	52	50	53
55-64 years old	52	52	55	60
65-74 years old	61	57	61	58
75+ years old	58	56	53	62
Level of education				
Low	39	31	33	38
Medium	37	39	43	43
High	53	59	56	61
Household income (in Swiss Francs)				
-3,000	39	33	34	35
3,001-5,000	36	39	41	44
5,001-9,000	45	44	48	47
9,001+	52	59	55	58
Political orientation				
Left wing	52	52	55	57
Centre	41	42	41	44
Right wing	57	51	59	58

Source: Swiss Electoral Studies (SELECTS), Lutz (2008: 8ff.)

Nevertheless, there are also some signs of improvement: First, as we can see in Table 1, the over-all voter turnout in Switzerland has been steadily increasing since 1995 from 42 to 48 percent, and it is more specifically the turnout among 18 and 24 years old voters, which has increased more than twice as much as the general voter turnout, from 21 to 35 percent. In addition, there have been several recent attempts to increase the quality of civic education.

National and cantonal governments have recently been moving to define the main content of political education in the curricula and to develop new materials such as textbooks, e-learning tools, etc. in collaboration with textbook publishers, research networks and others.

A related nongovernmental effort was the development of *smartvote*[1]. *smartvote* is a new type of *voting assistance application (VAA)*, which has become more and more popular in Western Europe and the United States (see Walgrave et al., 2008). The first one of these tools was the *Stemwijzer*,[2] a website which was introduced during the 1998 election campaign in the Netherlands to help undecided voters.

Since 1998 a steadily growing number of VAAs has been implemented in the run-up to many elections in Western Europe and the United States.[3]

smartvote shares the basic design and related features of other VAAs, though there are some differences to reflect the specificities of the electoral system. They all share the same key function: the issue-matching system. VAAs like *smartvote* provide each voter an individualized comparison between her or his policy preferences and those of the candidates or parties. To achieve this, the voters are asked to answer a questionnaire on the VAA website of typically 20 to 30 questions on policy issues and preferred solutions to particular political problems. The VAA then compares these answers with the corresponding answers of political parties and/or candidates and calculates the congruence between the particular voter and the parties or candidates. The result is returned to the voter in form of a list ranking candidates or parties according to how closely they match the voter's preferences.

smartvote first offered its service during the 2003 Swiss parliamentary election campaign and since then on the occasion of about twenty-five national, regional and local level elections. Originally *smartvote* was not designed for use as a tool of civic education in schools nor targeted at young voters. However, it soon became obvious that this on-line tool has a great potential to boost attentiveness to politics among students and young citizens by providing information about political parties and candidates in a modern and convenient way. Therefore between 2005 and 2007 two versions of *smartvote* were developed oriented to the specific needs of students, young voters and for civic education purposes.[4]

There were three websites available for use during the 2007 election campaign for the Swiss parliament and these websites seemed to respond to the needs of many voters. During the election campaign, from June to October 2007, *smartvote* and its civic education versions were used about 940'000 times. Since about 2.3 million voters cast a ballot, this is an impressive level of usage.

Given an increasing but still very low voter turnout and an insufficient level of political knowledge the widespread use of *smartvote* leads us to ask if the use of *smartvote* increased interest in politics and, thus, higher voter turnout? To be clear we do not encourage anyone to vote solely based on a computer generated voting recommendation. Therefore we are especially interested in determining whether the use of *smartvote* encouraged voters to look for additional information or to discuss the outcome of the "smart-voting" process with friends or the family. In other words, did *smartvote* contribute to an active political citizenship or did it result only to "couch potato voters"?

Before we address these questions, we first describe *smartvote* as well as its two civic education versions and their functions in greater detail.

SMARTVOTE – FEATURES AND FUNCTIONS

The *smartvote* website was developed for the specific needs of voters in Swiss elections. Due to the rather complex Swiss electoral system *smartvote* is also rather complex, at least compared to other VAAs. The *smartvote* website consists of three main elements: the *smartvote* module with the issue-matching system, a comprehensive database providing information on all candidates running for office, and a module allowing for a graphic visualisation of political positions.

The core of the *smartvote* website is the issue-matching module. The first step consists of all candidates completing the questionnaire consisting of up to 70 questions about the most important actual political issues. Only complete answer sets by candidates are included into the subsequent calculation of voting recommendations.

About six weeks before the election day the second, operational phase starts. The *smartvote* website is made accessible to voters in the form of the three steps arrive at their individual voting recommendation:

1. *Voters have to specify their political profile:* To do so they are asked to answer the same questionnaire as the candidates – except that they can choose either version: the "deluxe version" which includes all the questions, or the "rapid version", which consists of only 24 to 36 questions.
2. *Voters customize their voting recommendation:* After specifying their political profile voters have to indicate in which constituency (electoral district) they live and for which constituency they want to receive a voting recommendation. Due to the Swiss electoral system they have also to decide whether they wish to receive a voting recommendation for lists/parties or for individual candidates.[5]
3. *Calculation and presentation of the voting recommendation:* Based on this information *smartvote* generates an individual voting recommendation in the form of a list ranking of the candidates or parties for each voter.

If a voter wishes to receive a voting recommendation for lists/parties the procedure is the same with the exception that instead of the answers of single candidates the answers of lists or parties are used.

ADDITIONAL FEATURES

Apart from the *smartvote* module the website features offers additional services. The most important additional services are:

- The website contains a database with all candidates, including extensive portraits with a political and personal profile.
- The website provides tools for visual analysis of political preferences: the so-called *smartspider* and *smartmap* charts (see Figure 1). Both analytical graphs are based on the candidates' answers to the *smartvote* questionnaire. The *smartspider* shows the degree of agreement or disagreement on eight major political issue areas formulated as political goals in a spider net graph. The *smartmap* is based on a system of coordinates with two major ideological cleavages serving as axes – the "north-south axis" for the cleavage between liberal and conservative position and the "east-west axis" for the left-right cleavage.[6]

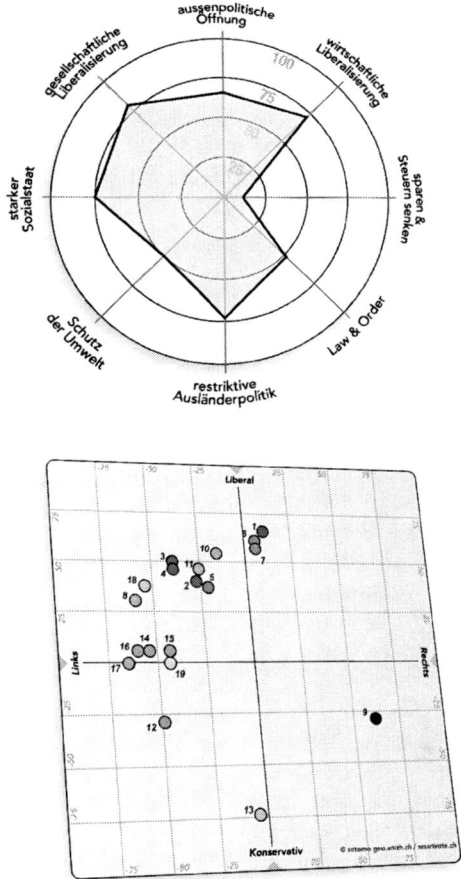

Figure 1. Examples of Smartspider (on the left) and Smartmap (on the right)

RUNNING SMARTVOTE – QUALITY CONTROL AND CREDIBILITY

The quality and credibility of the offered services is the key to successfully running a website like *smartvote*. This rests on a number of factors, in particular, the fact that *smartvote* was developed by *Politools,* a non-partisan network of researchers and computer scientists from different Swiss universities. It is responsible for running the website and also for the further development of the tool. No interest group or private corporation provides financial support; no political actor is directly engaged in the project. Hence there is wide confidence the methods used to calculate the voting recommendations.

The credibility of the *smartvote* questionnaire is also reinforced by its being updated before each election to reflect the political issues of the day and the regional/local context. Criteria underlying the selection of questions include coverage of a broad range of issues, relevance, comprehensibility, and an appropriate mixture of past, present and future issues. Although there are different sources that provide input toward the individual questions, the final responsibility for the composition of the questionnaire rests with the *Politools* network alone.

THE DIFFERENCE BETWEEN SMARTVOTE AND OTHER VAAS

smartvote is neither the first nor is it the best-known of all VAAs, but it is probably the most sophisticated of these tools. Its modular software architecture and its potential for incorporating further extensions make it possible for *smartvote* to offer its services for simultaneous multiple elections with overlapping constituencies (i.e. one national, one regional and two local elections). It also calculates specific voting recommendations for each constituency (electoral district) and not just one for the whole election (as does *Stemwijzer,* for example).

The questionnaire used by *smartvote* is more than twice as long as questionnaires used by other VAAs. The recommendation is thus based upon more empirical data and is therefore more reliable; however, all data from past elections are stored in the database, allowing for time series analysis.

The Use of smartvote *for Civic Education*

We can now turn to the use of *smartvote* for civic education. In the last few years, deficits in civic education have been held increasingly responsible for a lack of political interest and low political participation among younger citizens in Switzerland (as elsewhere). Any attempt to improve the situation however – we believe – has to consider the particular ways younger people these days use the media, i.e. the internet, and treat information. The closer a teaching tool reflects a real life situation – in our case the act of voting – the more likely is it to attract young people.

This is where VAAs like *smartvote* step in. These tools can help citizens to make up their minds, they are internet based and correspond to the way younger people gather and use information. Moreover, they are not simply games but touch upon a real life situation.

For of the Swiss parliamentary Elections in 2007 two projects, the *Parteienkompass* (*party compass*) and the VAA *myVote* were developed. Their aim was to increase the level of information about political parties, candidates and their political programs as well as to increase participation of young voters.

PARTEIENKOMPASS.CH (PARTY COMPASS): THE SCHOOL VERSION OF SMARTVOTE

In summer 2006, an adapted *smartvote* version for civic education, the so called *"party compass"*[7] was implemented in collaboration with one of the largest educational textbook publishers[8] in Switzerland. The *party compass* addresses itself primarily to teachers and students (upper secondary level) throughout Switzerland.

The *party compass* website consists of three main elements: an adapted version of the *smartvote* module with the issue-matching system, a comprehensive database providing information on the basic political positions and values of the five most important political parties in Switzerland as well as the party system in general and a download section where further information about the tool itself and the political parties is provided.

The issue-matching system used for the *party compass* has the same design and operates similarly to the one used by *smartvote*. A shorter questionnaire is used and the questions cannot be weighted. By answering a questionnaire on the most important political issues the *party compass* calculates an individual voting recommendation for each voter. Unlike the *smartvote* issue-matching system the *party compass* does not compare the answer to those of single candidates but to those of the five most important Swiss parties and calculates the congruence to each of them, ranking them in the order from the highest to the lowest.

In the database and the download section a great deal of background information is provided, such as general information about the party (name, president, secretary, website, etc.), a short summary of the party history, information about the voters profile (e.g. gender, age, income, education level etc.), statistics about the strength of the party, the questionnaire with the answers by party, a map indicating the number of voters per region in Switzerland, the *smartmap* and the *smartspider* portrait of the political position of the parties and the users.

What are the benefits of the *party compass* for civic education? The primary aim of the *"party compass"* is to give insights in the political positions and values of the Swiss political parties and into the party system in general in a non-partisan manner. Furthermore, by answering the questionnaire the student discovers his or her political position and the party which represents this position best. He or she can then compare the result with those of the political parties that match less and find out why. By discussing the results and presenting their own position to the rest of the class the future voters become more familiar with the basic political positions of the main Swiss political parties, and develop their capacity to arrive at a partisan political position.

For teachers the *party compass* is an additional instrument of civic education. The teacher can discuss and explain the most important political issues by presenting the questionnaire to his class. All the questions are accompanied by some background information and explanations including pros and cons. Discussing the pros and cons in class helps the future voters learn to come to a decision in an active and enjoyable way.

MYVOTE.CH

Electoral abstention, higher issue complexity and the lack of transparency in election campaigns were the main reasons why the project *myVote* was initiated. The primary aim of project *myVote* is to further interest in this democratic act, to inform young voters objectively and neutrally about the elections, and to help them identify preferred candidates in order to induce them to participate.

Young people aged 16 to 30 years have a different understanding and knowledge of the Swiss political landscape. Most are unaware of their own political position and this is a big obstacle to their choosing among the various candidates running for office. The first step is for voters to locate themselves in the political landscape and recognize that they have a political opinion. The second step is for the voters to be shown that there are candidates running for office who represent their opinion better than others.

The Swiss parliamentary election in October 2007 was the perfect opportunity to point out the importance of elections to future voters and to motivate them to participate. To take advantage of it, *Politools* initiated a civic education project group to establish the *myVote*[9] project. The main objective was to develop a specific website for the 2007 elections with the *smartvote* website as a model.

Though the *myVote* website consists of the same basic elements, it is specifically designed for young people and first time voters, offering an uncomplicated introduction to the themes "policy" and "elections". It seeks not only to provide guidance and stimulates thinking about politics, but is also designed to help to put the available political knowledge into action. By using *myVote* he or she should be able to answer: Where do I stand politically and which politicians or party running for office best represent my interests best?

The main differences distinguishing the *myVote* from smartvote website were:
- A new design;
- Only the short version of the questionnaire;
- Texts with a more common and understandable language;
- The program run of the *smartvote* module with the issue-matching system was changed. After the user has responded the questionnaire he first gets his own *smartspider* displaying his own political position so that he can locate himself in the political landscape. Only as a second step does the user get a voting recommendation for the candidates or lists/parties of a chosen constituency.

Even the best and most developed VAAs cannot contribute to civic education when they are not known by their target public. Developers have to collaborate with textbook publishers, teachers' associations, youth organisations and media partners in order to allow for the fact.

Collaboration with a media partner makes it possible to reach new and first time voters who do not attend an institution of learning offering courses in civic education. With "20 Minuten"[10] an ideal media partner was found for the project. "20 Minuten" is Switzerland's most popular free daily newspaper with a combined print run in German and a French of almost 650,000 copies and over 1,500,000 readers each day.[11] Moreover, "20 Minuten" runs the largest online community information platform in Switzerland and most of its readers and users are in the target age group, 14 to 34 years old.

Political websites should provide citizens with a wide variety of information about political issues, parties and candidates; and online forums, blogs and chats should foster deliberative discussions among citizens as well as between citizens and the political elite. In the run up to the Swiss parliamentary election such an online platform and the plan for its use was elaborated in collaboration with "20 Minuten".

Before the *myVote* website went online the civic education group of *Politools* organised together with Lernetz[12], another developer of e-learning tools, an advanced training course on the subject "politics in class". The primary aim of the course was to give the teachers an overview of the latest e-tools for civic education. After a short lecture about *smartvote* the project *myVote* was presented by explaining how it could be used for civic education. The teachers also had the opportunity to test the website and to give their feedback.

Two and a half months before the election the platform went online and the campaign started. During this period in the German print edition, a complete page was dedicated to the upcoming elections twice a week. In terms of content the printed articles and those posted on the Internet were similar. Among the items on the platform were:
- an inline-frame of the *smartvote* module with the issue-matching system;
- a problem-barometer where users can indicate their concerns;
- portraits of famous Swiss and their *smartspider* graphs;
- two kind of blogs, one by candidates running for office, the second by an ex-politician and an ex-editor-in-chief on which the user had the possibility to comment;
- e-talk section. Two candidates from opposing parties were invited to a discussion and the users could ask them questions online in real time;
- a public opinion poll (the results were also published in the print edition);
- a political quiz, where users could test their political know-how;
- a wide variety of information about political parties and the political and voting system in Switzerland.

During the campaign period flyers were distributed at chosen youth events and advertisements were placed to promote the "20 Minuten" online platform and the *myVote* website. The impact of the campaign and the promotion was remarkable. Slightly over 50,000 recommendations were generated on the "20 Minuten" platform and 27,000 on the *myVote* website which constituted 8% of all the recommendations generated in the lead time before the Swiss parliamentary elections by *smartvote*. After SRG SSR idée Suisse – the main media partner of *smartvote*[13] – "20 Minuten" was the media partner that generated the most recommendations.

USE AND IMPACT OF *SMARTVOTE*

The increasing popularity of *smartvote* convinces us believe of the vast potential of such tools to make politics more accessible and attractive to a younger and wider public.

INCREASE AND BREAKTHROUGH – THE USE OF SMARTVOTE IN RECENT YEARS

When *smartvote* was offered for the first time during the campaign for the 2003 parliament elections in Switzerland, it was used about 255,000 times by voters. Of course this does not mean that *smartvote* was used by 255,000 voters, because some used it more than once. The actual number of users can only be estimated. A realistic approach based on server statistics and post electoral surveys shows that the average user generates between two and four voting recommendations. Thus the effective number of voters using *smartvote* was 2003 between 60,000 and 125,000. In the 2007 elections *smartvote* and the *myVote* website were used about 940,000 times,[14] therefore the effective number of users can be estimated as between 250,000 and 450,000 voters. That means that about 15–20 percent of the voters were *smartvote* users. Initial findings from the 2007 Selects survey, which asked the voters if they had used *smartvote* or not lend credence to back up this estimate with between twelve and 15 percent of voters responding affirmatively.

Eliminating double counts out of the user statistics is very time consuming; instead we developed a very simple benchmarking method to compare the intensity of the use of *smartvote* between elections, namely to express the number of voting recommendations as a percentage of the number of votes cast. Note that this calculation does not reveal the actual number of *smartvote* users, but only of the increase or decrease over time.

Table 2 compares the use of *smartvote* over several parliamentarian elections in Switzerland between 2003 and 2007 and shows a clear increase. As we can see, the use of *smartvote* in national elections was almost four times as high in 2007 as in 2003.

During its first years the *smartvote* website was seen as an interesting innovation in election campaigns. But with its growing use, *smartvote*'s reputation grew, the

Table 2. Use of Smartvote by Voters, 2003-2007

Elections	*smartvote* use (number of voting recommendations)	*smartvote* use/voter turnout (in percent)
National level		
Swiss parliament 2003	255,000	11.7
Swiss parliament 2007	938,403	39.5
Regional parliaments		
Canton of St. Gall 2004	16,000	16.2
Canton of Thurgau 2004	7,750	13.7
Canton of Berne 2006	35,900	16.7
Canton of Zurich 2007	30,465	10.4

Canton of Lucerne 2007	9,864	9.1
Local parliaments		
City of St. Gall 2004	4,000	23.4
City of Berne 2004	9,500	28.9
City of Geneva 2005	22,900	24.9
City of Zurich 2006	15,100	22.8

Source: Ladner et al. (2008); Fivaz and Schwarz (2007)

run-up to the 2007 elections were a breakthrough with *smartvote* becoming seen as an essential component of every Swiss electoral campaign. A clear indicator of this change is the participation rate of candidates. In 2003 only 50% of the candidates running for a seat in the national parliament participated in *smartvote* and answered the questionnaire. In 2007 85% of the candidates participated.

This high rate of participation among candidates can be explained by risk non-participation in *smartvote* has come to constitute for the candidates; but what explains the rather impressive increase of use by voters? There are probably three answers to this question:

– First, the complexity of the Swiss electoral system. Swiss voters have the possibility to put together an individual ballot. In a constituency with 20 seats, each voter gets 20 votes. The voter can give all votes to just one party list or can split the votes and select specific candidates from different parties and put them together on his ballot. In the Canton of Zurich voters can thus choose among up to 1,000 candidates. Therefore a tool like *smartvote* offers a very useful service to voters by providing them an efficient means of scanning the political preferences of all candidates. Neither the media nor any other website is able to offer such a service.

– Second, *smartvote* seems to meet a real demand on the part of the voters by offering an individualized service. Every voter gets her or his individual voting recommendation based on her or his own political preferences.

– Third, *smartvote* is an instrument developed by the *Politools* network – a non-profit and non-partisan organisation. This fact lies at the base of the high level of trust voters have in *smartvote*.

IMPACT ON VOTER TURNOUT

The *smartvote* website is not only a popular instrument for informing potential voters in the run-up to elections in Switzerland. It is also the object of scientific research. As a part of a research framework at the University of Zurich[15] in 2005 a project was initiated to analyse the impact of the *smartvote* website on political participation, on voters' decision-making processes and on the strategies of candidates and party elites.[16] Before and after the 2007 elections this research project conducted several surveys among candidates and voters that used the *smartvote* website.

A first question which can be posed with the available data is what the typical *smartvote* user looks like. The findings are not really surprising and correspond to the findings of other research regarding the socio-demographic characteristics of Internet users. The typical *smartvote* user is young (average age of 37.5 years), male, with a higher level of education and income.

Table 3 shows some characteristics of *smartvote* users corresponding to categories from the Selects survey mentioned in Table 1. The Selects survey revealed that women, young citizens and citizens with a low or medium level of education and income have a below average turnout rate. The data displayed in Table 4 indicates that in itself providing *smartvote* does not appear likely to substantially boost voter turnout, since the groups with a below average turnout rate are clearly under represented among the *smartvote* users. This would mean that *smartvote* is inadequately addressing the "target groups", i.e. those among which the problem of insufficient political participation is most pressing. But there is one important exception: *smartvote* users are young. This means that for this group at least there is a real potential for a considerable impact on the level of political participation.

Table 3. Socio-demographic Characteristics of Smartvote Users, 2007

	Smartvote users
Gender	
Men	67
Women	33
Age	
18-24 years old	21
25-34 years old	28
35-44 years old	21
45-54 years old	15
55-64 years old	10
65-74 years old	4
75+ years old	1
Level of education	
Low	3
Medium	54
High	43
Household income (in Swiss Francs)	
-3'000	5
3'001-5'000	11
5'001-9'000	40
9'001+	44
Political orientation	
Left wing	31
Centre	55
Right wing	14

Source: NCCR "Democracy", IP16 "smart-voting", post electoral survey among voters.

Table 4 presents a somewhat different picture from the conclusions drawn above. It is based on responses to our survey, in which we asked the *smartvote* users if use of the tool had an influence on their decision to go to the polls. Just under 40% reported that the use of *smartvote* had a decisive or at least slight influence on their decision to vote. Based on the estimate of a total of about 300,000 *smartvote* users, that would mean that about 120,000 or 5% of Swiss voters were positively influenced by *smartvote* in their decision to participate at the 2007 elections. Of course these numbers should be treated with caution, but they indicate that *smartvote* does have an identifiable positive impact on voter turnout. More importantly, this impact is even clearer among the groups with a below average turnout rate: women and young voters seem to be more strongly influenced to vote by *smartvote* than are other groups (see Table 4). In sum, then, we arrive at an ambivalent response to the question of the impact of *smartvote* use on political participation. The socio-demographic characteristics of *smartvote* users are such as to indicate that it is used largely by those in groups likely to vote; but, on the other hand, when surveyed, these *smartvote* users themselves indicate a meaningful positive impact on their decision to vote. This suggests that *smartvote* has at least the potential for a significant effect on voter turnout.

Table 4. Impact of Using Smartvote on the Decision to Vote or Not

	Decisively motivated to vote	Slightly motivated to vote	No influence	Slightly detained to vote	Decisively detained to vote	N
Total	15.4	23.6	60.3	0.5	0.2	17,147
Gender						
Men	12.5	23.8	63.1	0.5	0.2	11,890
Women	22.0	23.3	54.0	0.6	0.1	5,226
Age Groups						
18-24	20.3	25.4	53.6	0.5	0.1	3,600
25-34	17.4	24.1	57.7	0.6	0.2	5,043
35-44	13.6	23.3	62.4	0.5	0.2	3,602
45-54	11.9	22.7	64.7	0.6	0.1	2,500
55-64	10.1	21.8	67.4	0.4	0.2	1,667
65-74	8.7	20.5	70.3	0.3	0.2	644
75+	15.4	19.8	63.7	1.1	0.0	91

Source: NCCR "Democracy", IP16 "smart-voting", post electoral survey among voters.

IMPACT ON OPINION FORMATION

The findings about the impact of *smartvote* on the voting decisions themselves are much clearer. Two thirds of *smartvote* users say that the *smartvote* voting recommendation had a clear impact on their decision for which parties and/or candidates they voted. And, again, this impact is strongest among women and younger voters (see Table 5).

Table 5. Impact of Using Smartvote on the Voting Decision

Did the *smartvote* voting recommendation have an impact on your voting decision?			
	Yes	No	N
Total	66.4	33.6	16,335
Gender			
Men	65.0	35.0	11,354
Women	69.9	30.1	4,949
Age Groups			

18-24	71.1	28.9	3,352
25-34	73.3	26.7	4,764
35-44	68.0	32.0	3,462
45-54	58.6	41.4	2,408
55-64	53.2	46.8	1,638
65-74	48.8	51.2	625
75+	41.9	58.1	86

Source: NCCR "Democracy", IP16 "smart-voting", post electoral survey among voters.

Table 6. Impact of Using Smartvote on Different Aspects of Opinion Formation

	18-24	25-34	35-44	45-54	55-64	65-74	74+	Average
Using smartvote helped to vote for candidates/parties on an improved information basis.								
Agree	56.4	57.5	56.6	49.8	47.6	42.9	46.4	54.5
Rather agree	31.4	30.3	28.9	30.5	28.6	30.9	23.8	30.1
Rather disagree	7.3	7.4	7.5	8.3	10.8	13.2	22.6	8.1
Disagree	4.8	4.8	7.0	11.5	12.9	13	22.6	7.4
Using smartvote motivated me to look for additional information about particular issues.								
Agree	18.4	14.8	14.6	16.3	16.4	16.1	17.6	15.9
Rather agree	33.1	30.8	32.0	32.2	34.4	36.1	31.8	32.3
Rather disagree	29.3	32.0	29.6	29.2	27.0	27.6	23.5	29.8
Disagree	19.2	22.5	23.8	22.3	22.2	20.2	27.1	22.0
Using smartvote motivated me to look for additional information about particular candidates/parties.								
Agree	23.9	21.8	19.9	17.7	16.5	13.2	15.3	20.4
Rather agree	37.2	36.4	36.4	34.6	31.4	33.0	24.7	35.6
Rather disagree	23.1	23.5	22.9	25.4	28.2	31.4	28.2	24.3
Disagree	15.9	18.3	20.8	22.3	23.9	22.4	31.8	19.7
Using smartvote motivated me to engage in discussions about particular issues with other people.								
Agree	35.1	30.5	24.8	23.3	20.8	16.9	16.9	27.7
Rather agree	35.6	38.0	37.3	38.5	37.5	36.8	28.9	37.3
Rather disagree	17.6	18.0	21.3	20.4	21.4	24.2	28.9	19.6
Disagree	11.7	13.6	16.6	17.7	20.2	22.1	25.3	15.4
Using smartvote motivated me to engage in discussions about particular candidates/parties.								
Agree	38.0	34.2	28.4	25.7	21.7	18.8	15.9	30.7
Rather agree	35.2	37.1	37.7	38.6	36.6	37.8	39.0	37.0
Rather disagree	15.2	17.0	18.0	19.6	21.7	20.8	19.5	17.8
Disagree	11.5	11.7	15.8	16.2	19.9	22.6	25.6	14.4

Source: NCCR "Democracy", IP16 "smart-voting", post electoral survey among voters; N = 16'683-16'731.

In order to get more information about the impact of *smartvote* on decision-making processes the *smartvote* users were asked to fill in a small battery of questions on different ways *smartvote* could have influenced their decision making (see Table 6).

The goal is not to have voters simply follow the computer generated voting recommendation, but rather to aid them in their decision. Therefore it is important to know just how *smartvote* impacts on voters' decision making processes. In Table 6 some of the ways the *smartvote* website influences voters are displayed. From it, we see

- First, *smartvote* seems to have had more impact on information about candidates or parties than about policy issues. Fifty-six percent of the users said that they

were looking for additional information about parties and/or candidates as a consequence of their *smartvote* voting recommendation.
- Second, *smartvote* seems to have a clear impact on the number of discussions about policy issues as well as about parties and candidates that its users had with their families and friends. About two thirds of the users said that the main impetus for such discussions was the use of *smartvote*.

The table also confirms the pattern already in the tables above: younger citizens are using the *smartvote* website more intensively than older ones.

CONCLUSIONS AND OUTLOOK

Civic education cannot only be limited to school-based activities seeking to promote democratic involvement by young people (see Milner et al., 2008). It must be seen in a wider context. Of course civic education of voters has to start at school but it should not only focus on young people and first time voters. Low political participation and insufficient political knowledge are not exclusive to younger citizens; they constitute a wider challenge for most modern democracies. Therefore civic education programs should be such as to also reach vulnerable older citizens.

The above presented Swiss website *smartvote* is one possible way to do so. It offers a real service to voters by preparing information (reduction of complexity and shrinking of the amount of available information) and assisting them in their decision making process. The website proved to be extremely popular among Swiss voters in the five years of its existence. Based on data from surveys among the *smartvote* users it is possible to do an initial evaluation. Our findings indicate that although *smartvote* will not boost voter turnout considerably, it does have positive effects on political interest, knowledge and participation of voters of every age – though by far strongest effects appear to be among the young voters.

The development of the supplementary *smartvote*-related e-tools, *party compass* and *myVote,* have been attempts to tap its potential for the civic education of students and young voters. Both *party compass* as well as the *myVote* website were pilot projects. All the project partners (Politools as the owner of *smartvote*, the text book publisher, the newspapers and universities) came to the same conclusion: they judged both projects as promising enough to invest more time and money in further development. Both projects received numerous very useful feedbacks from teachers (and students).

The feedbacks showed clearly that there is still room for improvement, especially in two areas. First, some of the questions of the *smartvote* questionnaire were too complex or otherwise not well suited for use in school classes. There is a need to further simplify the language of the questionnaire and to provide more background information about the policy issues mentioned (e.g. by an FAQ section or glossary). Secondly, teachers were critical of the lack of complementing didactic tools like text books, handouts and practical advice on how to integrate these new online tools into their curriculum.

Combined with the findings from the user surveys, the feedback from teachers confirmed that *smartvote* and its civic education applications were opening a door toward bringing Swiss politics closer to the citizens.

NOTES

1. See http://www.smarvote.ch (also partly available in English)
2. See http://www.stemwijzer.nl
3. The "Stemwijzer" was also implemented in Switzerland (http://www.politarena.ch) and Germany (http://www.wah-lo-mat.de). In Austria a similar website was developed (http://www.wahlkabine.at) as well as in the United Kingdom (http://www.whodoivotefor.co.uk), the United States (http://www.project-vote-smart.org; http://www.ontheissues.org), and one may find also a VAA for non-electoral comparisons with historical political figures from Stalin to Nelson Mandela (http://www.politicalcompass.org).
4. See http://www.parteienkompass.ch and http://www.my-vote.ch
5. The Swiss electoral system offers voters several options to express their preferences: they can vote for whole party lists or they can put together an individual ballot by choosing the candidates from different parties or lists they want to vote for.
6. Of course, the two axes are designed for the Swiss – or European at most – political context and would need to be adapted in other countries.
7. See http://www.parteienkompass.ch (only available in German)
8. See http://www.hep-verlag.ch
9. See http://www.my-vote.ch (only available in German, French and Italian)
10. See http://www.20min.ch
11. See (http://www.schweizerpresse.ch/fileadmin/schweizerpresse/brancheninfos/allgemein/15_gr.Tageszeit._Aufl_Le ser_08_1.pdf)
12. See http://www.lernetz.ch
13. See all media partners http://www.smartvote.ch/side_menu/partner/partners.php?who=v
14. About seven percent of the users were attracted by the *myVote* website.
15. This research network is the National Centre of Competence in Research (NCCR) "Challenges to Democracy in the 21st Century" (short NCCR "Democracy"; www.nccr-democracy.uzh.ch).
16. The project is called IP16 "smart-voting" (www.nccr-democracy.uzh.ch/nccr/knowledge_transfer/ip16) and is run by the Institut de hautes etudes en administration publique (IDHEAP) at the University of Lausanne, at the Universities of Zurich and Berne and at the European University Institute (EUI) at Florence, Italy.

REFERENCES

Bühlmann, M., Freitag, M., & Vatter, A. (2003). Die schweigende Mehrheit. Eine Typologie der Schweizer Nichtwählerschaft. In P. Sciarini, S.-b. Hardmeier, & A. Vatter (Eds.). (pp. 27–58). Bern: Schweizer Wahlen 1999.

Fivaz, J., & Schwarz, D. (2007, March 14–15). *Nailing the pudding to the wall – E-Democracy as catalyst for transparency and accountability*; paper presented at the International Conference on Direct Democracy in Latin America. Argentina: Buenos Aires.

Heanni Hoti, A. (2003b). Chancengleichheit und Gleichstellung von Migrantinnen und Migranten – Chancengleichheit und Gleichstellung von Frauen. In Jugend und Politik. Ergebnisse der IEA Studie zu politischem Wissen, Demokratieverständnis und gesellschaftlichem Engagement von Jugendlichen in der Schweiz im Vergleich mit 27 Ländern, ed. Fritz Oser and Horst Biedermann (pp. 101–127). Zürich, Chur: Verlag Rüegger.

Kersten, B. (2003). Politisches Verstehen der Schweizer Schülerinnen und Schüler. In Jugend und Politik. Ergebnisse der IEA Studie zu politischem Wissen, Demokratieverständnis und gesellschaftlichem Engagement von Jugendlichen in der Schweiz im Vergleich mit 27 Ländern, ed. Fritz Oser and Horst Biedermann (pp. 39–54). Zürich, Chur: Verlag Rüegger.

Kriesi, H. (1995). *Le système politique suisse*. Paris.
Ladner, A., Felder, G., & Fivaz, J. (2008). *Are Voting Advice Applications (VAAs) more than toys? First findings on impact and accountability of VAAs*; IDHEAP Working paper 2/2008; Lausanne.
Linder, W. (1999). *Schweizerische Demokratie. Institutionen, Prozesse, Perspektiven*. Bern.
Lutz, G. (2008). *EidgenössischeWahlen 2007. Wahlteilnahme und Wahlentscheid*. Lausanne.
Maiello, C. (2003). Politisches Engagement und politische Aktivität. In Jugend und Politik. Ergebnisse der IEA Studie zu politischem Wissen, Demokratieverständnis und gesellschaftlichem Engagement von Jugendlichen in der Schweiz im Vergleich mit 27 Ländern, ed. Fritz Oser, Fritz und Horst Biedermann (pp. 129–153). Zürich, Chur: Verlag Rüegger.
Milner, H., Nguyen, C., & Boylston, F. (2008). *Variations in civic education: The IDEA civic education database*. Montréal
Oser, F., & Biedermann, H. (2003). Jugend ohne Politik. Ergebnisse der IEA Studie zu politischem Wissen, Demokratieverständnis und gesellschaftlichem Engagement von Jugendlichen in der Schweiz im Vergleich mit 27 anderen Ländern; Zürich.
Reichenbach, R. (1998). Zwischen Polisidyll und massendemokratischem Realismus. Bemerkungen anlässlich der Ergebnisse einer Expertenbefragung zur Politische Bildung in der Schweiz. In Politische Bildung und staatsbürgerliche Erziehung in der Schweiz. Perspektiven aus der Deutschschweiz und der Westschweiz, ed. Fritz Oser and Roland Reichbach (pp. 15–35). Freiburg: Universitätsverlag Freiburg schweiz
Quesel Carsten und Dominik Allenspach (2007). Rahmenkonzept zur politischen Bildung in der Volksschule. Erarbeitet zuhanden des Departements für Bildung und Kultur des Kantons Solothurn. Solothurn, März 2007.

VINCENT TOURNIER

4. ATTITUDES TOWARD CITIZENSHIP AND POLITICAL PARTICIPATION UNDERLYING APPROACHES TO CIVIC EDUCATION

A Comparative Analysis[1]

INTRODUCTION

The aim of civic education is to produce good citizens. But this objective raises two major difficulties. The first one is to know if one can act directly on children or teenagers. Research in political socialization has shown that the impact of direct and explicit political teaching at school is quite low (Somit et al., 1958; Christenson & Capretta, 1968; Langton & Jennings, 1968). Even for the acquisition of political knowledge, school appears to have a minor impact (Dudley & Gitelson, 2003). Of course, education plays an important role in political socialization, but its influence seems to be more indirect than direct, and it passes essentially by acquisition of cognitive skills, political discussion, participation in classrooms, and relationships with peers or extra-curricular activities (Smith, 1999; Galston, 2001). Moreover, many years of research in political socialization have shown that the forming of political attitudes is a complex process in which informal agents like parents or peers and, more generally, the social environment, influence the children much more than explicit teaching at school. International surveys have confirmed, in the continuity of the seminal work of Almond and Verba (1963), that political and civic attitudes are rooted in cultural context and that they are relatively stable over time (Inglehart, 2000).

The second difficulty concerns the definition of civic virtue. What is a good citizen? Ancient Greek philosophers gave us a simple definition: a good citizen is one who participates in city life and respects the law. But modern political thought has seriously questioned this definition (Heather, 2004). In liberal philosophy, in which human rights are of crucial importance, a good citizen is educated and thereby independent from state and authorities (Condorcet); he is also capable of defending his religious beliefs (Constant) or his freedom of speech (Mill), and of joining associations (Tocqueville). The divide can be radical: is a good citizen one who obeys the law in the strict sense (Plato) or one who chooses to follow his conscience (Thoreau)? More generally, major political theories such as republicanism, liberalism or communitarianism, each defending diverging ideals of citizenship, tend to promote different and contradictory visions of civic virtue. There can thus be never-ending discussion on the notions usually employed to describe good citizenship. For example, trust in government and political engagement are traditionally seen as civic qualities, but one can also easily put forward that distrust is preferable to trust in order to keep the government under pressure – or that a certain passivity is better than an excess of participation which leads to instability and violence.

These normative difficulties invite us to ask the question differently. Scholars have suggested that we start not from an ideal notion of citizenship – which is necessarily normative and non-consensual – but from the way people themselves perceive citizenship (Conover, Crewe & Searing, 1991; Theisse-Morse, 1993; Dalton, 2008). This suggestion is very stimulating, especially since international surveys have given us the opportunity to compare civic attitudes among countries, notably in young people (Torney et al., 2001; Torney & Amadeo, 2003). Here, using the 2004 ISSP survey of representative samples in some forty countries, we shall demonstrate that different representations of the "good citizen" coexist in the world, and suggest that these representations, which are the product of specific national context, are relatively stable. Moreover, we shall see that the two main civic virtues, respect for the law and (unconventional) political participation, may, unexpectedly, turn out to be contradictory.

THE DATA

In 2004, the International Social Survey Program on Citizenship (ISSP) survey posed many questions about citizenship and political participation.

Civic conceptions The central question posed in the ISSP survey asked respondents to define their conception of citizenship. It provided a list of 10 characteristics, with answers from a scale of 1 to 7^2. Using these data Chart 1 displays the different statistical breakdowns for each characteristic, the content of which is explored below.

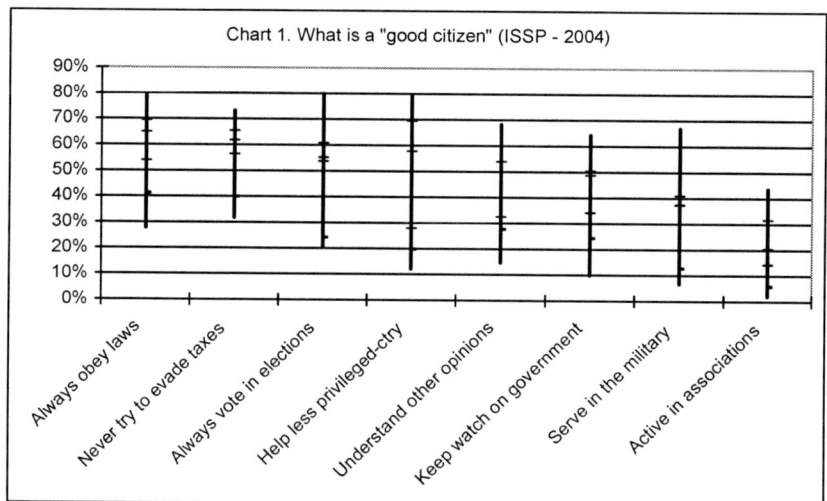

Political participation To measure political participation, the survey proposed six forms of engagement (sign a petition, boycott certain products, take part in a demonstration, attend political meetings, contact a politician and donate money or raise funds) and three types of associational engagement (political parties, trade unions and religious organisations).

Table 1. Dimensions of Political Participation

	I Unconventional participation	II Conventional participation
% variance explained	36.4%	11.9%
Sign a petition	.741	.081
Boycott certain products	.743	.011
Take part in demonstration	.734	.018
Attend political meeting	.607	.396
Contact a politician	.591	.415
Raise funds, donate money	.613	.225
Belong to political parties	.113	.728
Belong to trade unions	.299	.396
Belong to religious organisations	-.027	.669

ISSP 2004 Citizenship, 37 countries, weighted data.
Principal components analysis with varimax rotation.

A factor analysis reveals two distinct axes (Table 1). One is related to conventional participation (attend political meeting, contact a politician, donate money and engagement in associations: reliability = .64) and the other to unconventional participation (sign a petition, boycott certain products, take part in demonstration: reliability = .69). To create indicators for each, I used factor analysis. We can see great variety in the relative importance of each (Chart 2). For example, France and the United States represent two very different models of political participation: with conventional participation far more important in the US, while France has developed a strong tradition of unconventional engagement.

Control variables To test the relationships, we included a number of variables: sex, age (in years), education, marital status, active/inactive, subjective social class, rural/urban, church attendance, religious preferences (catholic or protestant), left-right wing, interest in politics (2 items, Cronbach = .72), interpersonal trust, trust in political leaders, satisfaction with democracy and proximity with government (2 items, Cronbach = 65).

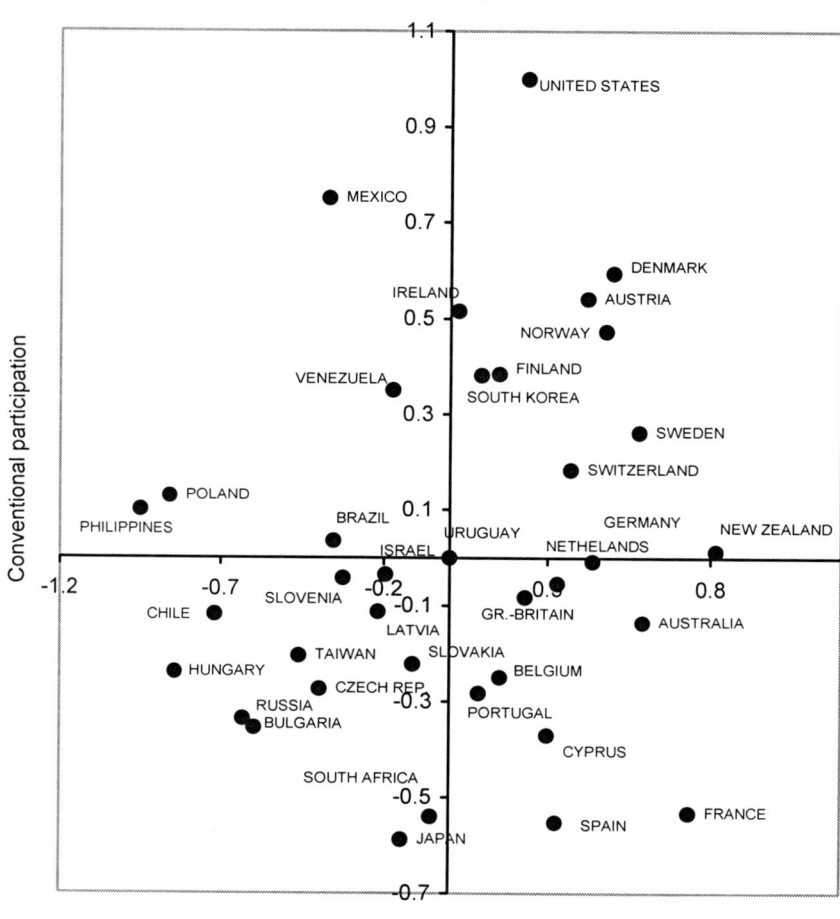

Graph 2. *Conventional and unconventional participation*
(ISSP - 2004)

THE DIMENSIONS OF CITIZENSHIP

A factor analysis of all the data on perceptions of citizenship from the participating countries allows us to identify three axes (Table 2). The first axis (34% of the variance) revolves around the political dimension, tied essentially to voting, volunteering in associations and keeping watch on the government (Cronbach = .66); the second (13%) around solidarity (helping poor people or poor countries; Cronbach = .77); and the third (10%) around legality and rules (obeying laws and paying taxes; Cronbach = .69).

There is a parallel to three steps of citizenship that were identified by Thomas Marshall in his seminal book: the civil dimension, political dimension and social dimension (Marshall, 1950), and we thus use the expressions of political citizenship, social citizenship and civil citizenship to designate the civic values. However, unlike Marshall, who took a historical approach to the three-fold classification of rights of citizens these, we see the three forms of citizenship to coexist; what differentiates in civic conceptions is less chronology than culture.

Different patterns are found as to the value placed on these three types of citizenship. At the aggregate level, there is no consistent correlation between these three dimensions. For example, some countries value the political dimension highly but do not value the civil dimension – and vice versa (see *appendices B1 and B2*).

Table 2. What is a "good citizen"?

	All countries			Factor analysis		
	Rank	% « very important »	Mean	I (Political)	II (Social)	III (Civil)
% variance explained				*34.5%*	*13.0%*	*10.1%*
Always obey the law	1	55.4%	6.18			**.835**
Never try to evade taxes	2	51.6%	5.97			**.815**
Always vote in elections	3	50.3%	5.77	**.619**		.409
Help less privileged people	4	38.7%	5.70		**.836**	
Understand other opinions	5	34.0%	5.65	.442	.460	
Keep watch on government	6	35.1%	5.43	**.707**		.294
Help less privileged countries	7	27.1%	5.03		**.855**	
Serve in the armed forces	8	24.6%	4.60		.228	.352
Choose environmental products	9	15.8%	4.44	.595	.337	
Active in associations	10	13.9%	4.17	**.728**	.245	

ISSP 2004 Citizenship, 37 countries, weighted data.
Principal components analysis with varimax rotation.

Further insight is provided by comparing the ISSP data with that from the previous ISSP survey of 1996 "Role of government" (Chart 4). In this study, a question asked respondents their preference: always obey the law or follow their conscience in exceptional cases. The comparison between these two studies revels a strong correlation at the aggregate level (Pearson's r = .41 or .66 without Spain and Czech Republic). This result confirms that the definition of good citizenship is quite different worldwide, and that these reflect profound attitudes about the role of the individual, and of the balance between rights and duties.

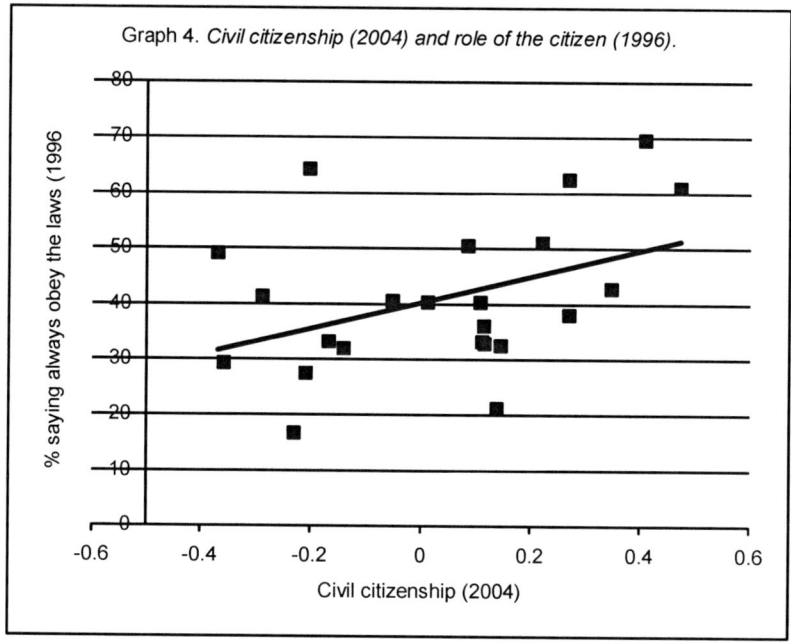

Graph 4. *Civil citizenship (2004) and role of the citizen (1996).*

THE SOCIO-CULTURAL ORIGINS OF CITIZENSHIP

Is it possible to explain this diversity of conceptions of citizenship? Why is one dimension of citizenship more developed in one country than in another? If we turn to the macro-level data (Table 3; see also *appendix A*), some visible trends emerge. Social citizenship is the most common form. It is more frequent in poor countries that lack equal opportunities for all, where education and interpersonal trust are weak, and where violence is widespread; it is also more frequent in countries where religion is strong (see *appendix C* for individual data on the influence of church attendance), particularly Catholicism, and in countries where the welfare state is underdeveloped. This last point should be noted: social citizenship should be seen not as the expression of the existence of the welfare state, but to the need for it due to the income gaps and social inequality.

Civil citizenship has common characteristics with social citizenship (GDP, inequality, welfare state, violence, trust), but it has some distinctive aspects. First, there is no connection with religion or education. Moreover, there is a negative correlation with civil liberties, which suggests that civil citizenship expresses a reaction to the lack of Rule of law.

Table 3. Bivariate Correlations Between Dimensions of Citizenship and Macro-Variables (aggregate level, 37 countries)

	Political citizenship	Social citizenship	Civil citizenship
GDP	.24	−.38*	−.38*
Inequalities	.21	.70***	.37*
Education	.06	−.50*	.02
Welfare state	.05	−.39*	−.48**
Civil liberty	.03	−.18	−.41*
Violence	−.09	.33*	.37*
Prison	.01	−.01	.31
Secularism	−.15	−.55***	−.28
Catholics	.09	.60***	−.12
Protestant	.09	−.29	−.12
Satisfied with democracy	.51***	−.07	−.24
Trust	.27	−.49**	−.37*

*** p < .001   ** p < .01   * p < .05

Table 4. Dimensions of Citizenship by Cultural Areas.

	Political citizenship	Social citizenship	Civil citizenship
Anglo-Saxon	,213	−,131	,178
North Europe	−,003	−,254	−,105
Continental Europe	,041	−,133	−,454
Post-war European Democracies	,141	,260	−,170
Former Communist states	−,413	−,195	,006
Asia	,237	−,246	,175
Latin America	−,048	,616	,130

Entries are factor scores (weighted data)

Anglo-Saxon: Australia, Great-Britain, United States, Ireland, New Zealand, Canada; *North Europe*: Norway, Sweden, Denmark, Finland; *Continental*: Netherlands, France, Switzerland, Belgium; *Post-war democracies*: Germany, Austria, Spain, Portugal; *Former communist states*: Hungary, Czech Republic, Slovenia, Poland, Bulgaria, Russia, Latvia, Slovak Republic; *Asia*: Philippines, Japan, Taiwan, South Korea; *Latin America*: Chile, Brazil, Venezuela, Mexico, Uruguay.

Political citizenship is more difficult to explain. The only factor which seems important is the satisfaction with democracy. To go further we need to look at where it is strong. Looking at Table 4, we see that political citizenship is strong in Anglo-Saxon countries (but not in Northern and Western Europe), and also in countries that became stable democracies after the war, both in Asia and in Europe. Former communist countries, whose democratization is still recent, do not have a strong political tradition in citizenship.

The geographical data confirms that social citizenship is strong is Latin America, and weak in the North of Europe, as expected, because of a long-standing social system. Civil citizenship is more powerful in Anglo-Saxon countries and in Asia, while it is weak in Europe.

The individual data (see *appendix D*) complete these results by underlining the importance of political factors in political citizenship. Political citizenship tends to be strong where satisfaction with democracy is widespread. As we see, however, individual factors do not explain social citizenship. The most important variables are religion and trust, and we can observe that these kinds of values often reflect a left-right divide. Civil citizenship is also correlated to satisfaction with democracy and trust in political leaders.

Education, i.e. length of schooling, has no discernible overall influence on social or political citizenship, but it is does have a negative influence of education on civil citizenship. This suggests that education produces critical citizens and, thereby, leads them to distance themselves from the laws. It can thus be suggested that the process of development, since it includes mass education, has an ambiguous influence on citizenship.

YOUTH AND CITIZENSHIP: CHANGES AND LIMITS TO CHANGE

Though different types of citizenship are historically rooted, they are nonetheless subject to change over time. The ISSP data do not allow us to compare the current results with the past, but they do allow for analysing the variations that are linked to age.

Table 5. Bivariate Correlations between Groups of Age (aggregate level, 37 countries)

	Political citizenship	Social citizenship	Civil citizenship
18-26 years/27-50 years	.92***	.89***	.88***
27-50 years/51 years and more	.94***	.97***	.86***
18-26 years/51 years and more	.85***	.88***	.76***

*** p < .001 ** p < .01 * p < .05

Variations with age exist, but, as we can see in *appendices C and D,* they are not the same for the three dimensions of citizenship. In most countries, it is civil citizenship that is most affected by age, but also, though somewhat less so, political citizenship. The relationship to social citizenship is weak and negative. Thus, the transmission of civic values over generations appears to be more problematic with political and civil citizenship than with social citizenship. This is especially the case for civil citizenship, suggesting that the need to respect the law is difficult to transmit, notably in modern and individualist societies such as ours.

We cannot be sure that this is an indication of generational change or just a matter of evolution over the life cycle. But it is important to underline that these changes have no influence on the hierarchy of the countries (Table 5). The correlations at the aggregate levels are always very strong, whatever the age groups. In most countries there is a certain continuity in civic attitudes. Variations are the most noticeable with civil citizenship, i.e. the learning of rules (r = .76). This field is also the one where the effects of age are the most telling, indicating that the learning of rules when young is a difficult process.

CITIZENSHIP AND POLITICAL PARTICIPATION

As we noted, political participation varies considerably between countries. These variations suggest that national context has an important influence. The ISSP survey confirmed the conclusions of previous research on the main causes of engagement, both at macro-level and micro-level (Inglehart and Catterberg, 2002; Kitschelt and Rehm, 2008). But what is newer and more original here is certainly the link between civic traditions and political participation.

MAIN CHARACTERISTICS OF POLITICAL PARTICIPATION.

Political engagement is globally much higher in Europe and in Anglo-Saxon countries than in the rest of the world (Table 6). But substantial differences do stand out. Northern European countries and Anglo-Saxon countries are those which have the highest levels of engagement on the two dimensions of participation, while continental Europe is less characterized by conventional participation. Contrary to Europe, South American countries have well developed degrees of conventional participation. Former communist countries and Asian countries have the lowest levels of both conventional and unconventional participation.

Table 6. Political Participation by Cultural Areas

	Conventional participation	Unconventional participation
Anglo-Saxon	.294	.456
North Europe	.427	.430
Continental Europe	−.156	.377
Post-war European Democracies	−.206	.302
Former Communist states	−.188	−.515
Asia	−.295	−.404
Latin America	.236	−.337
	$F = 474.23^{***}$ Eta = .26	$F = 1459.93^{***}$ Eta = .41

Entries are factor scores (weighted data).

Anglo-Saxon: Australia, Great-Britain, United States, Ireland, New Zealand, Canada; *North Europe*: Norway, Sweden, Denmark, Finland; *Continental*: Netherlands, France, Switzerland, Belgium; *Post-war democracies*: Germany, Austria, Spain, Portugal; *Former communist states*: Hungary, Czech Republic, Slovenia, Poland, Bulgaria, Russia, Latvia, Slovak Republic; *Asia*: Philippines, Japan, Taiwan, South Korea; *Latin America*: Chile, Brazil, Venezuela, Mexico, Uruguay.

Table 7. Bivariate Correlations for Political Participation (aggregate level, 37 countries)

	Conventional participation	Unconventional participation
GDP	.26	.70***
Inequalities	.09	−.34*
Education	.28	.40**
Welfare state	.02	.63***
Civil liberty	.07	.50**
Violence	.15	−.27
Prison	.16	−.25
Secularism	−.43**	.23
Catholics	.01	−.34*
Protestant	.50***	.48**
Satisfied with democracy	.40**	.73***
Interest in politics	.33*	.58***
Trust	.34*	.73***

*** $p < .001$ ** $p < .01$ * $p < .05$

The differences between conventional and unconventional participation are quite obvious. At the aggregate level, these two kinds of engagement are not correlated ($r = .19$). There are of course common factors: satisfaction with democracy, interest in politics, interpersonal trust. But the correlations with these variables are always much stronger with unconventional participation. Moreover, unconventional participation is always stronger in the wealthiest countries with the best educated populations, and also in the countries where inequalities are low, and where the welfare state and civil liberties are well developed – perhaps because the risks are also less serious (Table 7). By contrast, conventional participation is more present in religious countries. Thus, unconventional participation appears as a product of modernization, while conventional participation is more universal and more compatible with traditional forms of democracy.

YOUTH AND POLITICAL PARTICIPATION

At the individual level (see *appendix E*), the ISSP data confirms the role of political interest in explaining both conventional and unconventional participation. But micro-data has also confirmed that these two forms of participation are very distinct. Conventional participation is more associated with factors such as rurality and religiosity. The religious factor is generally known to have a strong impact on civic engagement (Smidt, 1999) but the data shows that this impact is strictly limited to conventional engagement. Indeed, religion is negatively correlated to unconventional participation, suggesting that being religious tends to entail some kind of conformism.

We can also note that conventional participation is more often found among men, contrary to unconventional participation. Moreover, there are two other important differences between conventional and unconventional participation: education and age. Educated people and the young are always more involved in unconventional participation, contrary to conventional participation which grows with age. But these variations with age do not appear in countries where political engagement is weak (former communist states and Latin American countries).

In sum, all these signs seem to indicate that conventional participation reflects a more traditional form of engagement. Unconventional participation is subject of a dynamic of change, contrary to conventional participation. In the developed world – with the exception of Japan and the United States – social conditions and the nature of political regimes probably create a more favourable context for unconventional engagement.

Table 8. Bivariate Correlations between Groups of Age (aggregate level, 37 countries)

	Conventional participation	Unconventional participation
18-26 years/27-50 years	.95***	.97***
27-50 years/51 years and more	.90***	.93***
18-26 years/51 years and more	.88***	.92***

*** $p < .001$ ** $p < .01$ * $p < .05$

Nevertheless, as with civic traditions, the differences with age do not alter the ranking of the countries (Table 8). The process of political socialization appears as a mix of change and continuity. Generational changes certainly exist, but their forms and rhythms are specific to national context. Moreover, the effects of age are largely a life cycle effect. Unconventional participation probably fascinates the young and appears much more attractive than conventional participation. The global context plays an important role. In old democracies, the personal risk from political engagement is very low.

CIVIC TRADITIONS, POLITICAL PARTICIPATION AND CIVIC EDUCATION

In what way is political participation related to civic traditions (Table 9)? Participation (both conventional and unconventional) is strongest in countries where political citizenship is highest. But unconventional participation is negatively correlated to civil citizenship. We find the same results at the individual level, and the link between civil citizenship and unconventional participation is still significant when controlled by other variables.

Table 9. Relationship between Political Participation and Civic Traditions

	Aggregate level		Individual level			
	Conventional participation	Unconventional participation	Conventional participation		Unconventional participation	
	R	R	R	ß	R	ß
Political citizenship	.34**	.37*	.16***	.03***	.23***	.13***
Social citizenship	.20	−.20	.04***		.04***	.08***
Civil citizenship	.12	−.36*	.08***	.02***	−.16***	−.12***
	$N = 37$ countries		$N = 52\,430$			

Entries: Pearson's r and standardised coefficients from stepwise regression (with 14 other variables of control).
*** p < .001   ** p < .01   * p < .05

This impact can be found in most countries (see also *appendix E2*), indicating that political citizenship tends to facilitate unconventional participation because it creates a normative context which is favourable to engagement. Conversely, civil citizenship discourages unconventional participation by pacing great stress on the need to respect legality. In this way, it can be said that civil citizenship discourages engagement.

What we have found thus suggests a contradiction between the two major dimensions of citizenship: engagement and legality. This brings us back to and underlines the divergences in the goals of civic education and the type of virtue that is to be encouraged. Moreover, it forces us to ask whether civic education can effectively counter the decline of social capital or the declining political interest of young people. This is not to deny thee findings of recent studies that have demonstrated that civic programs may have a significant impact (Slomszynski & Shabad, 1998; Finkel, 2002; Kahne & Sporte, 2007), but rather to suggest that the results from the specific countries or situations in which they take place cannot be generalized.

CONCLUSION

Nowadays, political attitudes still appear to have profound causes, and it is probably unrealistic to expect to transform them just by the introduction of civic courses into curricula. First, in light of our results and those of previous studies, it becomes clear that citizenship does not have the same definition everywhere in the world, and the question as to the appropriate goals of civic education is still open. Most salient here is our finding of a negative correlation between unconventional participation and what we termed civil citizenship. Contrary to McVeigh and Smith, who maintained that there is no difference between those who protest and those who engage only in institutionalized politics (McVeigh & Smith, 1999), we have found that weak attachment to the law is an important factor for engagement in forms of protest. Civil citizenship therefore appears to constitute an obstacle to unconventional participation. So the choice is what kind of "good citizenship" should be encouraged in a given country: engaged or respectful?

Given this choice, we are led to wonder if there can be universal goals for civic education. Can the role of civic education be to translate universal values, or is it rather to be conceived as "functional" to the society in which it is taught, going back to the old understanding, from Aristotle to Montesquieu, that civic virtue is a relative term, depending upon the features of any given constitution.

The question that thus needs to be posed in further research is what is the nature of the links between civic traditions and civic education? Generally, scholars are interested in the effect of civic education on political attitudes, i.e. the influence of institutions on society or values. But we would also learn from reversing this approach by examining the influence of society on civic education. In other words, by identifying civic education as a public policy, we would test the hypothesis that the approach to civic education reflects the social and cultural characteristics of the given country. We could investigate in which countries civic education is more developed, and how the form and content of civics courses reflect wider citizenship values. As it develops, the IDEA civic education database will certainly offer the possibility to engage in such a discussion.

NOTES

[1] The author wishes to thank Anna Jeannesson for her precious help in the proof-reading of this text.

[2] The exact question is: *"There are different opinions as to what it takes to be a good citizen. As far as you are concern personally, on a scale of one to seven, where 1 is not at all important and 7 is very important, how important is it...?"*

REFERENCES

Almond, G. A., & Verba, S. (1963). *The civic culture. Political attitudes and democracy in five nations* (p. 562). Princeton, NJ: Princeton University Press.

Baskerville, S. (1997). Civic education, political science, and education reform in central Europe. *Political Science and Politics, 30*(1), 114–115.

Christenson, R. M., & Capretta, P. J. (1968). The impact of college on political attitudes. A research note. *Social Science Quarterly, 49*(2), 315–320.

Conover, P. J., Crewe, I. M., & Searing, D. D. (1991). The nature of citizenship in the United States and Great-Britain: Empirical comments on theoritical themes. *Journal of Politics, 53*(3), 800–832.

Dalton, R. J. (2008). Citizenship, norms and the expansion of political participation. *Political Studies, 56*, 76–98.

Dudley, R. L., & Gitelson, A. R. (2003). Civic education, civic engagement, and youth civic development. *Political Science and Politics, 36*(2), 263–267.

Langton, K. P., & Jennings, M. K. (1968). Political socialization and the high school civics curriculum in the United States. *American Political Science Review, 62*(3), 852–867.

Finkel, S. E. (2002). Civic education and the mobilisation of political participation in developing democracies. *Journal of Politics, 64*(4), 994–1020.

Galston, W. A. (2001). Political knowledge, political engagement, and civic education. *Annual Review of Political Science, 4*, 217–234.

Heather, D. (2004). *Citizenship: The civic ideal in world history, politics and education* (p. 388). Manchester University Press.

Inglehart, R. (2000). Modernization, cultural change, and the persistence of traditional values. *American Sociological Review, 65*(1), 19–51.

Inglehart, R., & Catterberg, G. (2002). Trends in political action: The developmental trend and the post-honeymoon decline. *International Journal of Comparative Sociology, 43*, 300–316.

Kahne, J. E., & Sporte, S. E. (2007). *Developing citizens: The impact of civic learning opportunities on student's commitment to civic participation*. Paper Presented at the Annual Meeting of the American Political Science Association, Chicago, 2007.

Kitschelt, H., & Rehm, P. (2008). Political participation. In D. Caramini, *Comparative Politics* (pp. 445–472). Oxford University Press.

Marshall, T. H. (1950). *Citizenship and social class and other essays*, Cambridge, UK: Cambridge University Press.

McVeigh, R., & Smith, C. (1999). Who protests in America: An analysis of three political alternatives – inaction, institutionalized politics, or protest. *Sociological Forum, 14*(4), 685–702.

Langton, K. P., & Jennings, M. K. (1968). Political socialization and the high school civics curriculum in the United States. *American Political Science Review, 62*(3), 852–867.

Slomszynski, K. M., & Shabad, G. (1998). Can support for democracy and the market be learned in school? A natural experiment in post-communist poland. *Political Psychology, 19*(4), 749–779.

Smidt, C. (1999). Religion and civic engagement: A comparative analysis. *Annals of the American Academy of Political and Social Science, 565*, 176–192.

Smith, E. (1999). The effects of investments in the social capital of youth on political and civic behaviour in young adulthood: A longitudinal analysis. *Political Psychology, 20*(3), 553–580.

Somit, A., Tanenhaus, J., Wilke, W. H., & Cooley, R. W. (1958). The effect of the introductory political science course on student attitudes toward personal political participation. *American Political Science Review, 52*(4), 1129–1132.

Theisse-Morse, E. (1993). Conceptualizations of good citizenship and political participation. *Political Behavior, 15*(4), 355–380.

Torney-Purta, J., Lehman, R., Oswald, H., & Schulz, W. (2001). *Citizenship and education in twenty-eight countries: Civic knowledge and engagement at age fourteen* (p. 237). IEA.

Torney-Purta, J., & Amadeo, J-A. (2003). A cross-national analysis of political and civic involvement among adolescents. *Political Science and Politics, 36*(2), 269–274.

APPENDIX A. DESCRIPTION OF AGGREGATE DATA

Variable	Description	Source and year of reference
GDP	Gross domestic product based on purchasing-power-parity (PPP) per capita	International Monetary Fund, 2006
Inequalities	Gini Index	Human Development Report, 2007
Civil liberty	Index rank from 0 to 60	Freedom House, 2006
Violence	Homicides per 100 000 people	Human Development Report, 2000
Education	Average years of school (15 and over)	World Bank, 2000
Welfare state	Public expenditure on health in percentage of GDP	Human Development Report, 2004
Secularism	Percentage of people who declared themselves having "no religion"	ISSP Citizenship 2004
Catholics	Percentage of people who declared themselves as "catholic"	ISSP Citizenship 2004
Protestants	Percentage of people who declared themselves as "protestant"	ISSP Citizenship 2004
Interest in politics	Average of cumulative index (two items)	ISSP Citizenship 2004
Interpersonal trust	Average of cumulative index (two items)	ISSP Citizenship 2004
Satisfied with democracy	Average of single question	ISSP Citizenship 2004

APPENDIX B1. RANKING OF COUNTRIES ON THE 3 DIMENSIONS OF CITIZENSHIP

	Political citizenship	Social citizenship	Civil citizenship
1	Philippines	Venezuela	Bulgaria
2	Portugal	Brazil	Venezuela
3	Canada	Chile	Israel
4	Australia	Mexico	United States
5	South Korea	Uruguay	Great Britain
6	United States	Spain	Poland
7	Sweden	Portugal	Philippines
8	Uruguay	Poland	Taiwan
9	Austria	Slovenia	Chile
10	France	Ireland	Mexico
11	Denmark	Switzerland	Australia
12	Norway	Cyprus	Canada
13	Israel	Austria	Uruguay
14	Ireland	Slovak Republic	South Korea
15	Netherlands	Israel	Japan
16	Mexico	Philippines	Cyprus
17	Spain	United States	New Zealand
18	New Zealand	Germany	Russia
19	Switzerland	Australia	Hungary
20	Japan	Netherlands	Denmark
21	Taiwan	Denmark	Portugal
22	Brazil	Bulgaria	Ireland
23	Cyprus	Taiwan	Slovak Republic
24	Russia	Canada	Latvia
25	Poland	Norway	Brazil
26	Venezuela	Great Britain	Finland
27	Germany	Latvia	Norway
28	Belgium	Belgium	Sweden
29	Slovenia	France	Spain
30	Chile	Finland	France
31	Great Britain	Russia	Germany
32	Hungary	Sweden	Slovenia
33	Latvia	South Korea	Austria
34	Finland	Czech Republic	Czech Republic
35	Slovak Republic	Japan	Netherlands
36	Czech Republic	New Zealand	Switzerland
37	Bulgaria	Hungary	Belgium

APPENDIX B2. RANK (FROM 1 TO 37) FOR EACH COUNTRY ON THE 3 DIMENSIONS OF CITIZENSHIP

	Political citizenship	Social citizenship	Civil citizenship
Australia	4	19	11
Austria	9	13	33
Belgium	28	28	37
Brazil	22	2	25
Bulgaria	37	22	1
Canada	3	24	12
Chile	30	3	9
Cyprus	23	12	16
Czech Republic	36	34	34
Denmark	11	21	20
Finland	34	30	26
France	10	29	30
Germany	27	18	31
Great Britain	31	26	5
Hungary	32	37	19
Ireland	14	10	22
Israel	13	15	3
Japan	20	35	15
Latvia	33	27	24
Mexico	16	4	10
Netherlands	15	20	35
New Zealand	18	36	17
Norway	12	25	27
Philippines	1	16	7
Poland	25	8	6
Portugal	2	7	21
Russia	24	31	18
Slovak Republic	35	14	23
Slovenia	29	9	32
South Korea	5	33	14
Spain	17	6	29
Sweden	7	32	28
Switzerland	19	11	36
Taiwan	21	23	8
United States	6	17	4
Uruguay	8	5	13
Venezuela	26	1	2

APPENDIX C. BIVARIATE CORRELATIONS BETWEEN CIVIC TRADITIONS AND AGE (IN YEARS)

	Political citizenship	Social citizenship	Civil citizenship
Australia	.14***	−.02	.23***
Germany	.09**	−.02	.15***
Great Britain	.24***	−.07	.10*
United States	.08**	−.10***	.15***
Austria	.12***	−.06	.20***
Hungary	.03	−.01	.16***
Ireland	.09**	.01	.19***
Netherlands	.17***	−.01	.09**
Norway	.22***	−.04	.21***
Sweden	.18***	−.02	.26***
Czech Republic	.08**	−.04	.15***
Slovenia	.05	−.07*	.10**
Poland	.05	.04	.14***
Bulgaria	.11**	.00	.17***
Russia	.06*	−.00	.16***
New Zealand	.15***	−.05	.22***
Canada	.24***	−.03	.22***
Philippines	−.06	−.02	.05
Israel	.08**	−.01	.23***
Japan	.23***	−.09**	.33***
Spain	.07**	−.05*	.21***
Latvia	.12***	.01	.20***
Slovak Republic	.12***	−.01	.16***
France	.11***	−.03	.12***
Cyprus	.24***	−.02	.16***
Portugal	.07*	−.00	.17***
Chile	.14***	−.12***	.19***
Denmark	.13***	−.06*	.21***
Switzerland	.16***	−.06*	.23***
Belgium	−.00	.06	.14***
Brazil	.02	.00	.09***
Venezuela	.11***	−.02	.03*
Finland	.19***	−.10***	.27***
Mexico	.04	−.02	−.00
Taiwan	.11***	−.13***	.08**
South Korea	.02	.11***	.20***
Uruguay	.06	.02	.12***

*** p < .001 ** p < .01 * p < .05

APPENDIX D1. ANALYSIS OF POLITICAL CITIZENSHIP

	Australia	Belgium	Czech Repub.	Denmark	Finland	France	Germany	Great Britain	Japan	Latvia	Mexico	Netherlands	New Zealand	Norway	Russia	Spain	Sweden	Switzerland
Adjusted R2	.16	.26	.19	.15	.27	.20	.18	.22	.19	.17	.10	.19	.18	.15	.04	.06	.16	.21
Socio-demographics																		
Sex (1= male)	ooo	o										oo						ooo
Age	•••			•	•••		•	•••	•			••		•••		•	•••	••
Education		•••	•					•••										
Couple		••	•	•														
Actif	•	••				o												
Subjective status								–		oo			•		–			
Rural										••								
Church attendance		•••		•													•••	
Catholic										o								
Protestant		oo					••											
Politics																		
Left-right scale	•••	–													–			
Interest in politics	•••	•••	•••	•••	•••	•••	•••	•••		•••	••	•••	••	•••	•••	•••	•••	••
Government accessible				ooo								ooo						••
Satisfaction democracy		••			••	•••	•••			•••	••						•••	
Trust in others										oo								
Trust in political leaders	•••	••			•••	•••	••	o	••	oo		••		••	•••	•••	•	

Entries: standardized coefficients from a stepwise regression. Black: positive correlations White: negative correlations.
••• p < .001 •• p < .01 • p < .05   ooo p < .001 oo p < .01 o p < .05

APPENDIX D2. ANALYSIS OF SOCIAL CITIZENSHIP

	Australia	Belgium	Czech Repub.	Denmark	Finland	France	Germany	Great Britain	Japan	Latvia	Mexico	Netherlands	New Zealand	Norway	Russia	Spain	Sweden	Switzerland
Adjusted R2	.09	.02	.02	.12	.07	.15	.06	.09	.03	.03	.01	.10	.12	.12	.01	.02	.11	.02
Socio-demographics																		
Sex (1= male)	○○○		○○	○○○	○○○	○	○○	○	○○○				○○○	○○○		○○○	○○	
Age	●						●●	●●										
Education	○○				○○			○○				○○○	○○			○		
Couple	○○	○○○	●									○○						
Actif				○														
Subjective status	●●●		●●		●●	●●		●		●●		●●●	●●●	●●●			●●●	●
Church attendance						●●●		●●●		●●		●●●	●●●	●●●				
Catholic						○○○				○○		●						
Protestant																		
Politics																		
Left-right scale	○○○	–		○○○	○○	○○○	○○○	○○				○○○	○○○	○○○			○○	○○○
Interest in politics	●●			●●	●●		●						●	●●	●●		●●●	●●●
Government accessible	●						○○											
Satisfaction democracy					●●	●●●												
Trust in others	●	●●●				○○○			●●				●●	●			●●	
Trust in political leaders					○						○					○	●●	

Entries: standardized coefficients (stepwise regression). Black: positive correlations White: negative correlations.
●●● $p<.001$ ●● $p<.01$ ● $p<.05$ ○○○ $p<.001$ ○○ $p<.01$ ○ $p<.05$

APPENDIX D3. ANALYSIS OF CIVIL CITIZENSHIP

	Australia	Belgium	Czech Repub.	Denmark	Finland	France	Germany	Great Britain	Japan	Latvia	Mexico	Netherlands	New Zealand	Norway	Russia	Spain	Sweden	Switzerland
Adjusted R2	.10	.10	.15	.13	.16	.13	.07	.10	.12	.14	.05	.04	.14	.08	.05	.05	.17	.15
Socio-demographics																		
Sex (1= male)	○○	○○	○○○	○	○	○○○		○○○		○		○○		○○○			○○○	○○
Age	●●●	●●●	●●●	●●●	●●●	●●●	●●●		●●●	●●●			●●●	●●●	●●●	●●●	●●●	●●●
Education	●●●	○○		○○		●●●	○○○	○○		●●		○○	○○○				○○	○○
Couple					●	●●●		●					●					
Actif	●●●	●●●	●●●			●●●							●●					○
Subjective status								—							—		○○○	○
Rural											○		●●				○○	
Church attendance	●●		●●	●●	●●●	●●				●●●		●	●●	●●	—			●●
Catholic			●●	●			●●	●		○								●●
Protestant	●●●		●●															
Politics																		
Left-right scale	○○	—	○														○○○	
Interest in politics			●●●	○○	●●●		●●●			●●●	●●●	●●●	●●●	●●●		●●●	○	●●●
Government accessible	●●●	○	○○○	●●		○○				○○	●				—	●●		●●●
Satisfaction democracy		●●	●●●	●●	●●●	●				●●●	●				●●	●●		●●●
Trust in others		○○○			●●●													
Trust in political leaders		●●	●	●●●	●●●	●●●	●●	●●	●●	●●●	○		●●●				●●●	●●●

Entries: standardized coefficients from stepwise regression. Black: positive correlations White: negative correlations.
●●● p < .001 ●● p < .01 ● p < .05   ○○○ p < .001 ○○ p < .01 ○ p < .05

APPENDIX E1. ANALYSIS OF CONVENTIONAL PARTICIPATION

	Australia	Belgium	Czech Repub.	Denmark	Finland	France	Germany	Great Britain	Japan	Latvia	Mexico	Netherlands	New Zealand	Norway	Russia	Spain	Sweden	Switzerland
Adjusted R2	.33	.21	.25	.25	.27	.35	.32	.34	.08	.20	.31	.45	.40	.27	.07	.14	.27	.33
Socio-demographics																		
Sex (1=male)	•••	•••	•••	•••	••	•••	•	•••	•••	•••	•••	•••	•••	•••	•••	•••	•••	•••
Age	•	•••	•	•••	•••	•••	•••	•••	•••	•••	•••	•••	•••	•••	•••	•••	••	•••
Education	•••	•••	•••	•••	•••	•••	•••	•••			•••	•••		•••	•	•••	•	
Couple	•			•		•									–			•••
Actif	•••																	
Subjective status	•							–		•••					–			
Rural	•••	•••	•••	•••	•••	•••	•••	•••	•••	•••	•••	•••	•••	•••		•••	•••	•••
Church attendance	•••	•••	•••	•••	•••	•••	•••	•••			•••	•••		•••			•••	•••
Catholics	•••	•																•••
Protestant	•••																	
Politics																		
Left-right scale		–	○○															
Interest in politics	•••	•••	•••	•••	•••	•	•••	•••	•••	•••	•••	•••	•••	•••		•••	•••	•••
Government accessible	•		•		•••													
Satisfaction democracy										•			•	•••	•••	•••	•••	•••
Trust in others								○○○					•					•

ATTITUDES TOWARD CITIZENSHIP AND POLITICAL PARTICIPATION

	Australia	Belgium	Czech Repub.	Denmark	Finland	France	Germany	Great Britain	Japan	Latvia	Mexico	Netherlands	New Zealand	Norway	Russia	Spain	Sweden	Switzerland
Trust in political leaders									•									
Citizenship																		
Political					•	••					•	••	•••					•••
Social		○○○	○○○										○					
Civil																		

Entries: standardized coefficients from stepwise regression. Black: positive correlations White: negative correlations.
••• $p < .001$ •• $p < .01$ • $p < .05$ ○○○ $p < .001$ ○○ $p < .01$ ○ $p < .05$

APPENDIX E2. ANALYSIS OF UNCONVENTIONAL PARTICIPATION.

	Australia	Belgium	Czech Repub.	Denmark	Finland	France	Germany	Great Britain	Japan	Latvia	Mexico	Netherlands	New Zealand	Norway	Russia	Spain	Sweden	Switzerland
R2 adjusted	.32	.28	.22	.39	.45	.32	.39	.32	.21	.18	.21	.37	.28	.35	.12	.25	.35	.32
Socio-demographics																		
Sex (1= male)	○○○																	
Age	○○○	○○○		○○	○○		○○○							○			○○○	○○○
Education	•••	•	•••	•••	•••		••	•••	•••	•••		•••	•••	•••	•••	•••	•••	•••
Couple	•		•			•	•											
Actif			•															
Subjective status																		
Rural	○○○	○○				○○○	•	—				○○	○○○	○				○○
Church attendance	○○○	○○○	○○○	○○○	○○○		○○	○○	••	○	○○○	○○○	○○○	○○○	—	•	••	
Catholic	○						○○											
Protestant																		
Politics																		
Left-right scale	○○○	—		○								○○○	○	○○○	—		○○○	○○○
Interest in politics	•••	••	•••	•••	•••	•••	•••	•••	•••	•••	•••	•••	•••	•••	•••	•••	•••	•••
Government accessible		••	••				••	••	○○○		••							
Satisfaction democracy						○												
Trust in others	•••	•		•••		••			•••	•••	•••	•••					•••	
Trust in political leaders	○○○		•	○○○			○○○											
Citizenship																		
Political	•••	•••	•••	•••	•••	•••	•••	•••	•••	•••	•••	•••	•••	•••	•••	•••	•••	•••
Social	•••	•••	••	•••	•••	•••	•••		•••	•••	•••	•••	•••	•••	•	••	•••	•••
Civil	○○○			○○○	○○○		○○○	○○○					○○○	○○○	○		○○○	○○○

Entries: standardized coefficients from stepwise regression. Black: positive correlations White: negative correlations.

••• p < .001 •• p < .01 • p < .05   ○○○ p < .001 ○○ p < .01 ○ p < .05

ELLEN CLAES AND MARC HOOGHE

5. CITIZENSHIP EDUCATION AND POLITICAL INTEREST

Is there a Connection?

INTRODUCTION

Research suggests that young people know less about politics and participate less intensively than their parents and grandparents did when they had the same age (Putnam, 2000b; Zukin, Keeter, Andolina, Jenkins & Delli Carpini, 2006a). Citizenship education projects try to make adolescents more knowledgeable and participation-oriented in preparing them to take up their role as active citizens in society. There are few studies available, however, that confirm that civic education efforts are successful in this regard. Some sceptics have even argued that citizenship education might alienate young people from politics, instead of kindling their interest in the topic (Markus et al., 1993; Murphy, 2007). In most educational systems, the explicit goal of citizenship education is to promote political and civic engagement among young people (Torney-Purta, 2001; IDEA 2004). However, we also know that political interest is a crucial variable in determining levels of political participation: it is almost tautological to claim that those who are interested in politics will also be more inclined to participate in political life (Verba, Schlozman & Brady, 1995). Hence it becomes important to determine the exact relation between citizenship education and political interest.

Can citizenship education be expected to boost political interest, and thus also the likelihood of civic and political engagement, or is it the case, as a more sceptical view would have it, that citizenship education cannot make all that much difference, since the likelihood of participation is largely determined by pre-existing levels of political interest among young people. We also know that there are strong and structural differences in political interest, e.g., with regard to gender. If citizenship education efforts do not succeed in reducing these differences, citizenship education might just lead to a reproduction of already existing inequalities among the youth population (Schmid, 2003).

In this chapter, we test these assumptions about the role of political interest by distinguishing variations in the causal reasoning about citizenship education and political interest. Can we expect that citizenship education projects actually boost political interest, and thus indirectly also participation? Or should we expect rather that, once political interest is given, citizenship education will no longer have an independent effect on political participation?

CITIZENSHIP EDUCATION AND POLITICAL INTEREST

Despite strong national differences with regard to citizenship education practices, we can observe that most education systems share a rather broad concept of citizenship. Rights and responsibilities are considered as an essential prerequisite to maintain equality between citizens and to ensure the active role of the citizens in the political system and in society in general (Althof & Berkowitz, 2006). Citizenship can then be thought of as the willingness to "move beyond one's individual self-interest and to be committed to the well-being of some larger group of which one is a member" (Sherrod, Flanagan & Youniss, 2002, p. 270). This broadly based definition of citizenship also leads to a wide ranging definition of citizenship education. Citizenship education is here understood to comprise any effort of the education system with the goal to promote the development of citizenship norms among the students.

In the theoretical literature on moral development and character education, two different forms of citizenship education are distinguished (Solomon, Watson & Battistich, 2001). Traditional or direct citizenship education is mainly based on the transfer of cognitive abilities. Courses in citizenship education hence teach students about state structures or historical political facts. This approach can be traced back to the classic ideas of Emile Durkheim (1961). He argued that in order to reinforce social solidarity, schools should offer history lessons for students. Schools should moreover 'train' students for the social roles they would have to take up in later life. To facilitate this process, schools should preferably have the same hierarchical structure and expectations as society does (Durkheim, 1961). This direct approach can be found in schools in several forms such as classes in politics or visiting parliament or other political institutions. Direct forms of citizenship education indeed can have an effect on the development of civic attitudes. Kahne, Chi & Middaugh (2006) found that the civics curriculum could increase dispositions and capacities that support the development of social engagement and social capital. Niemi and Junn (1998, p. 145), too, demonstrated that the civic curriculum has an *"impact of a size and resilience that makes it a significant part of political learning"*. Following Morin (1996) one can argue that the more people know about politics the easier they will find it to acquire various political and participation skills. Halpern and Morris (2002), too, are quite optimistic about the potential impact of these direct forms of citizenship education.

An alternative approach to citizenship education is *indirect,* placing less emphasis on cognitive skills, and paying attention more explicitly to the development of moral reasoning and democratic values (Solomon, Watson & Battistich, 2001; Torney-Purta, 2004). This approach can be traced back to the views of John Dewey (1936) and Lawrence Kohlberg (1958). The central point in these theories is the school as an experimental garden for democracy: the school thus should not have to 'teach' children democratic skills and values; it should be democratic itself and in that way it will socialize children. So in order to be credible and successful, democracy must not only be the aim of education but also its means (Dewey, 1936; Kohlberg, 1958). This indirect approach can be measured in schools by assessing the democratic character of the school culture and by assessing the classroom climate (open or closed). In the classical research, Hartshorne and May (1928) found little indication for the success of traditional teaching on prosocial outcomes, but found profound support for the overall positive effects of school and classroom environment. More recently Torney-Purta (2002) reported that experiencing a climate in the classroom that encourages discussions of civic and political issues, stimulates the sense of engagement of the students. Because of the numerous indications of positive effects of school culture and classroom climate on students' social behaviour they should be taken into account in any model concerning citizenship education.

The distinction between direct and indirect forms of citizenship education is well-known in the literature. More recently however, various education practices have received attention that aim to bridge both approaches. Group projects, community service and participation in a school club have features of the direct approach (i.e., teachers show how it has to be done or directly introduce students to a project) and the indirect approach (students working together, discussing in a democratic manner). It has moreover been established that these kinds of service learning – that connect experience with academic study – may contribute to a deeper understanding of social problems (Batchelder & Root, 1994) and will lead to increased community involvement (Niemi et al., 1974; Metz & Youniss, 2003). It is expected that the experience with engagement will lead to higher participation levels in later life (Eyler, 2002). Given these distinctions in the research literature, it is of crucial importance to distinguish various elements of citizenship education in our analysis of the impact of school experiences on participation behaviour.

POLITICAL INTEREST

Fostering political knowledge and political participation are typically the main goals of citizenship education efforts in most liberal democracies. It is argued that the civic culture of a democratic political system will function better if citizens are informed about politics and more likely to become actively involved in political life (Galston, 2001).

When it comes to political knowledge, research (e.g. by Delli Carpini & Keeter, 1996) has shown that people with greater political knowledge are better able to link their personal interests with the appropriate public positions and therefore more capable of contacting the right person to meet their needs. This "enlightened self-interest' is important in a democratic society since people who know that they can have impact on the system are less likely to become politically alienated. The same authors also found that people with high political knowledge judge officials on the basis of how they carry out their responsibilities in the political system while people with a low score on the knowledge scale tend to judge officials on their personal character (Delli Carpini & Keeter, 1996). Secondly, political knowledge not only plays a role in people's 'feelings' towards officials and institutions, it also affects their views on public issues. For example, Popkin and Dimock (2000) found that political knowledge tends to dampen the level of fear toward immigrants. Overall the literature shows that political knowledge boosts support for democratic values and political participation (Baker, Sigmon & Nugent, 2001).

Next to political knowledge, political participation is the most commonly accepted policy goal for citizenship education. With political participation understood as an indispensable trait of democratic citizens, participation levels have attracted wide social and scientific concern as empirical research revealed that participation has been declining in most Western societies (Putnam, 2000a; Zukin, Keeter, Andolina, Jenkins & Delli Carpini, 2006b). Yet it is difficult to investigate the effects of citizenship education on political participation since the voting age in most Western countries is 18, the effect of which is that most students in high school cannot participate fully in political life. In response, evaluation usually relies on the proxy of expressed intention to participate as a dependent variable for citizenship education research of adolescents. In this regards, we need to take note of recent studies that suggest that the relationship between intended participation and actual participation behaviour is not one to one (Hooghe & Wilkenfeld, 2008).

In the currently available research about the effects of the different forms of citizenship education on political knowledge and participation, political interest is often used as an independent variable. It is assumed that those who are interested in political life, will automatically be able to acquire more knowledge, and will be more inclined to participate in political life (Verba, Schlozman & Brady, 1995). Of course, one can also argue it the other way around: if one knows more about political life, it is easier to claim that one is interested in politics (Glanville, 1999). It will require longitudinal studies, so far absent, to resolve these questions as to the relationship between participation and political interest.

In the literature, there is relatively little research available on the relationship between citizenship education and political interest. Schmid (2003) demonstrated that differences in political interest are clearly present before students are enrolled in a citizenship education course. While the course tended to raise the levels of political interest, it did not reduce the differences among the students. Mayer and Schmidt (2004) on the other hand, found little evidence of robust gender differences in political interest, implying that citizenship education can indeed function as the 'great equalizer': no matter what the initial levels of political interest, pupils stand to benefit from their participation in citizenship education courses.

In this paper, we argue that it does make sense to incorporate political interest more fully in the study of the effects of citizenship education. Research shows quite convincingly that there are persistent differences within the population with regard to political interest, especially those based on gender (Verba, Burns & Schlozman, 1997). If citizenship education fails to address these inequalities, one can wonder whether education efforts can indeed succeed in attaining the ideal of equal participation opportunities for the entire population.

Our analysis will focus on two different questions:
a. Can citizenship education (in whatever form) promote political interest among high-school students?
b. Does citizenship education lead to more political knowledge and willingness to participate, even when controlling for political interest?

DATA AND METHODS

The analyses presented in this paper are based on the McGill Youth Survey (MYS) conducted in 2005 and 2006 (Stolle et al., 2006) of 3,334 16 or 17-year olds (10th and 11th grade) in 81 schools. These were located in seven matched cities of different sizes in the two largest Canadian provinces, Quebec and Ontario. The response rate for schools was only 54 percent, as several schools declined to participate; despite this, the MYS data provide a representative sample of high school students in the two provinces.

The analysis proceeds in two steps: first, we look at the effects of citizenship education on political interest; then we assess the effect of citizenship education on political knowledge and political participation, controlling for political interest.

VARIABLES INCLUDED IN THE MODEL

As dependent variables, we focus on three different possible outcomes of citizenship education. First *political knowledge* is measured by including three questions on knowledge of politics in Canada and generally. The questions proved to form a reliable knowledge scale (see appendix II). To measure *intended future participation* we used the factor scores for conventional future intended participation (See appendix I). Intended future participation seems a good dependent variable in our quest to investigate whether citizenship education or only individual level characteristics like interest stimulate students to go to the polling booth in later life. The final dependent variable in our analysis is political interest itself. To operationalize this latent concept we use one question allowing respondents to indicate how interested they were in public issues and politics (see Appendix III).

An overview of all three dependent variables can be found in Table 1.

Table 1. Dependent Variables in the Analysis

Variable	All	French	English	Girls	Boys
Political Knowledge	.48	.53	.46	.46	.51
Intention Participation	.00	.18	-.10	-.09	.11
Political Interest	.46	.47	.45	.46	.46
N	3246	1174	2057	1803	1432

Entries are scale means. Source: MYS 2006

Among independent variables we are concerned in particular with those that indicate direct, indirect and mixed efforts at citizenship education. The extent of direct efforts at citizenship education at school was operationalized in the number of topics discussed during citizenship education classes. On the indirect side we use the factor scores reflecting the social and the affective school environment. These factor scores are derived from items assessing the school climate, an indicator used in other citizenship education studies getting at indirect efforts of citizenship education (Torney-Purta, 2002). To make mixed citizenship education efforts operational, community service is used. These indicators are all measured at the individual student level. In the regression analysis that follows, various individual characteristics that in earlier research have been shown to affect political knowledge and/or participation are included.

The first such explanatory variable is gender. In previous research it has been shown that boys perform better on political knowledge tests than girls, and that there is a clear gender bias in (intended) political participation (Verba; Schlozman, and Brady 1995; Hooghe and Stolle 2004a). In addition, we also expect that the socio-economic status (SES) of the individual has an effect on his/her propensity to acquire political information or to participate in political life. While in surveys among adults, questions about family income can be used to assess the socio-economic status of the family, this is not the case in research among adolescents. (In this survey 38 per cent of all respondents could or would not indicate their family's income). In line with earlier research (Torney-Purta et al., 2001) we therefore opted to include an estimation of the number of books in the home as a proxy variable for the SES of the home environment (Wößmann & Peterson, 2007). Because adolescents who regularly watch television news are known to have higher levels of political knowledge than those who do not, the variable watching television news is also taken into account (Hooghe, 2002).

Finally we include two variables that are intended to measure the most important parental and peer influences: if parents regularly discuss politics with their children, it can be assumed that this will contribute to their political knowledge and intention to participate. In the same way we assume that if respondents regularly discuss politics with their friends and peers, this too can strengthen their levels of political knowledge and participation (Niemi & Junn, 1998; Hillygus, 2005). All the independent variables are listed in Appendix III.

RESULTS: REGRESSION

We begin thus with political interest (Table 2). The model looks impressive, with an explained variance (R^2) of .38. It should be noted, however, that most of the variance indeed is explained by family and peer group variables: those who often discuss politics with their friends are more interested in politics and public life. Still, school experiences do show a significant relation with political interest, especially when it comes to the direct form of citizenship education (i.e., classes about politics). Interestingly, although it has long been taken for granted that there are significant gender differences with regard to political interest, in this model, we do not observe any significant differences between women and men in our sample. This first model confirms that political interest is a variable that should be included when considering the effects of citizenship education. But the causal reasoning about the relationship among citizenship education, interest, knowledge and participation is still unclear. Could it be that the expectation of citizenship education to stimulate knowledge or future participatory acts is too ambitious? To investigate this we need to look into more complex models that take these into

Table 2. Explaining Political Interest

	Political Interest	
	B (SE)	Beta
(Constant)	−.061 (.017)	
Gender	.003 (.009)	.005
SES	.052 (.017)	.046**
Discussing Politics with Peers	.396 (.020)	.317***
Discussing Politics with Parents	.218 (.018)	.193***
Watching News on Television	.318 (.017)	.290***
Community Service	.013 (.012)	.016
Classes about Politics	.078 (.018)	.068***
Social School Environment	−.001 (.004)	-.004
Affective School environment	.004 (.004)	.013
R^2	.38	

*p< 0.05   ** p<0.01   ***p<0.001

account. In table 3 we present a series of regression analyses, both with and without the political interest variable on the independent side of the spectrum.

Looking at both models we can see that the political interest variable explains a large part of the total variance of the model. We see moreover that other single level variables (the parental and peer characteristics) appear to be 'taking over' this variance in the analyses when the political interest variable is not included. This result serves to emphasize the importance of individual level variables, including the interest variable, in citizenship education research. Furthermore, in the knowledge models there seems to be a shift of the variance in interest toward the citizenship education measure 'classes about politics' in the model that includes the interest variable. To assess this claim in further detail, in Table 4 we introduce an interaction effect between classes about politics and political interest in the political knowledge model. As we can see, the interaction effect between interest and classes about politics proves insignificant. Hence the shift of the variance in interest to the citizenship education measure 'classes about politics' cannot be substantiated.

Table 3. Explaining Knowledge and Intention to Participate

	Political Knowledge				Future Intended Participation			
	Model I		Model II		Model I		Model II	
	B (SE)	Beta	B (SE)	Beta	B (SE)	Beta	B (SE)	Beta
(Constant)	.097 (.022)		.112 (.022)		-1.041 (.066)		-.964 (.062)	
Gender	.045 (.012)	.068***	.043 (.012)	.066***	.195 (.035)	.098***	.193 (.033)	.097***
SES	.075 (.023)	.059**	.065 (.023)	.051**	.196 (.069)	.051**	.124 (.065)	.032
Discussing Politics with Peers	.138 (.027)	.099***	.043 (.028)	.030	1.246 (.080)	.293***	.724 (.080)	,170***
Discussing Politics with Parents	.119 (.024)	.094***	.066 (.025)	.052**	.257 (.072)	.067***	-.023 (.070)	-.006
Watching News on Television	.222 (.023)	.181***	.145 (.024)	.118***	.353 (.067)	.095***	-.069 (.067)	-.019
Interest in Politics			.245 (.024)	.218***			1.313 (.069)	.386***
Community Service	.090 (.016)	.100***	.088 (.016)	.098***	.118 (.047)	.043*	.098 (.045)	.036*
Classes about Politics	.099 (.024)	.077***	.077 (.023)	.060**	.127 (.070)	.032	.037 (.067)	.010
Social School Environment	-.004 (.006)	-.012	-.004 (.006)	-.013	-.079 (.017)	-.079***	-.075 (.016)	-.075***
Affective School environment	.022 (.006)	.066***	.021 (.006)	.064***	-.041 (.017)	-.041*	-.049 (.016)	-.048**
R^2	.13		.16		.17		.26	

OLS Regression. *p< 0.05   ** p<0.01   ***p<0.001

Table 4. Explaining the Interaction of Classes about Politics and Political Interest

	Political Knowledge		
	B	Std. Error	Beta
(Constant)	.125	.026	
Gender	.043	.012	.065***
SES	.065	.023	.051**
Discussing Politics with Peers	.041	.028	.029
Discussing Politics with Parents	.067	.025	.053**
Watching News on Television	.146	.024	.119***
Interest in Politics	.211	.043	.188***
Community Service	.088	.016	.097***
Social School Environment	-.004	.006	-.013

(Continued)

Affective School environment	.021	.006	.063***
Classes about Politics	.045	.041	.035
Classes about Politics * Political Interest	.070	.073	.046
R²		.16	

OLS Regression. *p< 0.05   ** p<0.01   ***p<0.001

Overall, thus, the regression analyses lead us to conclude that political interest is an important but not predominant variable in citizenship education models, since other single level indicators seem to do the trick as well.

CONCLUSION AND DISCUSSION

At a time when education systems place more emphasis on citizenship education efforts, it becomes all the more crucial to determine the effects of various citizenship education models. Do they really succeed in making adolescents "better" citizens? Or can we support the sceptical view of James Murphy and some other authors that school-based efforts to strengthen political awareness can only be counter-productive?

We certainly do not claim to have provided a final answer to these questions, as this ideally would require longitudinal or panel data. For the McGill Youth Survey, and the corresponding Belgian Youth Survey, these panel data will be available for analysis in the future.

What we have made clear, we hope, is that the effects of citizenship education should be placed in perspective. Political interest, media consumption and discussions with peers and parents in most cases rank higher in explaining political knowledge. This does not mean, however, that the effects of citizenship education are insignificant.

The sceptical view is further weakened when we include the role of political interest. While it is no surprise that political interest boosts political knowledge and the intention to participate, our analyses indicate that citizenship education has a direct impact on political knowledge and the intention to participate, even after controlling for the effects of political interest. Or to put it slightly differently: even if students are not particularly interested in politics in the first place, they still tend to learn about politics in their classrooms. This would imply that the "Murphy view" is plainly wrong: citizenship education does promote political interest, political knowledge and political participation. The effect may not be as strong as we sometimes hope, but it is there.

The first purpose of this chapter was to determine how citizenship education interacts with political interest, not to identify which kind of citizenship education effort is most effective. If we return to this latter question, we find that our analysis implies that there is no unequivocal answer to this question. With regard to the cognitive outcomes, one can observe that traditional classes about politics still seem to matter, and therefore should not be neglected in the citizenship education curriculum. If one wants to encourage young people to become engaged in civic and political life, however, community service seems more promising. In noting this, the question shifts from the empirical ("which kind of education is most effective?") to the normative question ("what do we consider as crucial outcomes for citizenship education?"). If we place an emphasis on an informed and enlightened citizenry, this will require a different citizenship education approach than if one wants to promote an engaged citizenry. Where scepticism is justified, then, is toward the notion that there is a single form of citizenship education that will attain the divergent desired outcomes.

REFERENCES

Althof, W., & Berkowitz, M. W. (2006). Moral education and character education: the relationship and their roles in citizenship education. *Journal of Moral Education, 35*(4), 495–518.

Baker, M., Sigmon, J., & Nugent, M. E. (2001). *Truancy reduction: keeping students in school.* Washington, DC: Office of Juvenile Justice and Delinquency Prevention.

Batchelder, T. H., & Root, S. (1994). Effects of an undergraduate program to integrate academic learning and service: cognitive, prosocial cognitive and identity outcomes. *Journal of Adolescence, 17,* 341–356.

Baumrind, D. (1967). Child care practices anteceding three patterns of preschool behavior. *Genetic Psychology Monographs, 75,* 43–88.

Baumrind, D. (1978). Parental disciplinary patterns and social competence in children. *Youth and Society, 9,* 239–276.

Baumrind, D. (1991). Parenting styles and adolescent development. In J. Brooks-Gunn, R. Lerner, & A. C. Peterson (Eds.), *The encyclopaedia of adolescence.* New York: Garland.

Bennett, L. L., & Bennett, S. E. (1990). *Living with leviathan.* Lawrence, KS: University Press of Kansas.

Campbell, D. (2007). Sticking together. Classroom diversity and civic education. *American Politics Research, 35*(1), 57–78.

Coleman, J. S. (1988). Social capital in the creation of human capital. *American Journal of Sociology, 94*(1), 95–120.

Campbell, D. (2001). Making democratic education work. In P. E. Peterson & D. E. Campbell (Eds.), *Charters, Vouchers, and Public Education.* Washington, DC: Brookings Institution Press.

De Coninck, C., Maes, B., Sleurs, W., & Van Moensel, C. (2002). *Over de grenzen, vakoverschrijdende eindtermen in de tweede en de derde graad van het secundair onderwijs.* Brussel: Ministerie van de Vlaamse Gemeenschap.

Delli Carpini, M. X., & Keeter, S. (1996). *What Americans know about politics and why it matters.* New Haven, CT: Yale University Press.

Dewey, J. (1936). *The school and society.* Chicago: University of Chicago Press.

Dewey, J. (1966). *Democracy and education.* New York: Free Press.

Durkheim, E. (1961). *Moral education. A study in the theory and applications of the Sociology of education.* New York: Free Press.

Eyler, J. (2002). Reflection: Linking service and learning- linking students and communities. *Journal of Social Issues, 58*(3), 517–534.

Galston, W. (2001). Political knowledge, political engagement, and civic education. *Annual Review of Political Science, 4,* 217–234.

Galston, W. (2007). Civic knowledge, civic education, and civic engagement: A summary of recent research. *International Journal of Public Administration, 30*(6–7), 623–642.

Glanville, J. (1999). Political socialization or selection? Adolescent extracurricular participation and political activity in early adulthood. *Social Science Quarterly, 80*(2), 279–290.

Halpern, J. P. D., & Morris, Z. (2002). *Acquiring political knowledge through school curricula and practices.* Paper presented at the ECPR Joint Sessions, Turin, April.

Hartshorne, H., & May, M. A. (1928). *Studies in the nature of character. I. Studies in deceit. Book one: General methods and results. Book two: Statistical methods and results* (Vol. 1). New York: Macmillan.

Hooghe, M. (2002). Watching television and civic engagement: Disentangling the effects of time, programs, and stations. *Harvard International Journal of Press/Politics, 7*(2), 84–104.
Hooghe, M. (2004). Political socialization and the future of politics. *Acta Politica, 39*(4), 331–341.
Hooghe, M., & Stolle, D. (2004). Good girls go to the polling booth, Bad Boys go everywhere: Gender differences in anticipated political participation among American Fourteen-Year-Olds. *Women and Politics, 26*(3–4), 1–23.
Hooghe, M., & Wilkenfeld, B. (2008). The stability of political attitudes and behaviors across adolescence and early adulthood. A comparison of survey data on adolescents and young adults in eight countries. *Journal of Youth and Adolescence, 37*(2), 155–167.
IDEA (2004). Retrieved from http://civiced.idea.int/
Jennings, M. K., & Niemi, R. (1974). *The political character of adolescence*. Princeton, NJ: Princeton University Press.
Kahne, J., Chi, B., & Middaugh, E. (2006). Building social capital for civic and political engagement: the potential of high school civics courses. *Canadian journal of Education, 29*(2), 387–409.
Kohlberg, L. (1958). *The development of modes of moral thinking and choice in the years ten to sixteen*. Doctoral dissertation, Chicago, IL: University of Chicago.
Markus, G. B., Howard, J. P. F., & King, D. C. (1993). Integrating community service and classroom instruction enhances learning: Results from an experiment. *Educational Evaluation and Policy Analysis, 15*(4), 410–419.
Mayer, J., & Schmidt, H. (2004). Gendered political socialization in four contexts: political interest and values among junior high school students in China, Japan, Mexico, and the United States. *Social Science Journal, 41*(3), 393–407.
Morin, R. (1996, January 29). Who is in control? Many don't know or care. *The Washington Post*, 1–6.
Murphy, J. (2007). Against civic education in public schools. *International Journal of Public Administration, 30*(6–7), 651–670.
Niemi, R., & Junn, J. (1998). *Civic education. What makes students learn*. New Haven, CT: Yale University Press.
Niemi, R. et al. (1974). *The Politics of future citizens*. San Francisco: Jossey-Bass.
Pellerin, L. A. (2005). Applying Baumrind's parenting typology to high schools: toward a middle-range theory of authoritative socialisation. *Social Science Research, 34*, 283–303.
Popkin, S., & Dimock, M. (2000). Knowledge, trust and international reasoning. In A. Lupia, S. Popkin, & M. McCubbins (Eds.), *Elements of reason. Cognition, choice and the bounds of rationality*. Cambridge, UK: Cambridge University Press.
Putnam, R. (1995). Bowling alone: America's declining social capital. *Journal of Democracy, 6*(1), 65–78.
Putnam, R. (2000). *Bowling alone*. New York: Simon and Schuster.
Rahn, W. M., & Transue, J. (1998). Social trust and value change: The decline of social capital in American Youth. *Political Psychology*, 19, 545–565.
Schmid, C. (2003). Fördert der Schulunterricht an Gymnasien das politische Interesse von Jugendlichen? *Zeitschrift für Soziologie der Erziehung und Sozialisation, 23*(4), 371–384.
Sherrod, L. R., Flanagan, C., & Youniss, J. (2002). Dimensions of citizenship and opportunities for youth development. *Applied Developmental Science, 6*(4), 264–272.
Solomon, D., Watson, M., & Battistich, V. A. (2001). Teaching and schooling effects on moral/prosocial development. In V. Richardson (Ed.), *Handbook of research on teaching*. Washington, DC: American Educational Research Association.
Stolle, D., & Hooghe, M. (2004). The roots of social capital. Attitudinal and network mechanisms in the relation between youth and adult indicators of social Capital. *Acta Politica, 39*(4), 422–441.
Stolle, D., Harell, A., Maheo, V. A., & Nishikawa, L. (2006). *McGill youth survey dataset*. Montréal: McGill University.
Torney-Purta, J., Lehmann, R., Oswald, H., & Schulz, W. (2001). *Citizenship and education in twenty-eight countries: civic knowledge and engagement at age fourteen*. Amsterdam: IEA.
Torney-Purta, J. (2002). The school's role in developing civic engagement. A study of adolescents in twenty-eight countries. *Applied Developmental Science*, 6, 203–212.
Verba, S., Burns, N., & Schlozman, K. L. (1997). Knowing and caring about politics. Gender and political engagement. *Journal of Politics, 59*(4), 1051–1072.
Verba, S., Schlozman, K. L., & Brady, H. (1995). *Voice and equality. Civic voluntarism in American politics*. Cambridge, UK: Harvard University Press.

Wößmann, L., & Peterson, P. (Eds.). (2007). *Schools and the equal opportunity problem*. Cambridge, MA: MIT Press.
Zukin, C., Keeter, S., Andolina, M., Jenkins, K., & Delli Carpini, M. X. (2006). *A new engegament? political participation, civic life and the changing American citizen*. Oxford, UK: Oxford University Press.

APPENDIX I: FACTOR ANALYSIS FUTURE POLITICAL PARTICIPATION

	Factor	
	1 conventional	2 social movement
Will run office	**.670**	-.017
Will join party	**.768**	.131
Will raise/donate	-.011	**.832**
Will boycott/boycott	.436	**.509**
Will volunteer	.077	**.835**
Will follow campaign	**.572**	.370
Will protest legal	**.621**	.409
Will leadership community	.378	**.437**
Will protest illegal	**.593**	.048
Eigen value	3.30	1.20
Explained variance	37.1	14.1

Results of an exploratory factor analysis on the nine participation items. Varimax rotation. N=3, 218

APPENDIX II: DEPENDENT VARIABLES

Variables	Questions Questionnaire	Coding
Political Knowledge	3 questions in Canada Example: Who is the new Governor General of Canada? Who is the Provincial Premier of this province? The Supreme Court has the authority to...	Cumulative Scale 0-1
Future Intended (Conventional) Participation/Social Movement Participation	In the future would you..... run as a candidate for a public office join a political organization or party raise or donate money for a cause boycott or buy products for political, ethical or environmental reasons volunteer for a cause you believe in actively follow an election campaign take part in legal protest activities take on a leadership role in your community take part in illegal protest activities	Factor scores

APPENDIX III : EXPLAINATION VARIABLES

Variables	Questions Questionnaire	Coding
Gender	Are you: female male	Male = 0 Female = 1
SES	About how many books are in your family's home (excluding newspapers, magazines and books for school)? none 1-10 11-50 51-100 101-200 201-500 more than 500	Scale
TV news	What do you spend most of your time watching on television? news and current events	0 = No 1 = Yes
Parents discussing politics	How often do your parents discuss public issues and politics? never once in a while fairly often all the time	Scale
Friends discussing politics	When you are with your close friends, how often do you discuss public issues and politics? never once in a while fairly often all the time	Scale
Political interest	How interested are you in public issues and politics? not interested a little interested interested very interested	Scale

(Continued)

Classes about politics	Last school year, how often did you talk about the following topics in your classes :1)the way parliament works 2) the United Nations, 3) federalism 4) voting never once or twice several times many times		Scale
Community service	Were you required to do a community service project through your school? yes no If so, how many hours did the project involve overall? less than 10 hours between 10 and 20 hours more than 20 hours		Scale

		Component		Factorscores
Social School Environment (Component 1)		1	2	
Affective School environment (Component 2)	I do not feel alone in my class	-.064	.655	
	Student do have a strong impact on how affairs at this school are run	.400	-.028	
	Students are encouraged to make up their own minds about issues	.768	.078	
	Students feel free to express opinions in class even when their opinions are different from most of the other students	.739	.177	
	Teachers present several sides of an issue when explaining it to class	.723	.132	
	I feel treated fairly by my classmates	.089	.828	
	I feel treated fairly by my teachers	.346	.638	

All the scales were standardized 0-1

PART II: CIVIC EDUCATION APPLICATIONS AND PROGRAMS

HENRY MILNER, CHI NGUYEN AND FRANCES BOYLSTON

6. A WORLD PATTERN FOR CIVIC EDUCATION

From the IEA Civic Education Study to the IDEA CIVICED Database Project

INTRODUCTION

Democracy supposes a politically literate population. Political literacy can be described as a minimal familiarity with the relevant institutions of decision-making, combined with a basic knowledge of the key positions over relevant issues and the political actors holding them. Politically literate citizens need not be deliberators who assemble and weigh the pros and cons of alternative policies, but they do need to be (capable of being) adequately attentive to the political world. Attentive citizens, whether satisfied or critical, display significantly higher levels of political knowledge, participate more often, are less politically alienated, show a sense of political internal efficacy and are more likely to consider the defense of democracy as a civic duty (Geissel, 2008).

Being able to identify alternative positions is crucial to democracy. Citizens with access to only one view are naturally inclined to (follow leaders who) attribute malevolent motives to those who do not share it. Political censorship is the customary way of achieving this – but a similar result can be attained more gently via an inattentive, uninformed, i.e. politically illiterate, citizenry. The attainment of universal literacy through education has not assured political literacy. While it is true that better educated citizens are more likely to be informed and participate politically, and that the average number of years of education has risen significantly in the democratic countries, political knowledge and democratic participation have not kept pace. Indeed, there is good reason to believe that the proportion of politically illiterate citizens, or, political dropouts, has been increasing in recent years in most industrial democracies (See Milner forthcoming).

This is not to say that what goes on in the school is unimportant. Quite the opposite. It is the only institution available in a democracy to inhibit citizens to-be from becoming political dropouts. Controlling for characteristics associated with self-selection, Nie and Hillygus (2001) showed that American college students concentrating study in the social sciences and humanities were more likely to vote and discuss politics, as well as participate in community service and politics upon leaving college, a finding extended to longer term political engagement by

Hillygus (2005). She concludes that, more than anything else, a curriculum that develops language and civic skills contributes to democratic participation.

There is thus good reason to believe that education, both in fostering habits of literacy and teaching civic skills, contributes to informed political participation. But for the potential to be realized in the form of a virtually universally politically literate population, then these skills must be developed at the compulsory level. This is the challenge of civic education.

This challenge became more urgent and concrete in the late 1980s as the international political landscape began to undergo a process of considerable change. Democratic political institutions needed to be bolstered in new democracies in the former Eastern Bloc, while in more established democracies, observers and leaders began to refer to a "democratic deficit," especially among emerging generations. Attaining adulthood in the rapidly changing, globalised culture, this generation was increasingly "turned off" by the more traditional forms of civic participation, especially electoral politics. Young people were not only voting less than earlier generations but were less attentive to the political world around them. Civic education, which had been all but ignored since the 60s, began to find its way back to the agenda of researchers and policy makers.

Among the first to act on these concerns was Australia, despite its being sheltered from declining electoral participation by compulsory voting. Indications that many young Australians were far from politically literate led to the establishment, in the latter 1990s, of the then most up-to-date comparative study of civic education (Print, 2007). In setting out its research program, the Australian inquiry into Civics and Citizenship Education (Civics Expert Group, 1994) commissioned a survey of international best practices in civics education to guide it in its deliberations. Yet, unexpectedly, the survey results were meagre. Ultimately the report could do no better than provide a description of what it saw as the three alternate approaches to civic education, approaches it associated respectively with the US, Britain and France, noting that recognized instruments for comparing the three on the basis of their results simply did not exist. Clearly, systematic cross-national research was in order.

This chapter reports on two cross-national comparative studies related to civic education undertaken in recent years, the IEA Civic Education Study and the IDEA CIVICED database project. While the IEA study is well known, the latter is quite new and is the prime focus of this chapter. In setting out their contributions and limitations, we offer insight into what is known about civic education and its effects.

THE IEA CIVIC EDUCATION STUDY

The IEA (International Association for the Evaluation of Educational Achievement) Civic Education Study, completed in 2001, was based on a large international survey of secondary school-age students and their teachers. The study investigated the civic knowledge, attitudes, and engagement of young people, seeking to thus portray the conditions under which civic education was taking place in different settings, from Eastern and Western Europe, North and South America and Oceania.

A rigorous data-based approach, it was felt, could best address questions central to understanding the international drop in youth civic engagement, as well as lead to a better understanding of the effects of policies and practices on youth engagement.

The study surveyed 90,000 14 year old students in 28 countries, as well as 50,000 17-19 year old students in 16 countries, in 1999 and 2000. It sought to understand how young people learn about civic responsibilities, and how they become involved in political communities both in and beyond their school environment. A preliminary phase, carried out in 1996 and 1997, sought to collect comprehensive information regarding civic education provision in the participating countries. Country experts were asked to identify what they felt 14 year old students should know about civic education. In addition, researchers from several of the countries carried out qualitative case studies. From the observations thus assembled an information-gathering instrument to assess students' civic knowledge and their civic attitudes and levels of civic engagement was produced (see Torney-Purta et al., 1999).

The main phase was built around a quantitative test and survey of representative groups of 3,000 students aged 14 and 15 in the participating countries, (as well as a number of civics teachers and principals (see Torney-Purta et al., 2001).[1] The study was organized into three themes: the first focused on the organisation of educational programs, the status of citizenship education in the school program, and the goals it was to address (the students' civic identity, or the resolution of social conflicts and tensions, etc); the second focused on how students define concepts of citizenship, whether or not these conceptions correspond to gender or socioeconomic cleavages, and the approach taken to rights and responsibilities; the final theme was concerned with the attitudes and techniques teachers used in teaching civic education, how these techniques influenced the students' perceptions and understanding of the topic, and the degree to which teachers were trained for the role.

The study identified four main streams through which civics was taught: History, History/Civics, Social Sciences, and Social Sciences framed by Religion/ Ethics, and listed the 20 subject areas it could encompass, clustered under headings such as National History, Constitution and Political Systems, Citizen and Human Rights, International Organizations and Relations, Economics and Welfare, and Media. Overall, it found that instruction in civic education was much less structured than instruction in other subjects, leaving greater discretion to the teachers to set the civic education curriculum. Related to this was the finding that teachers' confidence levels was lower for teaching civic education than other subjects and the consensus that teachers require better teaching materials, more subject-matter training, and more instructional time for civic education. Civic education was generally understood to be integrated into the social sciences, but this tended to leave it in a precarious position in the schools. Given these weaknesses, a significant degree of scepticism prevailed regarding the apparent broad societal consensus on civic education and its importance.

The student respondents in most countries were found to exhibit a basic level of understanding of fundamental democratic values and institutions. Although males outperformed females, particularly in the area of economic knowledge, gender differences were less significant in civic knowledge than in attitudes. For example, girls were often more sympathetic to the plight of women and immigrants than were boys. The students were, on the whole, quite sceptical in their attitudes towards conventional forms of civic engagement – though usually not toward voting – but, at the same time, tended to be open to alternative forms of engagement, such as attending a protest or collecting money for a cause.

Despite constituting the central element of the student study, the findings with regard to civic knowledge are problematic. As a result, the study did not succeed in its effort to produce an appropriate dependent variable, i.e. a quantitative measure to compare countries as to the effectiveness of their approach to civic education. The dependent variables in the study were a combination of the students' future intention of whether to be an informed voter and an active participant in the community, and, most importantly, scores on a test of what was termed but did not in fact constitute civic knowledge.

The first indication that the latter was unsatisfactory for the purposes of cross-national comparison of political knowledge came when the report ranking countries by average civic knowledge score were made public, since the rankings failed to correspond to the findings of other political knowledge studies. The source of the problem was evident once the content of the questions were made known. The selection process resulted in any questions that could possibly place a participating country at a disadvantage, i.e. all factual questions, were eliminated. What remained were items measuring the students' familiarity with democratic concepts and skills in interpreting political communication. Thus, rather than testing factual knowledge, the questionnaire tested vocabulary, logic, and, especially, appreciation for democratic principles.[2]

This left responses to the questions that surveyed the students' future intention to be an informed voter and expectations of community participation to serve as dependent variable. But it is also problematic to use a 14 year-old's expressed intentions as a predictor of future behaviour rather than as a reflection of culturally-based expectations.[3] At the individual level, however, the study does show that intended future informed political participation correlates notably with the degree to which students believe that they and the groups they join can make a difference in what happens at school. Moreover, this relationship is stronger than simple membership in a governance organization like student council, or taking a civic education course, though these, too, contribute. When it comes to attitudes toward future citizen responsibilities what happens in the school, both in the classroom and beyond it, matters. This is an important contribution, confirming that what happens in the school, both in the classroom and beyond it, matters when it comes to the exercise of citizen responsibilities.

Returning to the independent variable, i.e. the various factors distinguishing approaches to the provision of civic education, a few useful generations emerged. For example, civics teaching favoured history and human rights over economic and international affairs, with little attention to topics like migration and trade unions. But the IEA limited itself in the breadth and applicability of such findings since it explicitly steered clear of trying to extract numerical values allowing for cross-national comparison,[4] as explained by Torney-Purta:

> In spite of the rich detail provided by this mass of information, when the CIVED coordinating team needed numerical values for country-level inputs to be related to student test outcomes, it was clear that this material was not suitable for that purpose. It was much more valid to use information provided by the nationally representative samples of principals or teachers in the schools where the testing took place; these values could be averaged to the national level (for example, the average of the availability of certain organizations or certain curricular topics in schools). The international coordinating team decided that deriving a single number or set of numbers to represent a country based on one or two respondents would be risky even with methodological safeguards such as those described (Torney-Purta, 2008: 6).

The problem was that while averaged information provided by the representative samples of principals and teachers in the tested schools would be more valid, the information was not directly applicable to many of the questions that needed to be asked.

Similar limitations apply to the report entitled *Citizenship at School in Europe: A Comparative Study* prepared by the European Commission about civic-education related policies and curriculum in 29 countries.[5] Chapters for the participating countries describe approaches to citizenship education in the primary and secondary school curricula, in fostering participation by pupils in the school and community, in the assessment of students and in the training of teachers. While some effort is made to have a similar general presentation for each country, there is no numerical comparison undertaken, and indeed no basis for one.

The absence of numerical data for such comparison constituted an important motivating factor for the development of the IDEA CIVICED database. The context, as noted, was evidence of a secular decline in civic duty to participate in electoral politics, which, in turn, gave rise to a call for more systematic research into civic education. Among those taking up the challenge were specialists in education who could see how, with declining parental and community sources of authority, the school had inherited a greater socialising burden, that of forming citizens by improving and increasing youth political knowledge and skills.

The effort encompassed in the IEA Civic Education Study is evidence of this interest among education specialists. But it was exceptional in its rigor and international scope. Political scientists were slower to take an interest in civic education, and this held back development of a systematic research literature that transcends individual case studies, It is in this context that the IDEA CIVICED Database Project was conceived.

FROM THE IEA CIVIC EDUCATION STUDY TO THE IDEA CIVICED DATABASE PROJECT

An important development among political scientists, during this period, was research carries out in many different democratic countries confirming that more politically knowledgeable citizens are significantly more likely to vote – even when controlling for education, age, political interest, associational participation, and trust. A number of those researchers came together at a workshop of the European Consortium on Political Research on political knowledge and political participation in Turin in March 2002, from which an informal network emerged. In the following years, data assembled from a number of countries (Franklin, 2004, Phelps, 2004; Howe, 2006; Wattenberg, 2007; Milner, 2005) brought the age dimension into the forefront: turnout decline was in good part a generational phenomenon coinciding with a decline in levels of political knowledge.

At the ECPR general conference in Budapest in September 2005, two well-attended sections reflecting these concerns were organized. Participants in these sections formed the nucleus of a network of interested persons that first met in Budapest with the support of International IDEA. Participants expressed a shared concern with the political literacy of the new generations and agreed that priority needed to be placed on research into civic education. A coordinating group, which included two of the authors of this chapter, was set up with a mandate, building on the work of the IEA Civic Education Study, to comparatively study youth political participation, political knowledge and civic education. The key obstacle to progress in this area was identified to be lack of systematic data about civic education required for cross-national comparisons. The concrete task, it was agreed, was thus to develop a questionnaire and a list of country experts who would be asked to complete it. International IDEA took on the task of coordinating the work and agreed to host a "database" in which the information from the completed questionnaires could be compiled and made available to researchers and scholars.

The questionnaire asked respondents to answer a range of questions on various components of a country's civic education program. The questions asked how countries structured civic education; which bodies set the civic education curriculum; how civic education is delivered; the range of content; methods for teaching civic education; teacher qualifications; and student evaluation. By spring of 2006, the website was up and running and the questionnaires distributed to an initial list of over 55 civic education specialists in over 45 countries. Gradually, over a period of two and half years – until development of the entire network IDEA databases suspended late in 2008 to undergo reconstruction – data from the filled-in questionnaires was regularly incorporated into the database.

Although no formal criteria with regard to the inclusion of countries were established, there was an understanding that those countries where civic education was not available, either due to domestic conflict or the absence of any kind of arms length distance between the educational system and the country's regime, would not be included. The benefit of the doubt would be extended to countries at the margin, on the understanding that inappropriate data could always be excluded at a later stage. Hence an important difference with the IEA was that

A WORLD PATTERN FOR CIVIC EDUCATION

many more countries could be included since the IDEA CIVICED database would not be limited, like the IEA, by the capacity and willingness to carry out an intensive and rigorous survey.

With development suspended for IDEA database reconstruction, the CIVICED website remains incomplete. More countries still need to be added to the database; a Spanish-language version of the questionnaire remains to be put into circulation in Latin America. And much of the existing data has to be verified. Meanwhile, civic education continues to change, remodel, and evolve as new policies are implemented, regimes change, and further research is brought to light, developments that will have to be incorporated.

As far as method is concerned, the fundamental difference with the IEA was the decisions to create an instrument in the form of a questionnaire that would lend itself to numerical coding and, thus, cross-national, aggregate comparisons. The IEA had ruled out asking its expert respondents to be subject to such constraints when describing civic education in their countries. As noted (in the citation from Torney-Purta above) they feared that deriving a single number or set of numbers to represent a country based on one or two respondents would be risky. While we were fully aware of the limitations of an indicator based on assessments by only one or two respondents from a given country, we felt that these limitations were, on balance, more than offset by the advantages of allowing for such comparisons, however crude, of many different countries. This meant, of course, that when the data would be made publically available, users would have to be clearly informed that the IDEA civic education database represents only a "snapshot" at a given moment and from a given perspective of the state of affairs in participating countries. This is even more the case at present, with the database suspended in incomplete form – and the reader is reminded to keep this in mind in the summary of findings from the database presented below.

In approaching the subject, the designers of the IDEA CIVICED decided first that while citizenship education and civic education are sometimes used interchangeably, the use of the latter was preferred in order to make it clear that the focus was on activity that takes place in and around the school. (That activity can take the form of a specific course termed "civics", but it need not be limited to this.) This led to the following working definition:

> Civic education consists of school-based activities seeking to promote democratic involvement by young people. These seek to increase knowledge of and interest in politics and public affairs and, thus, to reinforce the individual's sense of efficacy as a citizen. That efficacy can take the form of identifying and pursuing one's political interests and articulating these in the public realm to participating in groups and networks that are civically engaged in their communities, to protesting injustices.

An immediate decision concerned how to deal with federal countries in which education is under the jurisdiction of the states or provinces. The clearest cases here were the United States and Canada. In the case of the latter, it was decided to include separate entries for 4 (of 10) provinces. (Note that below, therefore, when for simplicity sake when we refer to countries, we are, strictly speaking, being inaccurate, since these include the four Canadian provinces.) Choosing such a small number was a more difficult proposition for the United States, given the large number of states, so that, provisionally, it was decided to treat the US separately (see epilogue). For the other federal and quasi-federal countries it was possible to use one set of data to reflect country wide patterns, though some variation is noted in the section of the questionnaire in which respondents provide explanatory notes. For example, for Spain, the data is based on the requirements set by the state which allow the provinces to themselves decide over the remaining part of the mandated curriculum.[6]

Another complication was the fact that the very structure of education differed as to the number of years students spend in school at different levels. In order to maximize comparability, we attempted to provide guidelines. This was done by using what appeared to be the most common breakdown, namely into three levels which we termed primary, intermediate, and secondary, asking respondents to associated these as closely as possible with the following categorization:

Primary level – students aged up to 11 years.

Intermediate level – students aged 12 to 14 years.

Secondary level – students aged 15 years and over.

This was, of course, not always easy, and we received explanatory notes in a number of cases about how the categorization was applied. The cut-off between 14 and 15 is particularly problematic, since, for example, students are typically 15 or even 16 when arriving at the end of compulsory schooling in certain Nordic countries. Overall, the result was that almost all respondents answered the questionnaire for the secondary level, many of those also answered for the intermediate level, and a few for the primary level. In many cases the answers for secondary and intermediate were the same, but when only one could be entered where they differed, we used the answers for the secondary level, except for the two countries which did not offer responses for the secondary level, for which we used the answers for the intermediate level.

The most complex problem was the inevitable subjectivity that entered, less in the responses to questions about structural factors (at what level civic education is offered, whether it is compulsory, etc), than to questions related to course content and method, where the respondent is asked to weigh the importance given to different elements. This becomes especially salient and needs to be taken into account when we compare countries.[7]

PRELIMINARY GENERALIZATIONS FROM THE IDEA CIVICED DATABASE

From the existing data (see Table 1) we learn that civic education related courses are targeted just only slightly more at the secondary (or upper secondary) level (aged 15-18) than at the intermediate level (12-14). A number of countries concentrate resources on the younger group because many students leave school at age 15.[8] Almost all countries offer some form of civic education, which is compulsory in three quarters of them, and authorities tend to give it importance – at least verbally. Yet, we found also that in just under two-thirds, civic education teachers do not have specific training related to the subject. Among important exceptions in this regard are the Scandinavian countries, where there is a special subfield in the university undergraduate teacher training program for civics teachers in which social science professors are directly involved.

Table 1. Structuring Civic Education

Civic education curriculum is determined at the national level (67%)
Civic education is compulsory within the curriculum (75%)
Civic education course time is specified in the curriculum (67%)
Civic education is a part of the school at the Intermediate and Secondary Levels (87%)
Civic education teachers do not have specific training in CE (64%)
Civic education is a specific/stand-alone course (56%)

Two profiles of how civic education is delivered and structured emerge from the above table, which we term "formal" and "informal". The ideal-type of a formal system is one in which civic education is compulsory for all students, in which the civic education curriculum is determined at the national level, the time allotted for instruction of civic education is specified within the curriculum, and teachers are required to possess and given specific training in civic education. It should be kept in mind that the formality here is a matter of regulations and rules; what actually happens in the classroom may be another matter.

The ideal-type of an informal structure features the opposite characteristics: civic education is not compulsory for students; teachers do not have specific teacher training opportunities; the civic education curriculum is determined at the local level; and there are no requirements for the time allotted for teaching civic education. Because informal systems allow more discretion at the local level, with individual teachers and schools determining the range of the civic education, it is more difficult to generalize since we can be sure of significant regional or in-school variations as to the characteristics of what is actually delivered and in the ways this is done.

As we can see, civic education is a specific/stand-alone course in just over half the countries (56%).[9] The responses to the question of whether countries delivered civic education as a stand-alone course, or whether it was incorporated into a wider curriculum (social studies, history, political science…) does not seem to correspond particularly to the other indicators of the formality or indeed the importance of civic education in a given country. This suggests that the choice is more a matter of packaging the content in a way to best present it in the national cultural and historical context.

This question has generated some discussion especially in the United Kingdom where it is decided locally.[10] In the end, the advantages of offering civic education in a particular set of courses, rather than spreading it out over different ones, is not intrinsic but rather procedural, in that it allows specific civic education-related goals to be more readily be assigned, outcomes monitored, and adjustments made when the targets are clearer. On the other hand, there is a risk that an ineffective civics course can produce results inferior to that when history and other classes encourage keeping up with political issues and discussing them in class.

Breaking down responses to the questions getting at the formality of civic education structures, i.e. whether civic education is compulsory for all students, curriculum is determined at the national level, time allotted is specified within the curriculum, and teachers are required to possess and given specific training in civic education, we get two profiles, with the countries displayed in the chart below most clearly fitting into each.

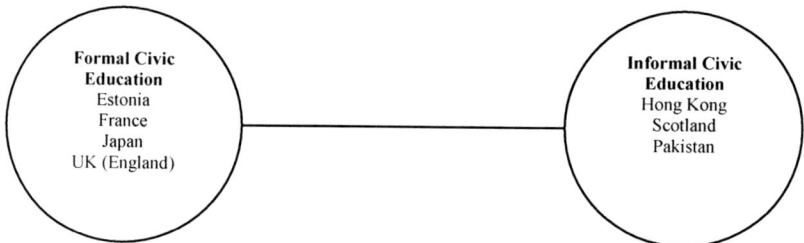

One related finding shows that the former communist countries participating in the survey (listed below) shared certain basic formal structural characteristics: civic education compulsory for all students, time for teaching specified, the curriculum determined at the national level, and teachers receiving training in civics education. Moreover, with the exception of Russia, in all of these cases, civic education is delivered as a stand-alone course in the curriculum. This regularity reflects historical patterns tied to communist regimes and possibly also similar external influences in the process of transforming civic education in the transition to post-communism.

Post-Communist countries	
Czech Republic	Slovenia
Estonia	Russia
Latvia	Ukraine
Lithuania	Vietnam
Serbia	

CIVIC EDUCATION AND ITS CONTENTS

In the questionnaire, respondents were asked to rank the importance of various components in the civic education curriculum, from no importance to very high importance (scale of 1-6). In the questionnaire, these included the following:

Components of Civic Education
Politics (National, Regional, Local)
International Affairs
Democratic Values
History
Community Involvement
Voting Procedures
Constitutional Principles
Good Citizenship
Civic Values

After some discussion, we chose to simplify by collapsing and combining them into five combined categories. The questions allowed for responses ranging from (1) for no importance to (6) for high importance. Countries where the average importance given to a curriculum component was 3.5 or higher are considered to rate this as important. We also created a similar breakdown based on two other characteristics, which are more related to methods than to content (found at the top of Table 2).

Table 2. Percentage Asserting Components of Course Content and Methodology to be Important

Methodology Questions
Is teaching civic education through classroom instruction important? (82%)
Is teaching civic education through out-of class, community-based opportunities important? (28%)
Content Questions
Are Politics and International Affairs an important component in civic education curriculum? (66%)
Are History and Constitutional Principles an important component in civic education curriculum? (69%)
69% of countries ranked this as important (average ranking: 3.9)
Are Democratic Values, Good Citizenship and Civic Values an important component in civic education curriculum? (76%)
Is Community Involvement an important component in civic education curriculum? (72%)
Is Voting Procedures an important component in civic education curriculum? (52%)

While we initially had thought that looking at the methods of instruction would shed light on varying country practices on civic education, and that, more specifically, there would be a link between countries emphasizing out-of-class activities and those more formally structured and more likely to stress community involvement, this is not the case.[11] On the characteristics related more to curriculum, we identified two distinctions that appear to be meaningful, though we need to keep in mind that in these questions the classifications are relative and subjective: seldom do respondents draw clear-cut distinctions.

The first contrast that emerged is between, on the one hand, countries that focused more strongly on *institutional knowledge* (politics, international affairs, history and constitutional principles) versus those that emphasized *values* (democratic values, good citizenship and civic values). The latter list is quite a bit longer than the former, on which we find only Japan, New Zealand, and Ukraine.

A second type of distinction that emerged is set out in the chart below. It is tied to the kinds of political participation emphasized in the curriculum. One group of countries appear to focus more on the mechanics and traditional forms of political participation; while another group focuses more on non-traditional forms of participation, specifically community involvement.

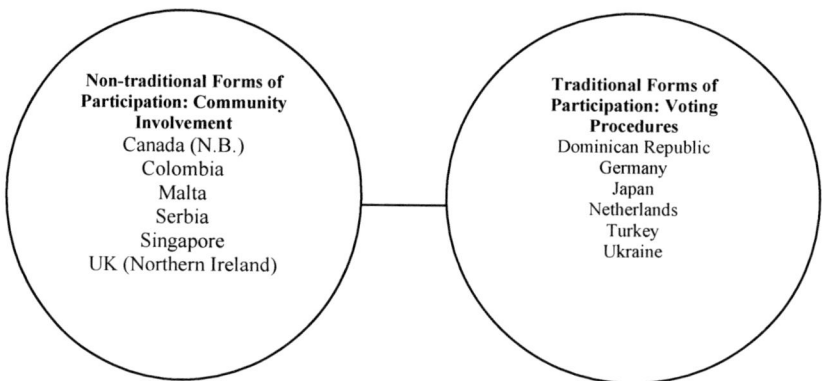

This was manifested also in the responses to the question about voting procedures. The first group gave higher scores of importance to teaching about such procedures, while the second rated community involvement as more important. The importance of this distinction can be seen in the fact that while, overall, of the five content elements, a notably lower percentage of countries rate voting procedures as important (52%) compared to community involvement (72%).

A glance at the above charts reveals that one country occurs repeatedly, namely Japan, which has a formal structure, emphasizing institutional knowledge and traditional forms of participation. It is also the only country using only written examinations and assignments for assessment.[12] The starkest contrast is with Serbia, which limits assessment to classroom performance and projects, and emphasizes community involvement and values.

There are, of course, more distinctions of this kind that can be drawn from the existing data – but the above serves the purposes of this paper.

FUTURE DIRECTIONS AND INITIAL POLICY RECOMMENDATIONS

The IDEA CIVICED database has the potential to develop into an important tool that will enable policy makers around the globe to make informed decisions based on best practices internationally from comprehensive, up-to-date, comparative data submitted and maintained by country experts, who would periodically review and update the material in the database in the context of both the national agenda and the latest research and developments in the field. To complement the data, there could be a web-based forum to enable researchers and policymakers to share insights. Should this potential be realized, it could create a virtuous circle, with up-to-date information incorporated into innovative policy-making the results of which is made available in the form of information on best practices in civic education.

If and when the database develops, we would get greater insight into the factors explaining the political attentiveness and participation of citizens. One area requiring further refinement is identification of forms and sources of funding on civic education. Of the initial participating countries in the database, 12 indicated specific funding allotted to civic education. In some instances, countries noted that it was an official government education authority, often in the form of dedicated funds for teacher training and specific in-service opportunities. In others, a third party, occasionally an NGO, provided training opportunities, as well as project funding for schools. One important outstanding research question thus concerns the impact and role that third parties, national or international, play on civic education.

As more sophisticated measures of comparative factual political knowledge are developed (see Milner forthcoming), it will be possible to more conclusively link the relationship between various elements of civic education and political knowledge levels. Researchers will be able to test whether countries that invest in civic education and make it compulsory boost youth political knowledge, and bring into the analysis contextual factors such as the voting age and compulsory voting.

But we are not there yet. In the meantime there are improvements to be made in the instrument, to take into account ideas offered in response to a request for respondents' comments and suggestions, especially about innovative practices, programs, and tools. One of these, already mentioned, concerns the role of third parties in civic education, such as Student Vote (Canada), the Citizenship Foundation (the United Kingdom). This aspect complements what seems to us an important, if tentative, conclusion from the data so far gathered. Generally speaking, civic education gives inadequate attention to the knowledge and understanding of how and why the government and political system function: of the mechanisms of government at all levels, and how the citizens-to-be can exercise their responsibilities. It is not surprising that these elements are neglected given the often lack of formal training of instructors in the context of a generally apolitical youth culture.

This is not a call for rote learning of constitutional principles and institutional procedures, which could only be counter-productive. *Ensuring that the education system plays a hand in introducing young people to how politics directly affects their own circumstance is critical for accruing the political knowledge needed for active citizenship.* Instead, it is a call for adopting and adapting innovative practices that can incorporate the kinds of electronic sources of information that are most promising in terms of the patterns and expectations of emerging generations. It entails identifying, using and creating materials for websites in a format attractive to young people that can be readily incorporated into modules of civics education courses and adapting the curriculum to be much more relevant for young people's own experiences. Role playing is an effective way to bring in politics, for example in mock elections, mock parliamentary committees or press conferences with a political figure in which the students' play the journalists (see Milner forthcoming). A more direct experience with the political system for young Canadians was a Students' Assembly that paralleled a Citizens' Assembly on electoral reform. This gave students a firsthand opportunity to engage directly in a policy-making capacity (see http://www.studentsassembly.ca/en/faq.php). In further developing the instrument to gather information about best practices in civic education, these are the kinds of engaging activities and methods that should be emphasized.

An important dimension in devising and adapting such techniques, is openness to bringing discussion of partisan politics into the classroom. This diverges from the mainstream American approach in which partisan politics is played down in favour of American history and the US constitution in the civics classroom and community-based volunteer activities outside it. We look briefly at these practices in the final section.

EPILOGUE: CIVIC EDUCATION IN THE UNITED STATES

As evidence of declining youth interest participation in and attentiveness to politics mounted in the 1990s, many American states developed or refined standards in high-school civics or government courses. The goal was to ensure that students acquired at least a minimal understanding of how their government works, and of its basic democratic values and fundamental historical documents and events.

Impetus came in 2003, in a Conference on Civic Education hosted by the Joint Congressional Leadership with the purpose of strengthening civic education at the state and local level. By the time of the fourth annual congress in 2006, some 26 states had conducted thorough surveys of their civic education practices at the state and district level; 14 states had established state commissions on civic education or civic literacy, and 36 states had introduced legislation to strengthen civic education[13]. At the formal educational level, in its education department's mission statement or in its statement of educational regulations, standards and codes, every state identifies civics as an important component of the education curriculum. Beyond this there is a vast network of civic education initiatives to be found in and also outside of the formal education system, some directed at youth generally, some to specific vulnerable groups (for example, the campaign of the Hispanic Federation).[14] And there is a plethora of private, non-profit foundations providing resources and model programs to schools.

To coordinate efforts, the Education Commission of the States created the National Center for Learning and Citizenship, which compiles and makes available quantitative information about such aspects as whether Citizenship Education is offered, any standards and curriculum requirements, whether it is required for high-school graduation, whether the courses are included in state assessments, and statutes, and whether there is a specific state website. The data reveal a certain progress, but also the distance yet to be travelled, for example, in establishing state-wide assessments aligned with their civics standards. A 2006 policy scan conducted by the National Center for Learning and Citizenship (see Lopez & Kirby 2007) found that while all 50 states and the District of Columbia required high schools teach civics or government, a substantial rise since 2003, there has been no parallel improvement in accountability measures. Only 21 states examinations for civics and/or social studies, a proportion slightly lower than that for the countries in the IDEA database.

Despite the states explicit requirement that there be a civics component in the curriculum, the reality is far more mixed as civic learning is often deemphasized as the curriculum becomes overcrowded with other courses (ranging from driver education to health to technology). The interpretation of this civics component varies: some states emphasize "character education", one stipulates that civics courses teach the mechanics of using voting machines, while others still stress service learning and civic engagement.

In high schools, until the 1960s, three courses in civics and government were common, and two of them ("civics" and "problems of democracy") explored the role of citizens and encouraged students to discuss current issues (Galston, 2004). Today, those courses have in most cases been replaced by a course on "American government" that places the priority on structure rather than process, and by civic engagement experiences that emphasize emotional connection rather than knowledge base. In a 2005 study of school district policies and practices, the New Jersey Campaign for the Civic Mission of Schools found that only 39 percent of districts in fact offered a required course in civic education.

Below we try to identify certain patterns in US states' approach to civic education. The information in this section has been primarily gathered from the information provided in and through the ECS from state departments of education, as well as from specific studies assessing civic education programs in the United States. One still useful compilation is provided by Gagnon (1999), categorizing the curriculum requirements for a "civic core" of subjects as set out by the board of education in each state. In the study he rated each state on five criteria: 1) content (does curriculum provide for a common core of learning about democracy for the political education of citizens?), 2) teachability (can the required or suggested topics be taught within the school year?), 3) scope and sequence (do the standards mandate a sequence of courses across the middle and high school curriculum?), 4) courses required (are all students required to partake in the civic core course or does it apply only to a limited stream?), and 5) content connection (are the concepts from civics, economics, geography and history linked where appropriate). His findings are reflected in the summaries below. While many states were judged as having an appropriate content or scope, this was undermined by no state having allocated sufficient time for the topics actually to be taught during the school year.

Training of Teachers

No state has a certification program for civics teachers. But extensive in-service training is part of the teachers' experience in most states. Many require that to maintain their teaching license they must take a specific number of in-service courses. Civics training or workshops in civics (some as one-day workshops, some as "summer institutes) are offered in many states. These are not limited to civics teachers and can be taken by any teacher to upgrade their certificates. Most are offered through various non-profit networks, such as the North Carolina Consortium on Civic Education and CIRCLE. But there is some uncertainty over how widespread this practice is: the previously cited 2005 New Jersey study found that just 35 percent of districts offered in-service training opportunities for teachers in civic learning, while a 2005 study of Arizona school districts, the Arizona Campaign for the Civic Mission of Schools, found that 53 percent of teachers had never undergone in-service professional development in civic learning (www.civiced.org/index).

Control over Curriculum Content

Control over the curriculum can be conceived as being exercised in three ways: 1) content; 2) time allocation; and 3) testing. Most states leave course arrangement and specific content to the districts, only providing guidelines. Though 20 states have recently conducted benchmark surveys of current policies and practices with the aim of identifying civic education needs, and legislators in 31 states have passed resolutions designed to strengthen civic education (Quigley, 2005), much variation persists. One type is represented by Alabama, which views methods and implementation as a local prerogative, with course order and content as a state responsibility. Other types are exemplified by Massachusetts, which requires all students to complete a course in history and civics but does not specify the actual number of hours required, and Nebraska, which leaves it to the local school district to determine time and content.

Some states identify specific content and competency skills; e.g. students must show that they understand the election process, while some states specify particular civic competencies but do not direct in which sort of course they are to be taught. For example, Iowa stipulates "that all students in grades nine through twelve complete, as a condition of graduation, instruction in American history and the governments of Iowa and the United States, including instruction in voting statutes and procedures, voter registration requirements, the use of paper ballots and voting machines in the election process, as well as the method of acquiring and casting an absentee ballot" (Iowa Code §280.9A).

Testing

No formal testing of civic education at the elementary level is required, and only about half of the states have state assessments in social studies and/or civic education. While most states and the District of Columbia have a course or credit requirement in government or civics for high school graduation (see previous table), only a few (Alabama, Georgia, Louisiana, New Mexico and New York) require students to pass an exit exam to graduate, though Delaware and Illinois require a graduation exam in social studies. Most states indicate that schools are to ensure that students show competencies in civic action but do not specify how this is to be measured and documented.

Time Allocation: At the elementary level civic education is understood to be woven throughout the curriculum. At the secondary level most states specify a particular amount of time in the school schedule for social studies and/or civic education. This is generally formulated in terms of periods per term. Where civic education is combined with social studies, however, the number of hours is usually specified. The most common allocation is a half course dedicated to civics education and two course credits to history/social studies.

COMMUNITY SERVICE

In response to the perceived lack of civic engagement by young people there has been a rush to provide and require community service as part of the secondary school experience. This is often presented as the major component of the student's civic education, yet it is not a testable component of the educational experience (showing up for the task is sufficient to pass). Moreover, providing this experience is often contracted out to community groups which can range from church groups that provide for the elderly, to welfare groups, to environmental groups. Almost half of public high schools in 1999 offered formal service-learning programs that were part of the curriculum (Skinner and Chapman, 1999) and the trend has increased in the last ten years. Some states differentiate between community service and service learning, the latter having a content basis. The community service component usually is overseen by outside agencies and is rarely systematically evaluated. For example: the District of Columbia specifies that the student must complete 100 hours of service; Washington State requires students to complete 60 hours of community service; the Maryland secondary school curriculum has a 75-hour community service component of which a minimum of 60 hours must be completed before the student can graduate. Notably absent is involvement in any kind of partisan political activities.

INVOLVEMENT OF OUTSIDE AGENCIES

Significantly, civic education – unlike other core courses – is often contracted out to other agencies. For example the Law Association in Texas is the primary trainer and determiner of content for civic education courses in that state. In the state of Washington, Americorps is a prime player in conducting civic engagement experiences. In North Carolina it is the NC Civic Education consortium based at UNC Chapel Hill which coordinates and directs grants obtained from foundations that fund civic education projects in the schools. Supervision of students in the service component may be conducted by private groups such as Rotary, social service centers, religious groups, and the like.

To this overall, and rather mixed, picture one element needs to be added. Though education is a state jurisdiction, with the federal government having no direct involvement, the states have found their autonomy encroached upon in recent years, notably through the 'No Child Left Behind' Act (NCLB). This is aimed at improving the performance of schools by increasing the standards of accountability for states, districts, and schools, especially in reading and math. Some educators have felt that this focus has had a detrimental effect on civic education. In a 2006 study by the Center for Education Policy (CEP – www.cep-dc.org) of 299 representative school districts in all fifty states, 71 percent of the surveyed districts reported reduced instructional time in at least one other subject to make more time for reading and math: civic education, with its less rigidly-determined content, makes an especially easy target. Some districts struggling to meet the requirements of the NCLB Act, (a poor score has detrimental effects not only for the school but for individual teachers) resort to doubling the amount of time allotted for reading and math, sometimes cutting out other subjects altogether.

In gathering this information, we have relied on secondary sources. It is hoped that the next round of questionnaires can also be sent to American educators, and that combined with the above sources, we will be able to develop a small number of profiles which would do justice the main approaches to civic education in the United States, while avoiding swamping the database with US data.

NOTES

[1] The following countries participated in the study: Australia, Belgium (French), Bulgaria, Canada, Chile, Colombia, Cyprus, Czech Republic, Denmark, England, Estonia, Finland, Germany, Greece, Hong Kong (SAR), Hungary, Israel, Italy, Latvia, Lithuania, Netherlands, Norway, Poland, Portugal, Romania, Russian Federation, Slovak Republic, Slovenia, Sweden, Switzerland, United States. Canada and the Netherlands participated in Phase 1 and Chile, Denmark, Estonia, Latvia, Norway, the Slovak Republic, and Sweden in Phase 2 only. Israel collected data only for upper secondary students.

[2] For the next round, planned for the end of the decade, the civic knowledge instrument is slated to have 80 questions, with 19 actually testing the cognitive domain of "knowing," as opposed to 61 testing that of "analyzing and reasoning". (*www.iea.nl/uploads/media/ICCS_01.ppt*)

[3] An indication of the culturally bounded nature of intention to participate in the future is the fact that Claes and Hooghe (2008) could find no relationship between what was reported to have gone on in the classroom and intention to participate among Canadian students.

[4] For the next round, planned for the end of the decade, the civic knowledge instrument is slated to have 80 questions, with 19 actually testing the cognitive domain of "knowing," as opposed to 61 testing that of "analyzing and reasoning". (*www.iea.nl/uploads/media/ICCS_01.ppt*)

[5] European Commission (Brussels, Belgium) published in 2004. Report entitled Citizenship Education at School in Europe. : http://www.eurydice.org/portal/page/portal/Eurydice/EuryStructureResult?chapId=141

[6] The state law (LOE, 2006) requirements must take up at least 55% of the time in regions that have a language of their own (Cataluña, País Vasco, Galicia, Comunidad Valenciana, Navarra e Islas Baleares) and 65% in the rest.

[7] For example, an observer in one country (A) will characterize the various elements that comprise the content of a civic education course as varying between moderately and highly important, while in another country (B) might do so as varying between of little importance and moderately important. In such a case, when we compare the importance of two of these elements, X and Y, A may very well classify X as moderately important and Y as highly important, and B may classify X as of little

importance and Y to be of no importance. Depending on how we do the comparison, we can conclude that either A or B assigns greater importance to X.

[8] In countries where the great majority of young people are still in school at 16 and 17, the evidence suggests that limited resources should go primarily toward students at that age, rather than at early adolescence, a stage of life not especially conducive to the kind of learning provided in civics courses. The effects of civics courses taken one hour weekly from grade 7 or 8 by almost all German students seem to have little effect (Händle et al, 1999). On Australia, Hugh MacKay concludes, "typically, teenagers find little to interest or inspire them in the political process, and they often report that politics is the most boring subject discussed at home" (quoted in Civics Expert Group, 1994:182). See also Dekker and Portengen (2000).

[9] In the decentralized educational systems in North America, only a minority of states and provinces have a compulsory civics education course as such. That is why the ECS (see Appendix 1) always refers to courses in civics, citizenship education or social studies.

[10] Kerr et al (2007) concluded that citizenship education is best delivered as a discrete element of the curriculum, while, Whiteley, also using data from a survey of British students, comes to a somewhat different conclusion. If citizenship is taught in dedicated classes, it weakens voting intentions compared to being spread widely among different subjects, such as history, geography or politics. Still, he concludes, what matters in the end is less where it is taught, than that it cover a wide variety of topics.

[11] The list of countries giving at least as much importance to out-of-class as to in-class activities is a short one: Colombia, Hong Kong, India, and Morocco.

[12] Pakistan goes even further, using only written examinations.

[13] See http://www.representativedemocracy.org/detail.asp?repdemPLinks_ID=12.

[14] For further information, consult the website of the Center for Education www.civiced.org and CIRCLE at www.civicyouth.org.

REFERENCES

Civics Expert Group. (1994). *Whereas the people: Civics and citizenship education*. Report of the Australian Commission on Civics and Citizenship. Canberra, ACT: Australian Government Publishing Service.

Dekker, H., & Portengen, R. (2000). Political knowledge: Theories and empirical research. In R. F. Farnen et al. (Eds.), *Democracies in transition: Political culture and socialization transformed in west and east*. Oldenburg: Bibliothek der Universitat.

Eurydice. (2005). *Citizenship education at school in Europe. Background note*. Brussels: European Commission Directorate-General for Education and Culture.

Franklin, M. N. (2004). *Voter turnout and the dynamics of electoral competition in established democracies since 1945*. Cambridge, UK: Cambridge University Press.

Gagnon, P. (2003). *Educating democracy: state standards to ensure a civic core*. Washington, DC: Albert Shanker Institute.

Galston, W. A. (2004). Civic education and political participation. PS Online. Retrieved April. From http://www.apsanet.org

Geissel, B. (2008). Reflections and findings on the critical citizen: Civic education – what for? *European Journal of Political Research, 47*(1), 34–63.

Händle, C., Oesterreich, D., & Trommer, L. (1999). Concepts of civic education in Germany based on a survey of expert opinion. In J. Torney-Purta, J. Schwille, & J.-A. Amadeo (Eds.), *Civic education across countries*. Amsterdam: International Association for the Evaluation of Educational Achievement.

Hillygus, D. S. (2005). The missing link: Exploring the relationship between higher education and political engagement. *Political Behavior, 27*(1).

Kerr, D., Joana, L., Julie, N., Kerensa, W., Elizabeth, C., & Tom, B. (2007). *Vision versus pragmatism: Citizenship in the secondary school curriculum in England*. Nottingham. United Kingdom: National Foundation for Educational Research.

Kleiner, B., & Chris, C. (2000). *Youth service-learning and community service among 6th through 12-Grade students in the United States: 1996 and 1999*. Washington, DC: U.S. Department of Education, Office of Educational Research and Improvement.

Lopez, M. H., & Emily, H. K. (2007, August). U.S. civics instruction: content and teaching strategies. *CIRCLE*.

Milner, H. (2002). *Civic literacy in today's world: How to make democracy work*. Hanover, NH: University Press of New England.

Milner, H. (Forthcoming). *Political dropouts or netizens: Democracy and the Internet generation*. Hanover, NH: University Press of New England.

Nie, N. H., & Sunshine, H. D. (2001). Education and democratic citizenship: Explorations into the effects of what happens in pursuit of the baccalaureate. In D. Ravitch & J. Viteritti (Eds.), *Education and civil society*. New Haven, CT: Yale University Press.

Print, M. (2007). Citizenship education and youth participation in democracy. *British Journal of Educational Studies, 55*(3), 325–345.

Quigley, C. E. (2005, September 25). *Keynote lecture. Third international conference on civic education*. Washington DC.

Skinner, R., & Chapman, C. (1999). *Service-learning and community service in K-12 public schools* (NCES 1999-043). U.S. Department of Education. Washington, DC: U.S. Government Printing Office.

Torney-Purta, J., Schwille, J., & Amadeo, J. (1999). *Civic education*

Torney-Purta, J. (2008). The IEA civic education study: Looking backward and looking forward. Presented at the civic education and political participation workshop, Université de Montréal, Montréal, Québec.

Torney-Purta, J., Schwille, J., & Amadeo, J. (1999). *Civic education across countries: Twenty-four national case studies from the IEA civic education project*. Delft, Netherlands: Eburon Publishers.

Torney-Purta, J. R., Oswald, L. H., & Schulz, W. (2001). *Citizenship and education in twenty-eight countries: Civic knowledge and engagement at aged fourteen*. Amsterdam: IEA.

Whiteley, P. (2005). Citizenship education longitudinal study: Second literature review. *Citizenship Education: The Political Science Perspective*. University of Essex Research Report RR631 2005.

MURRAY PRINT

7. CONNECTING YOUTH POLITICAL PARTICIPATION AND CIVIC EDUCATION IN SCHOOLS*

Modern democracies face a significant challenge to their viability and future sustainability. Dalton (2004) argues that "This challenge does not come from enemies within or outside the nation. Instead, the challenge comes from democracy's own citizens, who have grown distrustful of politicians, sceptical about democratic institutions, and disillusioned about how the democratic process functions" (p. 1). Similarly. Milner, Nguyen and Boylston (2008) note that "It is well established that the democratic world in the past 30 years has seen a secular decline in the sense of civic duty to vote, and, more generally, participate in politics." (p. 1)

While this is a general phenomenon that spans recent generations in most western democracies, for more than a decade the international literature has focussed its expression among the youngest adult generation and identified the need for that generation to become engaged in modern, formal democracy (Crick, 1998; Dalton, 2004; Galston, 2004; Forbig, 2005; Macedo, 2005; Print & Saha, 2006; Power Inquiry, 2006). Such engagement, the Power Inquiry (2006) argued, is necessary to avoid weakening the legitimacy of elected governments as they struggle with falling election turnouts as well as to counter the rise of undemocratic political forces and the growth of 'quiet authoritarianism' within government.

The literature has drawn attention to widespread disenchantment and disengagement of youth with political participation. Researchers have expressed concern with the lack of formal political participation of young people in modern democracies, primarily evident in declining voting turnout amongst young people, but also seen in other indicators such as joining political parties, contacting politicians and engaging with media (IDEA, 1999, 2002; CIRCLE, 2002; Galston, 2004; Macedo, 2005; Forbig, 2005; Print & Saha, 2006; Print, 2007; Wattenberg, 2007). Are there ways to address this situation through the education system? What can be done in the schools through civic education? Unlike certain observers who take a pessimistic view, this paper argues that civic education can facilitate youth participation in democracy. Essentially it takes an educational perspective to

---

* data presented in this paper come from the Youth Electoral Study conducted in Australia. The author wishes to thank the Australian Research Council for its support and his co-researcher, Larry Saha, for his contribution to the project. The author wishes to thank the editorial contributions of Andre Blais and Henry Milner.

illustrate how young people in schools might become more engaged in democratic behaviour especially voting.

This paper, I should add, also takes a normative perspective in arguing that participating in politics is good for democracies and an important component of being a democratic citizen. Hence it is assumed that civic education can, and should, be used to encourage young people to participate providing them with a positive civic education experience which enables young people to think and reflect about political participation and the reasons why they would, or would not, participate.

ALTERNATIVE FORMS OF POLITICAL PARTICIPATION

A first question to pose is does such a problem exist? Many argue that declining youth political participation is not a problem at all. Rather the current situation is merely young people changing their forms of participation from traditional forms (enrolling, voting, joining political parties, contacting politicians) to alternative forms such as a myriad of activities on the internet, boycotting, and buycotting (Print & Saha, 2007). Certainly evidence exists that young people do have political views, some with strong views and some participate in alternative political behaviour (Norris, 2002; O'Toole, 2003; O'Toole et al., 2003). Norris has argued that "In sum, indicators point more strongly toward the evolution, transformation, and reinvention of civic engagement than to its premature death." (2002, p. 4).

Although this argument has appeal the evidence, what exists, is far from compelling. In terms of the Internet for example, Wattenberg (2007) reported research indicating that few young people used the internet for reading online versions of newspapers. The argument does find some support from Jennings & Zeitner (2003) who found evidence of a digital divide and the internet having a positive effect on some indicators of civic engagement. However, they also found limited use of the internet for political reasons amongst the young. Considering the highly significant, general impact of the internet on youth this suggests a negative, relative impact in this context in terms of political participation.

In recent studies of political participation in the United States, Zukin, et al., (2006) supported by Wattenberg (2007) have made the case for a civic resurgence in the American polity. Adult Americans are participating more and comparatively they are amongst the highest in the world. But, as Wattenberg clearly shows, this does not apply to young Americans. Excluding the anomaly of school level 'volunteering' or service learning, he concludes "there is little evidence of exceptional youth participation." (2007, p. 195).

The assertion of alternative democratic participation of youth, therefore, must be tempered with caution. Several reasons support this caution. Even if young people do hold political views, by not being engaged through formalized activities such as voting, they have little ability to influence major political decisions and election outcomes. Second, participation in alternative political activities for the young is typically episodic or idiosyncratic in nature, usually located around a single/ limited, and often, topical issues. Moreover, such 'participation' demonstrates little evidence of sustainability in political terms, being driven by the immediacy mantra of this generation ... "we want it now." (Print, 2007).

A recent development also deserves comment. The Obama campaign to gain the Democratic nomination effectively utilized the Internet to gain support, engagement and finance. This was apparently the case during the US presidential elections, which took place too late to be incorporated into this chapter.

KEY CONCEPTS

There is widespread support for the notion that democracy is well grounded in the concept of public participation in political matters. Citizen participation, it is understood, is the very rationale of democracy, essential if democracies are to be viable, sustainable and healthy (Crick, 1998, 2002; International IDEA, 1999, 2002; Norris, 2002; Putnam, 2000; Power, 2006). As Dalton reminds us, "Democracy is a process and a set of political expectations that elevate democracy above other political forms.... Otherwise, we should praise authoritarian regimes..., but we do not..." (2004, p. 10).

Political participation connotes something more than political interest and political knowledge, though both may be necessary requirements to subsequent participation. Dalton (2004) distinguishes between different forms of political action, arguing that conventional participation (voting, contacting politicians) derives from a more positive view of politics and parliamentary democracy. By contrast, alternative forms of political participation, characterized by protest, boycotts, buycotts, and demonstrations, which challenge elites and institutionalised processes are more likely an outlet for those who distrust politicians and political parties. The essence of political participation, however, is citizen action in the political process, regardless of positive or negative views of politicians, parties or parliamentary democracy.

Drawing upon the IDEA Civic Education database, Milner, et al., (2008) note that citizenship education and civic education are sometimes used interchangeably, with the latter more commonly associated with activities such as subjects or courses taken at school in most countries. In terms of content civic education seeks to promote citizen engagement, involvement, and interest in politics and public affairs (see Crick Report, 1998), and to increase knowledge and reinforce the individual's sense of efficacy as a citizen (Verba et al., 1995). Often known as education for democratic citizenship, civic education may be defined as the opportunity to learn about our system of government, democracy, rule of law, rights and responsibilities, democratic values, and political issues (Patrick, 1999; Print, 2007). As such, its direct intention is to prepare young people for active citizenship, which implies voting in elections as well as more diverse democratic activities.

IS VOTING IMPORTANT?

The assumption is often made that voting is important to sustaining democracies. Voting in an election is an important contribution to maintaining the principle of popular sovereignty, a cornerstone of representative democracy. It is also the legitimate manner by which citizens can change their government. Of the various forms of political engagement, voting has a special role as it is the only form of political participation in which each citizen has an equal voice. While in principle the right to vote is a great equalizer of political influence in practice it is only shared by those who make the effort to exercise that right. Voting encourages effective dialogue between the governed and those who govern, at least in election campaigns. Perhaps most importantly voting in an election provides a mandate and legitimacy for the elected government and for the democratic system as a whole. Unlike other forms of participation, voting can directly change a government and is the ultimate form of accountability to the electorate.

It is reasonable to consider voting as a significant indicator of democratic engagement, a minimal sign of an individual's democratic participation as a citizen and, as Franklin (2004) notes, a useful indicator of the health of a democracy. Though there is some debate about the importance of voter turnout in a democracy, there exists widespread support for voting as a valuable expression of one's participation in a political entity (International IDEA, 2002). All in all then, it is clear that young people need to participate in their democracy and to vote.

However, international studies of youth voting show, in most established democracies, clear declines in youth turnout over the past two decades. In the United States, for example, since the introduction of voting at age eighteen in 1972 the percentage of young people (18-24 years) voting in presidential and non-presidential elections, steadily declined in every election until 2004 (CIRCLE, 2004). It is estimated that in the 2000 Presidential Elections only 32% of young people (18-24 years) voted, a record low turnout (CIRCLE, 2002). A concentrated effort to increase the youth turnout, particularly by the major political parties, produced an increased vote in the 2004 election to 47% of that youth group (CIRCLE, 2004) which will probably be sustained for the 2008 presidential election given the high level of youth support for the Democratic nominee and his campaign for change. However, it is too early to say if the downward turnout trend is merely temporarily suspended or will continue to be reversed in the future.

Participation of young people in UK elections presents a similar pattern. Over the past two decades there has been a noticeable decline in young people voting in general elections as well as local and European Union elections. The 2001 UK general election showed the youth vote had declined to 39% of the age cohort (The Electoral Commission, 2002). While voter turnout in the 2005 UK election increased marginally overall, the youth vote dropped to an all time low of 37%. (The Electoral Commission, 2005).

In Canada the situation is apparently worse, with the lowest youth turnout figures amongst the established democracies. In summary, O' Neill argued that "If legitimacy of a democratic political system rests on the number of citizens who participate is in its elections, then Canadian democracy is in some danger" (2001, p. 42). More specifically in terms of young Canadians Pammett and LeDuc (2003) found that in the 2000 Canadian elections youth turnout (18-20 year olds) was barely 22% compared with in excess of 80% for those over 58 years of age. For the

21-24 age group turnout increased marginally to 27.5%, while the turnout rate doubled for the thirties group and reached 83% for those 68 and older. By the 2004 elections youth voting has risen to 37%, but still barely one in three young people bothered to vote and participate.

Part of the explanation note Blais, et al., (2004), as they showed in the Canadian Electoral Study, is that young people have less sense of civic duty as well as less interest in and pay less attention to formal politics. For O'Neill, "The most worrying trend is the increased political disengagement apparent among younger Canadians, a trend unlikely to be overcome as they age because it is rooted in generational effects (2001, pp. 41-42).

In European Union elections voter turnout among young people is also declining, though the decline varies considerably across countries (International IDEA, 1999; 2002; Franklin, 2004). European youth tend to vote moderately highly at national elections, with a lower turnout at provincial, state or local levels. But the lowest level of voter turnout is clearly the European Union elections.

If voting is important to democracies then citizens need to participate. While some may argue for compulsory voting (Wattenberg, 2008) changing political cultures of this nature is highly problematic. Besides, the phenomenon of lower than expected voter turnout exists even in countries with compulsory voting (Print & Saha, 2006; Hallett, 2007).

WHAT IS THE CONNECTION?

Delli-Carpini and Keeter (1996) contend that informed American citizens are demonstrably better citizens, as judged by the accepted standards of democratic theory and practice. They are more likely to participate in politics, more likely to have meaningful, stable attitudes on issues, better able to link their interests with their attitudes, more likely to choose candidates who are consistent with their own attitudes, and more likely to support democratic norms, such as extending basic civil liberties to members of unpopular groups. Furthermore, "The differences between best – and least-informed citizens on all of these dimensions are dramatic." (1996, p. 272).

Nie, Junn and Stehlik-Barry (1996) noted a strong positive relationship between formal educational attainment (measured in years of completed schooling) and political behaviour, cognition and attitudes:

> Well-educated citizens display substantially greater levels of understanding of the principles of democratic government, have a much better ability to identify incumbent local and national leaders, …….. pay much closer attention to political life……. More likely to participate in political life, including those difficult activities of contacting public officials, working on political campaigns, serving on local boards…..are also more likely to vote in both local and presidential elections than their less educated counterparts (1996, p. 31).

Similarly in Canada, Blais et al., (2004) noted that "... the better educated are more prone to vote than the less-educated. We also know that the overall level of educational attainment has increased over time. Theoretically, the latter should have produced an increase in electoral participation. Yet, we observe precisely the opposite." (p. 222).

In Australia youth political participation and civic education in schools have been investigated extensively through the Youth Electoral Study (YES). More specifically YES is investigating the declining participation and increasing disengagement of young people in Australian democracy and elections. In the process the study has sought to understand how young adults become politically informed about and engaged in Australian democracy and identify why so many fail to vote. Using a mixed-method approach over a five-year period data were collected through in-depth group and individual interviews with youth aged 17-25 in school and non-school sites. A national cross sectional survey of nearly 5,000 Year 12 senior secondary students investigated student behaviour and attitudes towards democracy and voting as well as information about type of school, enrolments and citizenship education programs.

A formidable body of recent research on political socialization (Verba et al., 1995; Delli-Carpini & Keeter, 1996; Saha, 2000; Torney-Purta, 2002; Hooghie, 2004; Forbig, 2005; Zukin, et al., 2006; Print & Saha, 2008) identifies three primary sources of influence on young people's learning about politics and democracy – the family, through role modelling, discussion, and media use; the media, mostly television, radio and newspapers; and third, school experience providing knowledge, skills and values from non-partisan educators. Other potential sources of influence, such as peers, the extended family, community, and church, count for little.

Of these sources it has been widely argued that the school offers the best chance of building an informed, balanced sense of democratic worth, political knowledge and democratic values and skills (Nie, et al., 1996; Niemi & Junn, 1998; Patrick, 1999; Saha, 2000; Torney-Purta et al., 2001; Print, et al., 2002; Forbrig, 2005). Indeed, the best predictor of adult voting and democratic engagement available is the course taken in civics or citizenship education at school (Niemi & Junn, 1998).

EXPERIENCING CIVIC EDUCATION

It may be argued that in modern societies all students need to experience civic education in schools so they may become competent citizens in a representative democracy (Crick, 1998). It has become abundantly clear that the family does not, or cannot, provide this educative experience, even though research indicates that parents and television are influential sources of political information for young people. (Niemi & Junn, 1998; Torney-Purta, 2002; Print, Saha and Edwards 2004; Print & Saha, 2006, 2008). That leaves the school as the most logical source for conducting sustained and non-partisan civic education.

For young people much learning of political engagement is incidental, idiosyncratic and frequently superficial. Niemi and Junn (1998) acknowledged that even students in the later years of school developed most of their knowledge of government and politics from parents, friends, the media and even through direct contacts with government agencies. "Indeed, political scientists have largely ignored the high school civics curriculum, having concluded that efforts to teach civic knowledge in the schools are largely redundant and therefore ineffectual." (1998, p. 62). Therefore, learning civic education in a formalized, non-partisan, educational environment could lay sound foundations for future active citizenship.

American research by Niemi and Junn (1998) and Niemi and Finkel (2006) shows that studying civic education can make a difference to student civic knowledge, student civic values and student civic participation. In Australia, McAllister (1998) noted that education produced higher levels of political knowledge that, in turn, made people a 'better democratic citizen.' More broadly, citizenship education, which encourages students to acquire civic knowledge, civic skills and civic values, is widely acknowledged as more likely to produce engaged citizens (Niemi & Junn, 1998; Patrick, 1999; Saha, 2000; Torney-Purta, et al., 2001; Wattenberg, 2008) as well as to assist with the formation of social capital (Print & Coleman, 2003). Of course the form that civic education takes, and whether it makes a difference to political participation, may depend upon what type of citizen one wanted to produce (Westheimer & Kahne, 2004) and this has not sufficiently been accounted for in civics education curricula.

The first issue in experiencing civic education in schools is the necessary opportunity to learn through the school curriculum. That is, students should have the opportunity to experience learning about politics, democracy and civic engagement through taking a civics education subject. Milner, et al., (2008) using the IDEA Civic Education database found that, in the countries involved in the database, such opportunity was highly likely, though far from certain. In summary, the study found that:
- Civic education curriculum is determined at the national level (67%)
- Civic education is often compulsory within the curriculum (75%)
- Course time for civics is specified in the curriculum (67%)
- Civic education is usually located in the school at the Intermediate and Secondary Levels (87%)
- Civic education teachers do not have specific training in civics (64%)
- Civic education is often a specific/stand-alone course (56%)

The authors argue that ideal-type of formal education system is one where civic education is compulsory for all students. The characteristics of that civic education include a nationally determined curriculum, specified time is allocated for instruction within the curriculum, and specific training in civic education is required of teachers. However, while the formality reflects national regulations and rules the authors suggest what actually happens in the classroom may be another matter.

The Formal School Curriculum

In schools and educational systems the formal curriculum is usually conceptualised as school subjects. The critical feature is that these are the planned learning activities for students for which there are anticipated outcomes (Print & Coleman, 2003). Evidence indicates that opportunity to learn enhances political knowledge and political engagement. Niemi & Junn, for example, found in the 1988 NAEP Civics Study that for Years 4 and 8 a correlation existed between levels of student civic knowledge and the amount and frequency of civics studies in subjects such as Social Studies, American Government and Civics. Yet, in Year 12, they found that the amount of civics study is unrelated to student achievement in political knowledge.

The school, nevertheless, can make a difference to young people. Through the formal curriculum it can build levels of civic and political knowledge which can positively influence engagement and participation. School subjects which address civics and political issues are a necessary first step, but they are not sufficient to ensure political engagement (Youniss, et al., 1997; Patrick, 1999; Print, et al., 2003; Print & Saha, 2008).

There is, however, widespread research evidence showing that while opportunity to learn civics and democracy through the formal curriculum of schools is common (mostly through civics or social studies subjects), this subject is considered unimportant compared with other school subjects, has low status in the school curriculum, and is often found only near the end of compulsory schooling (Niemi & Junn, 1998; Torney-Purta, 2001; Galston, 2001; Print, Saha & Edwards, 2004). While the study of history is important by itself, and can contribute to civic education, it is not sufficient. The subject matter of history is substantively different from democratic citizenship. The role and perceived importance of education for democracy through the formal curriculum will need to be enhanced considerably if it is to make a significant impact on student knowledge, skills and participation.

So what did we find in Australia? Despite the existence of compulsory voting, well known by the young (Print, et al., 2004), the presence of civic education in the formal school curriculum is limited and haphazard. First we wanted to determine what students had studied in terms of school subjects where they could learn about civics. Like many countries, the study of civic education in schools is not undertaken in a subject called civics education. We found, as seen in Table 1, a range of subjects in the formal curriculum that students identified as a source for civics.

Table 1 also shows that students generally did not find these subjects particularly interesting that suggests different subjects are likely to produce different student outcomes in terms of political participation. We need to identify and nuance the nature of the curricula experience more precisely to identify if this is the case. The table also linked the identified school subjects to whether students indicated if they would vote (in a Federal election when 18 even if they did not have to), whether they were interested in the subjects which taught about the government, and the per cent who could correctly name both Houses of Parliament.

Table 1. Civics subjects Ranked by Voting Intention, Subject Interest and Knowledge. (N=3883)

	Would Vote Found % (Total N)	Found Study Interesting %(Total N)	Named Both House of Parl %(Total N)
Civics, Politics and International Relations	77.8 (153)	38.0 (160)	50.3 (161)
Geography	68.8 (109)	23.0 (113)	47.8 (113)
Australian Studies	68.7 (275)	24.7 (288)	42.6 (291)
Business, Economics and Commerce	64.5 (431)	27.1 (442)	50.1 (445)
Legal Studies	64.1 (460)	34.3 (481)	48.0 (485)
History	63.5 (875)	19.7 (899)	45.5 (913)
SOSE and Social Studies	57.4 (1032)	15.8 (1075)	29.8 (1089)
Humanities	54.4 (195)	21.6 (199)	32.9 (207)
No Response or Uncodable	52.9 (87)	25.0 (72)	27.8 (90)
Other (VET, Work Studies, Religion, etc)*	45.9 (85)	22.1 (86)	27.0 (89)

Source: Print & Saha, 2008

It is evident from the data in Table 1 that the school subject in which the student recalls having learned about the government does make a significant difference in voting commitment, in the level that the student found the study of government interesting, and in the level of political knowledge (naming the Houses of Parliament). However, we need to keep in mind that some subjects were compulsory while others were optional. As SOSE is a compulsory subject, while civics, politics and international relations are electives, it may be that the conditions under which subjects were taken might be a factor regarding the impact on students. Nevertheless, these differences do provide important information regarding the study of government in the curriculum.

The Youth Electoral Study has found a relationship between taking civic education courses in the formal curriculum and political participation in the form of intention to vote, voting in school elections, and standing for office in school elections. Figure 3 shows the relationship between studying civics and intention to vote, even if it were not compulsory. The difference in voting intention between those who have and have not studied about government may appear small, but the difference is statistically significant. Consequently the study of government does make a difference for students' commitment to voting when they reach voting age. What we don't know and would be helpful is how different forms of study of government are likely to affect intention to participate.

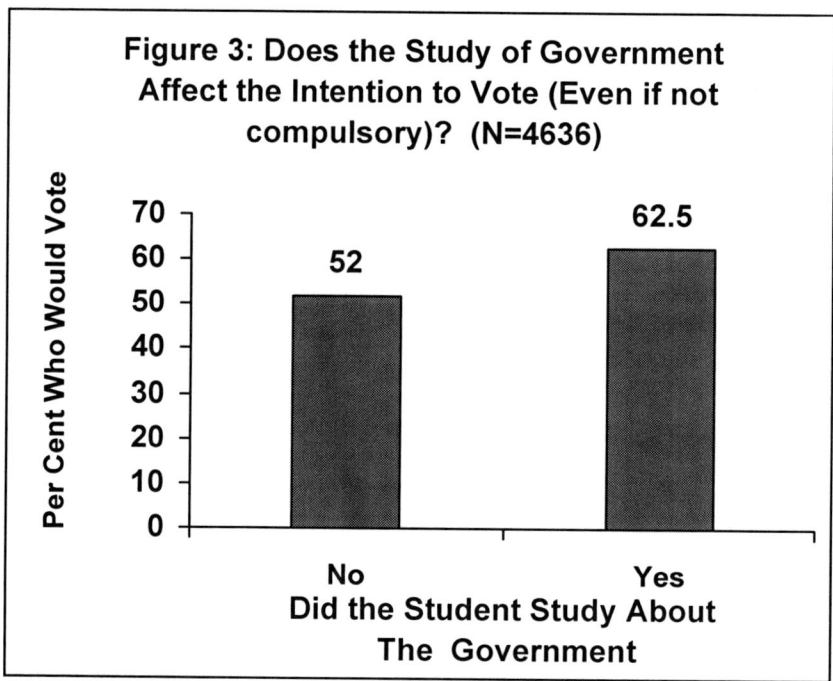

Source: Print & Saha, 2008

While it is comforting to know that the study of civics, in whatever form, does make a difference in voting intention, a more relevant question is whether the timing of the study of the government makes a difference. Like many countries, civics in Australia could be studied at several times in a student's school career. Would political engagement, especially voting, be more effectively promoted if taught in Years 11 or 12, closer to the time that students will be required to vote? We found very little difference between the grade level in which the students studied civics and their intention to vote. We found no correlation between the grade level of the study of government and intention to vote; the main significant correlation is between those who studied government and those who did not, the correlation (Pearson r) being 0.14 Thus the main issue regarding the study of government seems to be *whether* the students studied it, not *when* the students studied it.

We then considered, as seen in Figure 4, to what extent interest in government affects the extent to which students are committed to voting. It is clear that the more interesting the study of civics is found to be, the more likely the student is committed to voting. We further found that when the grade level of taking a government course is included in a regression equation, with interest and whether the student takes such a subject, the level of interest is by far the most important variable. The relative importance of these three variables is shown in Figure 5, which displays the standardized regression coefficients for each variable.

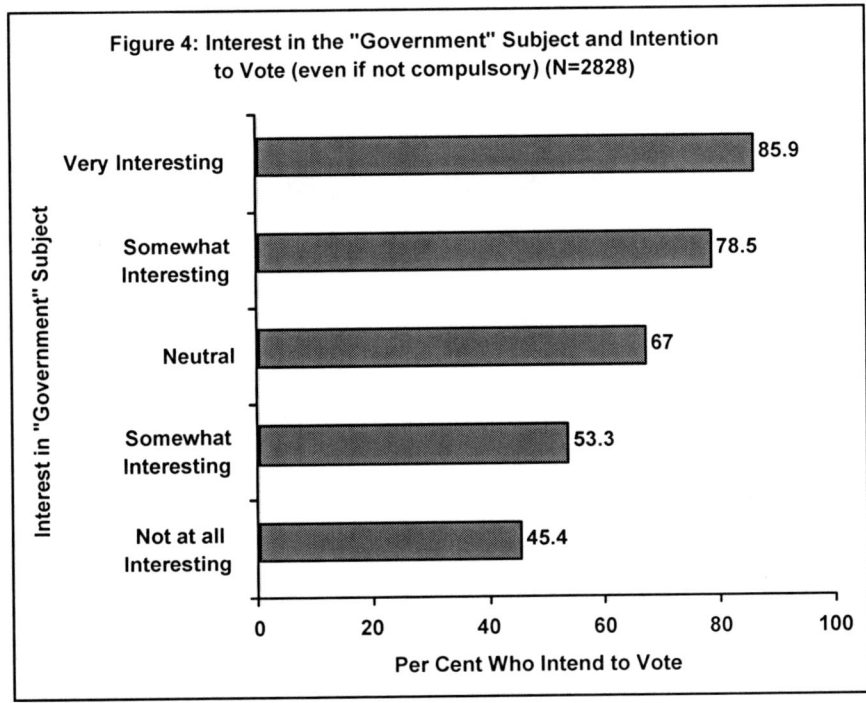

Figure 4: Interest in the "Government" Subject and Intention to Vote (even if not compulsory) (N=2828)

Source: Print & Saha, 2008

Although this is a simple model it does reveal that having taken civics, and being interested in government are important in political participation. At what time the student studied civics, in primary or any high school grade, is not related. As the figures represent standard units they are comparable and it is possible to say that being interested in government is four times more important than studying civics or not. For educators the message is that it is more important to teach civics in an engaging manner, than to teach it at all (though teaching civics is still better than not doing so). What makes the study of government interesting for students therefore becomes a major concern for policy makers, schools and teachers.

In summary, taking civics affects voting intention and political participation more generally. Clearly Figure 5 also reveals that engendering interest in government, through the means of the civics course, is highly important in encouraging political participation. Also we know that taking civics boosts civic knowledge and that a connection exists between knowledge and participation. But is all this enough? Why do many young people still not participate even if they study civics and their knowledge levels are good? In all, the YES data suggest that attending civic education classes in school may be a necessary, but not sufficient, stimulus to engage young people in political participation.

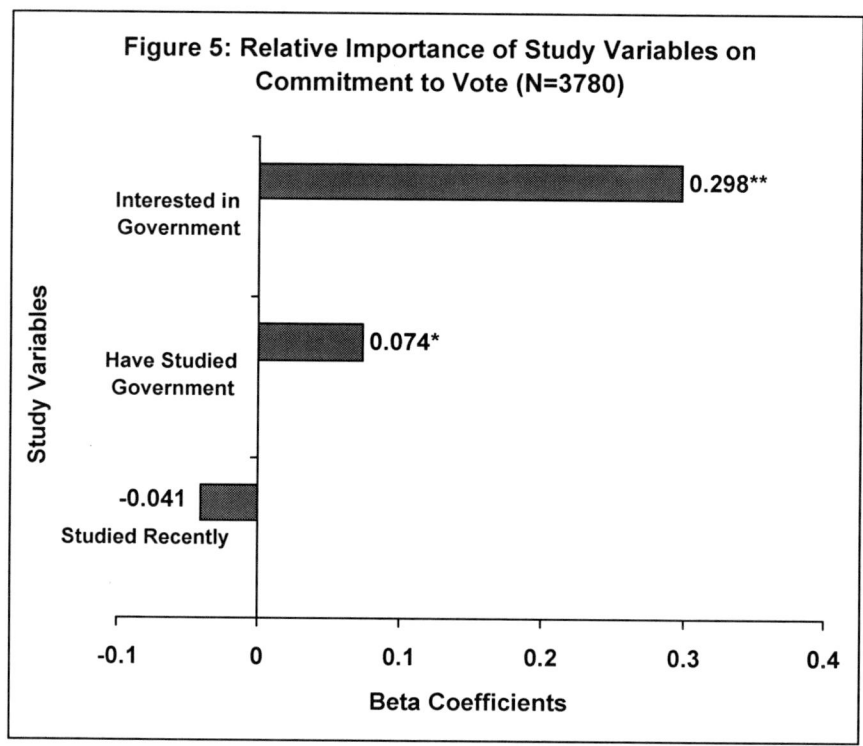

Figure 5: Relative Importance of Study Variables on Commitment to Vote (N=3780)

$R^2 = .09$
*** p > .000
** p > .01

A logical outcome then would be to require students to attend civics education courses at strategic times in their schooling. There are, however, three important caveats to consider in promoting civic education classes which, if not addressed through the formal curriculum, will undermine school attempts to engage young people with democracy. These factors are also likely to contribute significantly to making the study of government interesting for students. First, research shows that participatory pedagogy is generally weak in civic education classes. Rather, instruction in civics is characterized by textbooks, rote learning and non-participatory, non-critical strategies, as well as inadequate teacher preparation (Niemi & Junn, 1998; Hahn, 1998; Torney-Purta et al., 2001).

Second, substantial research shows that participatory approaches such as class voting, group inquiry, simulations, fieldwork and co-operative learning, are more likely to engage learners in experiential learning and aspects of democratic values and practice (Youniss et al., 1997; Niemi & Junn, 1998; Hahn, 1998; Torney-Purta et al., 2001; Print et al., 2002; Print & Saha, 2006). The EPPI review in Britain, for example, showed that engaged pedagogy can enhance student learning and achievement, especially when characterized by a facilitative, conversational pedagogy

(Deakin Crick et al., 2005). Such pedagogy can increase student participation, improve communication skills and empower students to become more engaged.

Finally, open, informed, meaningful and critical discussion with non-partisan teachers is highly significant in engaging students (Youniss et al., 1997; Hahn, 1998; Niemi & Junn, 1998; Torney-Purta et al., 2001; Torney-Purta, 2002; Deakin Crick et al., 2005). These approaches offer opportunities for learning about politics and building political participation.

Informal Curriculum

The YES research also found that civic education, when understood through the informal curriculum, also contributes to building political participation. The informal curriculum includes learning from non-school subject experiences. These activities are informal in that while they are recognized by the school they are characterized as non-subjects, low status and low value. Potentially, however, these activities constitute powerful means for educating about democracy and developing political participation. As Patrick argues "Participation in democratically run student organizations, and especially in student government activities, provides opportunities to practice the habits and skills of democracy." (1999, p. 53).

Two sets of related activities constitute the informal curriculum: instrumental activities and expressive activities. The former, which develop civic engagement, such as student governance, newspapers, debating, student elections, fundraising and political clubs (Kirlin, 2002; Print, Ornstrom & Neilsen, 2002; Print, 2007) are real, meaningful activities which encourage active participation by students and are positively correlated with later civic engagement. They are, potentially, the best predictor of adult political engagement. (Verba et al., 1995; Kirlin, 2002; Keeter et al., 2003). The latter, expressive activities, such as sports, clubs, bands and social activities, are seen as contributing less to building civic engagement, though they do fall along the same participation continuum. (Kirlin, 2002; Keeter, 2003).

Much has been made in recent years of volunteering and service learning particularly in relation to building civic engagement. This 'component' of the school curriculum is problematic as it is located at the crossroads between the formal curriculum (a 'required subject'?), the informal curriculum (within school volunteering) and the extra-curricular (volunteering outside the school). Volunteering drops sharply once young people enter the paid workforce and it is often characterized by young people as an alternative to formal politics (Galston, 2004). In his overview of participation by the young, Galston noted the problematic relationship between volunteering and political engagement. "They have confidence in personalized acts with consequences they can see for themselves; they have less confidence in collective actions...whose consequences they see as remote, opaque, and impossible to control." (p. 263). Others, however, argue that community service seems to assist civic engagement, generates pro-civic attitudes and is linked with civic knowledge (Kirlin, 2002; Keeter et al., 2002; Zukin et al., 2006).

A growing, body of literature contends that student participation in the informal curriculum is positively related to engaging young people in later political and civic life (Verba, Scholzman & Brady, 1995; Youniss, McClellan & Yates, 1997; Niemi & Chapman, 1999; Patrick, 1999). Over the past decade American research has demonstrated that participation in both student government and school interest groups is related to adult engagement in political and civic life (Verba, et al, 1995; Youniss, McLellan & Yates, 1997; Putnam, 2000). Verba and his colleagues (1995) argued that institutions in which individuals have an opportunity to practice democratic governance are 'schools of democracy'. In their retrospective study of adults, participation in student government while in high school was the most important school variable in predicting later adult political activity (Verba et al., 1995).

International research using the IEA Civics Study shows that the culture of the school is indeed significant in engaging young people (Torney-Purta et al., 2001). Schools, she suggests, are effective places for developing student engagement through ".... supporting effective participation opportunities such as school councils." (2002, p. 210). Yet these findings need qualification from the perspective of young Australians. The YES project found that while students appreciate these activities, they do not value them highly, largely because the school appears not to value them. In particular student government, for most students, and for the same reasons, was perceived as inconsequential. The most common student comment on student government was that the results were manipulated by teachers and could not be taken seriously (Saha, Print & Edwards, 2005). Students perceived they had little influence over important decisions, their opinions were not valued and student government had no or negligible power, unlike the case in Scandinavian countries (Print et al., 2002).

Yet the YES data show students who have voted in school elections are significantly more likely to vote, while those who have stood for a student election are even more likely to say they would vote as an adult (Saha, Print & Edwards, 2005). In the YES national survey, students were asked whether they had ever run for a school position, for example in the student association, school council, school parliament, or as a school prefect. They were also asked whether they had voted in elections for any of these positions. Figure 10 shows the difference between students who have and who have not voted in school elections, or who have or have not stood for office in school elections, and whether they would vote when 18 even if voting were not compulsory. These findings reinforce the argument that young people's political participation is likely to be significantly influenced by prior experience with student elections, even if they do not recognize the association.

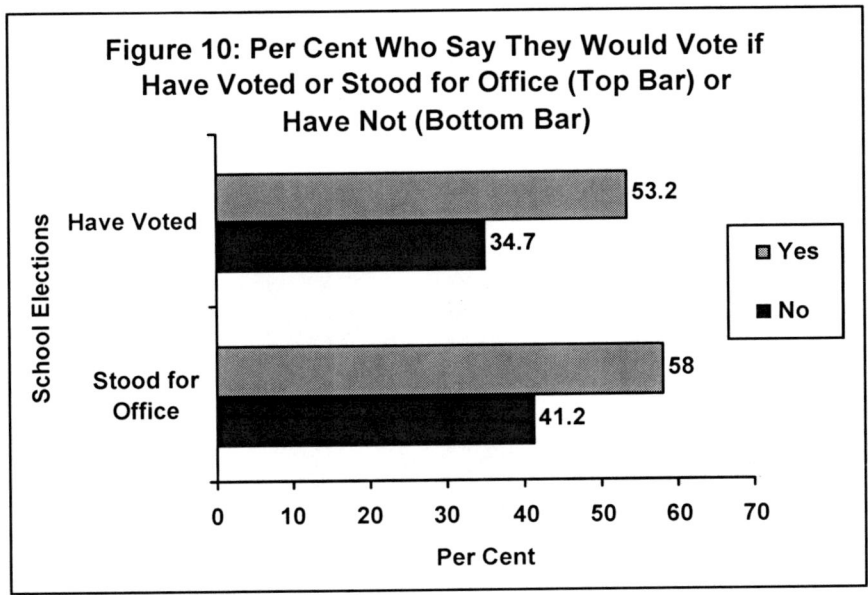

Source: Saha, Print & Edwards, 2005

A statistically significant difference exists between the attitudes to compulsory voting of those who have voted or not in student elections. A similar difference exists when students were asked if they had stood for office in school elections. These findings reinforce the argument that young people's electoral behaviour is likely to be significantly influenced by prior experience with voting.

Is participation in school elections related to the intention to vote? In YES Report 2 we briefly examined this question and concluded that it did (see Saha, Print, & Edwards, 2005) as seen in Figure 10 above. Here we examine the effects of student government involvement on potential voting more thoroughly. Figure 15 shows that the relationship between school election variables and commitment to vote is quite strong, with Pearson correlation coefficients of .16 and .17, for voting and standing for office respectively.

The data in Figure 15 are clear, revealing statistically significant differences. For those students who have stood for office, 65 per cent say they will vote when 18, compared with 48 per cent who have not. A similar relationship is found for those who have voted in school elections, with 60 per cent saying they will vote compared with 40 per cent who have not voted in a school election.

These data reveal that participating in school elections has a beneficial positive effect on political participation of secondary school students. The pattern is very clear, voting in and standing for school elections are strongly related to active political behaviour, which is consistent with the findings reported by Verba and his colleagues (1995), using retrospective data on a sample of American adults.

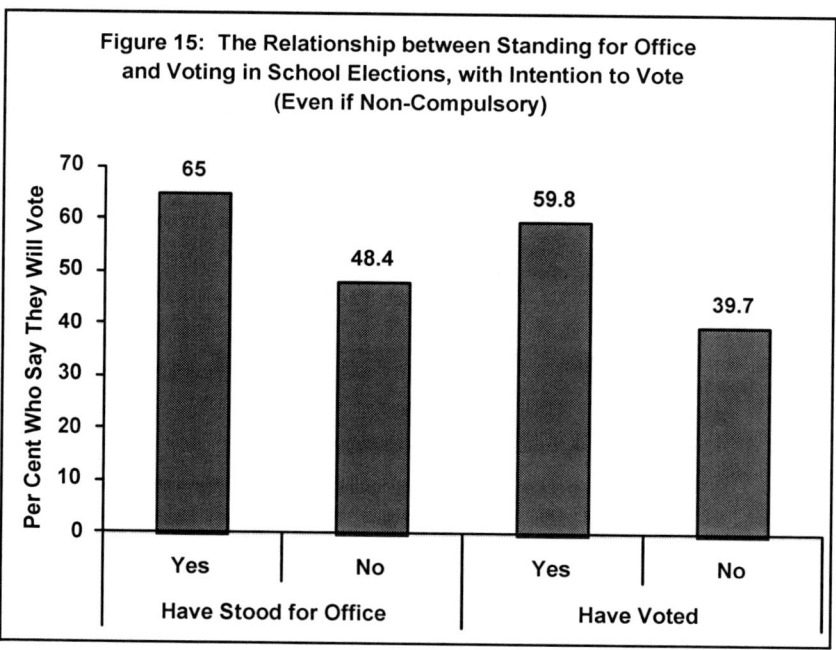

Figure 15: The Relationship between Standing for Office and Voting in School Elections, with Intention to Vote (Even if Non-Compulsory)

There are, however, several reservations to consider in relation to political participation and the informal curriculum. First, while student governance is undervalued by schools and students its power for building student political participation is diminished. Second, within the informal curriculum it appears that instrumental activities need to be encouraged more than expressive activities to develop participation. Third, volunteering and service learning need to be treated with caution. They may assist civic engagement but their problematic application (episodic, event-related) and 'required' status in many school contexts may diminish their positive impact on political participation.

YES REGRESSION MODEL

Looking at the YES data overall and along with the data from our comprehensive survey, we constructed a model that integrated a set of demographic and background variables (not discussed here) together with a set of school variables (not all discussed here). Table 2 presents Beta regression coefficients in standard deviation units from the same regression model, grouped separately for family and school and ranked by size and indicating statistical significance. The excluded variables are not statistically significant and cannot be regarded as having any direct independent influence.

As these figures came from the one regression model, each figure indicates the impact of that variable on voting commitment, controlling for all the other variables in the model. In the full model the school variables that exercise the largest impact on political participation are interest in the study of government and having voted in school elections. Furthermore, this impact occurs irrespective of the value of the other variables, such as gender, parental educational or occupational level, whether students like school or get along with their teachers, and whether they attended a government or private school.

Table 2. Beta Coefficients for the Full Simultaneous Multiple Regression Model, Family and School Variables on Commitment to Vote

Demographic/Background Variables Beta		School Variables Beta	
Info from parents - politics	.139*	Interest Study of Gov	.216*
Info from parents - voting	.118*	Voted in elections	.115*
Father's education	.091*	Get along with teachers	.088*
Father's occupation	-.053*	Like school	.058*
Sex of student	-.026	Stood for office	.046*
Mother's occupation	.017	Studied Government	.022
Mother's education	.014	Attend private school	.008

* $p > .05$
$R^2 = .21$.

We learn that taking a course about Australian government does not have a statistically significant impact on commitment to voting. Whatever relationship might exist at the bivariate level disappears when the other variables are taken into account. On the other hand, the variable with the strongest unique impact, for both the school and family variables, is interest in the study of government. The next most important school variable is voting in a school election. Clearly school elections, and the general satisfaction of the student with the school, have significant impacts on student political participation, irrespective of whether the student's gender or socioeconomic background.

Also interesting in this model is the coexisting impact of the family. The student's commitment to voting is not a function of only the family, or only the school, but a combination of both. In the family, both the extent to which the student learns about politics from their parents, and the extent to which the student claims to be influenced about voting by parents, appear very important in affecting the student's commitment to voting. Again, these effects occur independently of the student's relationship with the school. Using these school and family variables it is possible to make some strong statements about the effect of the school on political participation. The regression model explained 21 per cent of the variance, which by sociological standards, indicates a fairly strong model.

CONCLUSIONS

Research has identified widespread disenchantment and disengagement of youth with formal political participation, expressed through declining turnout amongst young people, but also in other indicators such as joining political parties and contacting politicians. Explanations claiming their being replaced by alternative forms of political participation by the young, however, must be treated cautiously. There is, however, now even more evidence that civic education can make a contribution to enhancing political participation in young people. This contribution may be seen in both the formal and informal curricula. However, civic education could make a greater contribution in both areas. In itself, taking a civics subject at school is helpful, but not sufficient to build strong participation.

Now that interest in the study of government has been identified as a key factor in boosting political participation educational systems need to pay more attention to making civics education more interesting for young people as do schools and teachers. They also need to take school elections more seriously. The data indicate that students who participate in school elections, by voting or standing for office, are more politically engaged. Furthermore this effect is not explained by other variables in our model.

Finally educators need to appeal to parents to involve their children in family political life by encouraging them to register to vote and accompanying them to vote, as well as through family discussions on political issues. Combined with the efforts through the schools, the total effect on building political participation amongst the young would be substantial.

REFERENCES

Blais, A., Gidengil, E., Nevitte, N., & Nadeau, R. (2004). Where does turnout decline come from? *European Journal of Political Research, 43*, 221–236.

Centre for Information and Research on Civic Learning and Engagement (CIRCLE). (2002). *Youth civic engagement: Facts and trends.* Maryland: CIRCLE

Centre for Information and Research on Civic Learning and Engagement (CIRCLE) (2004). *The Youth Vote in 2004.* Maryland: CIRCLE

Crick, B. (1998). *(Chair) Education for citizenship and the teaching of democracy in schools.* London: Qualifications and Curriculum Authority.

Crick, B. (2002). *Democracy.* Oxford, UK: Oxford University Press.

Dalton, R. (2004). *Democratic challenges, democratic choices: The erosion of political support in advanced industrial democracies.* Oxford, UK: Oxford University Press

Deakin, C. R., Taylor, M., Tew, M., Samuel, E., Durant, K., & Ritchie, S. (2005). A Systematic review of the impact of citizenship education on student learning and achievement. In: *Research evidence in education library.* London: EPPI-Centre, Institute of Education

Delli, C. M., & Keeter, S. (1996). *What Americans know about politics and why it matters.* New Haven, CT: Yale University Press.

Forbrig, J. (Ed.). (2005). *Revisiting youth political participation.* Strasbourg: Council of Europe.

Franklin, M. (2004). *Voter Turnout and the dynamics of electoral competition in established democracies since 1945.* Cambridge, UK: Cambridge University Press.

Galston, W. (2004, April). Civic education and political participation. *PS: Political Science and Politics,* 263–266.

Hahn, C. (1998). *Becoming Political.* Albany, NY: State University of New York.

Hallet, B. (2007). Legislation on youth enrolment and voting. In L. Saha, M. Print, & K. Edwards (Eds.), *Youth and political participation.* Amsterdam: Sense Publishers

Hooghe, M. (2004). Political socialization and the future of politics. *Acta Politica, 39,* 331–341.

International IDEA. (1999). Youth voter participation. Stockholm: International Institute for Democracy and Electoral Assistance.

International IDEA. (2002). *Voter Turnout Since 1945*. Stockholm: International Institute for Democracy and Electoral Assistance.
Jennings, K., & Zeitner, V. (2003). Internet use and civic engagement. *Public Opinion Quarterly, 67*, 311–334.
Keeter, S., Zukin, C., Andolina, M., & Jenkins, K. (2002). *The civic and political health of a nation: A generational portrait*. Maryland: CIRCLE.
Kirlin, M. (2002). Civic skill building: The missing component in Service learning? *PS: Political Science and Politics, 3*(35), 571–575.
McAllister, I. (1998). Civic education and political knowledge in Australia. *Australian Journal of Political Science, 33*(2), 7–23.
Macedo, S. et al. (2005). *Democracy at Risk*. Washington, DC: Brookings Institute
Milner, H. (2002). *Civic literacy in today's world: How to make democracy work*. Hanover, NH: University Press of New England.
Milner, H., Nguyen, C., & Boylston, F. (2008). Variations in civic education: The IDEA civic education database. Discussion paper from http:// www.civiced.idea.int
Nie, N., Junn, J., & Stehlik-Barry, K. (1996). *Education and democratic citizenship in America*. Chicago: University of Chicago Press.
Niemi, R., & Junn, J. (1998). *Civic education: What makes students learn*. New Haven, CT.: Yale University Press.
Niemi, R. G., & Finkel, S. E. (2006). Civic education and the development of civic knowledge and attitudes. In L. Harrison & J. Kagen (Eds.), *Essays on cultural change*. Routledge.
Norris, P. (2002). *Democratic phoenix: Reinventing political activism*. Cambridge, UK: Cambridge University Press.
O'Toole, T. (2003). Engaging with young people's conceptions of the political. *Children's Geographies, 1*(1), 71–90.
O'Toole, T., Lister, M., Marsh, D., Jones, S., & McDonagh (2003). Tuning out or left out? Participation and non-partiicpation among young people. *Contemporary Politics, 9*(1), 45–61.
Pammett, J., & LeDuc, L. (2003). *Explaining the turnout decline in Canadian federal elections: A new survey of non-voters*. Ottawa, ON: Elections Canada.
Patrick, J. (1999). Education for constructive engagement of citizens in democratic civil Society. In C. Bahmueller & J. Patrick (Eds.), *Principles and practices of education for democratic citizenship*. Bloomington, IN: ERIC Clearinghouse.
Print, M. (2007). Citizenship education and youth participation in democracy. *British Journal of Educational Studies, 55*(3), 325–345.
Print, M., Ornstrom, S., & Nielsen, H. (2002). Education for democratic processes in schools and classrooms. *European Journal of Education, 37*(2), 193–210.
Print, M., & Coleman, D. (2003). Towards understanding social capital and citizenship education. *Cambridge Journal of Education, 33*(1), 123–149.
Print, M., Saha, L., & Edwards, K. (2004). *Youth electoral study: Report 1*. Canberra, ACT: Australian Electoral Commission
Print, M., & Saha, L. (2006). *Adequacy of civics and electoral education in Australia .Invited submission to the joint standing committee on electoral matters*. Canberra, ACT: Parliament of Australia
Print, M., & Saha, L. (2007). Youth, democracy and politics: Issues in Australia. In, L. Saha, M. Print, and K. Edwards (Eds.) (2005), *Youth and political participation*. Rotterdam, The Netherlands: Sense Publishers.
Print, M., & Saha, L. (2008). *Youth, schools and learning about politics*. Report 5. Canberra, ACT: Australian Electoral Commission.
Saha, L. (2000). Political activism and civic education among Australian secondary school students. *Australian Journal of Education, 44*(2), 155–174.
Saha, L., Print, M., & Edwards, K. (2005). *Youth, political engagement and voting*. Report 2. Canberra, ACT: Australian Electoral Commission.
The Electoral Commission. (2002). *Voter engagement and young people*. London: The Electoral Commission.
The Electoral Commission. (2005). *Election 2005: Turnout*. London: The Electoral Commission
The Power Inquiry. (2006). *Power to the people*. York: York Publishing Distribution

Torney-Purta, J., Lehaman, R., Oswald, H., & Schulz, W. (2001). *Citizenship and education in twenty-eight countries: Civic knowledge and engagement at age fourteen.* Amsterdam: International Association for the Evaluation of Educational Achievement.

Torney-Purta, J. (2002). The school's role in developing civic engagement: A study of adolescents in twenty-eight countries. *Applied Developmental Science, 5*(4), 203–212.

Verba, S., Scholzman, K., & Brady, H. (1995). *Voice and equality: Civic voluntarism in American politics.* Cambridge, MA: Harvard University Press

Wattenberg, M. (2007). *Is voting for young people?* New York: Longman

Westheimer, J., & Kahne, J. (2004). What kind of citizen? The politics of educating for democracy. *American Educational Research Journal, 41*(2), 237–269.

Youniss, J., McClelland, A., & Yates, M. (1997). What we know about engendering civic identity. *American Behavioural Scientist, 40,* 620–631.

Zukin, C., Keeter, S., Andolina, M., Jenkins, K., & Delli Carpini, M. (2006). *A new engagement? Political participation, Civic life, and the Changing American Citizen.* New York: Oxford University Press.

ALAN SEARS

8. CHILDREN'S UNDERSTANDINGS OF DEMOCRATIC PARTICIPATION: LESSONS FOR CIVIC EDUCATION

INTRODUCTION

In recent years the perception of growing levels of disengagement of young people from democratic civic participation has generated significant levels of concern around the world. This is often manifested in academic and public discourse as a crisis or, a set of "overlapping crises" which a colleague and I have described elsewhere as the crises of "ignorance, alienation and agnosticism" (Sears & Hyslop-Margison, 2007, 46; Faulks, 2006). These concerns have led to a flurry of activity in a range of areas including a greatly expanding body of academic and scholarly work as well as a plethora of public policy debates and initiatives around the world (See, Arthur, Davies & Hahn, 2008). Perhaps the most recent of the latter is the revised National Curriculum in Citizenship that England implement in the fall of 2008 (Qualifications and Curriculum Authority, 2007).

This revision follows on from years of very substantial policy development and implementation in England beginning with the work of the Advisory Group on Citizenship (1998), the so-called 'Crick Commission,' in the 1990s and continuing with the first national curriculum order being implemented in the fall of 2002, and a considerable range of complimentary work in pre and in-service teacher education as well as materials development and research. While England is arguably the jurisdiction with the most comprehensive and well funded set of initiatives in the field, it is by no means alone in making this a priority area. Australia, for example, has made participatory citizenship one of its key national goals for schooling, spent 28 million Australian dollars on the Developing Democracy Program for schools and provided significant funding for the Youth Electoral Study (YES) to gage the civic involvement of young people in that country (Saha, Print & Edwards, 2007). Indeed, virtually every democratic jurisdiction in the world as well as a number of multilateral and international organizations such as the Council of Europe and the International Association for the Evaluation of Educational Achievement (IEA) have launched significant initiatives in civic education in the past two decades.

While this flurry of interest and reform is heartening for those involved in civic education, there are clear dangers involved in developing and implementing public policy as a response to perceived crises. As Stein (2001) points out, policy debates in that kind of atmosphere are often overly ideological and lack for analysis regarding both what the actual issues are and possible solutions might be. The field of education generally and civics and citizenship education in particular has certainly not been immune to this kind of ill-advised rush to reform. Indeed, one scholar describes the history of education as a failed "search for panaceas" largely driven by ideology rather than evidence (Hunt, 2002).

Space does not permit full discussion of why education is particularly vulnerable to this approach to policy making but it certainly has something to do with the fact that everyone has been to school and has a commonsense view of how learning happens and what shape schooling should take to facilitate that. As educational psychologist Howard Gardner (2006, 3) points out, however, what we know about how children learn is often "deeply counterintuitive" and commonsense views about learning "are often common nonsense."

In this chapter I argue that research in the area of cognition and prior knowledge generally and related to civic education in particular provide us with important lessons for the development of policy and practice in the field. Many of these lessons are "deeply counterintuitive" which means, somewhat ironically, if the central findings of cognitive science over the past century are true, both academics and the wider public will find them difficult to accept. It is essential, however, that we at least let these findings create the dissonance necessary to challenge our taken for granted assumptions about what may or may not work in civic education.

Caveats

In considering these arguments a couple of caveats should be kept in mind. First, the idea of drawing 'lessons' from research can be deceptive. Despite what some researchers might say, "One can never proceed directly and unambiguously from a scientific finding to an educational practice" (Gardner, 2006, 219). Context matters very much in education both in terms of shaping the knowledge students come to school with and in terms of what form schooling, including teaching and learning, can and should take. Educational policy is always made in political and social contexts with complex combinations of perceived needs, priorities and resources. Any research lessons have to be examined in light of those sometimes competing concerns (Barton & Levstik, 2004).

Second, an overly prescriptive approach by researchers to the application of their research findings discounts the experience and role of educational practitioners in shaping policy making and practice. From a purely pragmatic point of view this has been shown to be disastrous for educational reform. More than a century of evidence clearly demonstrates that teachers, schools and school systems can and will thwart reform efforts from which they feel alienated (Tyack & Cuban, 1995). More importantly, practitioners should not be regarded simply as implementers of policies developed by others but as colleagues in a process of deciding what to do and how to do it. Hargreaves (2003) argues that over the past twenty years educational reformers have discounted teacher professional autonomy to the great detriment of progressive reform. He contends that good teachers have "the competence and confidence to engage critically, not compliantly, with the research that informs their practice" (p. 29). In light of these caveats the 'lessons' that follow are intended as starting points for broader discussion rather than end points for implementation.

Lesson One: Prior Knowledge Matters

In 1909 Charles Doolittle Walcott, director of the Smithsonian Institution, discovered what came to be known as the Burgess Shale high in the mountains of British Columbia, Canada. The rocky outcropping is one of the richest deposits of fossils in the world and its discovery precipitated a significant rethinking of evolutionary theory. This rethinking did not begin right away, however, but was delayed more than fifty years because the scientists who first worked on the shale did not see what was there but what they wanted to be there. In his book *Wonderful Life: The Burgess Shale and the Nature of History* the late Harvard palaeontologist Stephen J. Gould (Gould, 1989, 24) argues that Walcott and his immediate successors were so locked into the evolutionary framework of the day they "shoehorned" the evidence into that framework rather than letting it speak for itself. It was decades before another group of scientists allowed the fossil evidence to challenge their prior conceptions of evolution.

This story is illustrative of a central tenet of what Gardner (2006, 74) calls the "cognitive revolution" of the twentieth century; that people come to any learning situation with a set of cognitive structures that filter and shape new information in powerful ways. He calls these structures "mental representations" and argues they underlie the fact that "individuals do not just react to or perform in the world; they possess minds and these minds contain images, schemes, pictures, frames, languages, ideas, and the like" (p. 76). The literature uses a range of different terms but generally refers to this phenomenon as prior knowledge; meaning the knowledge learners brings with them to the classroom or any other learning situation.

As in the case of Walcott and other early scientists working with fossils from the Burgess Shale, these mental representations or frameworks are often incomplete, "naïve," or just plain wrong (Byrnes & Torney-Purta, 1995). In the words of Gardner (2006, 227), "Many of the theories espoused by young children are wonderful; some are charming; some of them are dead wrong from the point of view of physics, biology, psychology, history."

Research demonstrates not only that learners bring mental frameworks or schemata with them to learning situations, but that these filter and shape new learning. When presented with information that does not fit existing frameworks learners will often distort it or discard it completely rather than doing the difficult work necessary to restructure their frameworks (See, Hughes & Sears, 2004). Research on prior knowledge consistently shows cognitive schema to be persistent and resistant to change.

Barton and Levstik (2004) provide a clear example from their research on children's understandings of history of how pre-existing frameworks shape new knowledge. A large body of work in this field demonstrates that American students have a conception of the history of the United States framed by the twin themes of freedom and progress. This view allows for slight deviations from the nation's commitment to freedom or minor set backs on the road to progress in the American story, but the overall direction of American history is toward greater freedom as well as social and economic progress. As part of their work Barton and Levstik exposed students to historical material that countered these preconceptions and found, "so powerful was the narrative of progress that it led students to distort the historical evidence to fit their preconceptions" (p. 170).

Barton and Levstik's findings illustrate the central implication of research on prior knowledge; in order to be effective curricula and teaching must take the cognitive schema of students into account and operate to create the cognitive dissonance necessary to foster the reframing of those schema in line with more accurate and sophisticated understandings of the concepts and/or process being studied. If this is not done, teaching all the right information in the world will be largely ineffective. As Gardner (2006, 77) writes, "If one wants to educate for genuine understanding, then, it is important to identify these early representations, appreciate their power, and confront them directly and repeatedly."

An obvious implication for civic education is that it is necessary to build a body of work on how students understand key ideas and processes related to democracy and democratic participation. Compared to the areas of mathematics and science, social educators have been slow to build a body of knowledge about how children and young people understand the social and political world (Hughes & Sears, 1996; Peck, Sears & Donaldson, 2008). A significant exception to this is history education where researchers around the world have made a significant start at building a knowledge base for how students understand historical ideas and processes and the implications of these understandings for policy and practice (See, for example, Stearns, Seixas & Wineburg, 2000; Wineburg, 2001; Seixas, 2004; Sandwell, 2006; Lévesque, 2008). Much of their work, such as that cited by Barton and Levstik above, has direct implications for civic education.

While the knowledge base for young people's understandings of the key concepts and processes related to democratic citizenship is not nearly as comprehensive as that in history education, it is growing and has important implications for practice in the field. A number of studies, for example, indicate young people across the world have a very strong orientation away from conventional forms of political participation associated with formal political systems and toward more unconventional or grassroots engagement. For example, the IEA study of 90,000 14 year-olds in 28 countries found that "the generation of young people represented by the study's 14-year-olds is gravitating to affiliation and action connected to social movement groups and not to political discussions or formal relations with political parties" (Torney-Purta, Lehmann, Oswald & Schulz, 2001, 81). Similarly, a range of work from Australia and the United States shows young people generally moving away from engagement in the formal political realm but participating in a range of other ways (Vromen, 2003a; Zukin, Keeter, Andolina & Carpini, 2006; Dalton, 2008). In these cases the research demonstrates not only that young people behave in particular ways but that they understand good citizenship and participation in distinct ways. Dalton (2008, 75), for example, argues that "different images of citizenship" have more to do with shaping civic behaviour than levels of interest or apathy.

This kind of understanding is clearly demonstrated in phenomenographic research on understandings of democratic participation conducted by Chareka and Sears (2005; 2006). As part of this work participants were shown sets of pictures "depicting various kinds of civic participation ranging from community based activities such as volunteering in a food bank through more formal political activities like voting or running for office" (Chareka & Sears, 2005, 52). They were asked to select pictures or sets of pictures they wanted to talk about and then interviewed about their choices.

Virtually all of the participants separated the pictures into two groups clearly identifying one group as political and the other as non-political. In looking at the pictures of people voting, participating in party meetings, or running for office participants said things like, "Now we are talking politics" or "This is politics, are you political?" (Chareka & Sears, 2005, 53). All participants were also explicit and forceful in saying that they saw their own participation as falling in the realm they considered non-political. One even said about pictures showing grassroots community involvement, "Things like this are real citizen involvement, not politics" (p. 54).

It is clear that a significant number of young people across democratic jurisdictions have a conception of participation that privileges forms of engagement other than those associated with formal political systems. Some have argued that this is not necessarily a problem for democratic societies but I disagree for at least two reasons. First, I share concerns raised by the directors of the YES in Australia that disengagement from formal politics is a threat to the legitimacy and long term health of democratic governments (Print & Saha, 2007). Second, I share concerns raised by feminist scholars and others about the depoliticizing or privatizing of certain kinds of participation (Arnot & Dillabough, 2000; Vromen, 2003b). In other words, the fact that young people seem to both discount political involvement and too narrowly construe it should be addressed by civic education.

The area of civic involvement that has raised the most concern for political theorists and civic educators is the decline of voting rates among young people across the democratic world. This has precipitated a flood of voter education programs that often focus on voting as a civic duty and/or the mechanics of voting. A range of research demonstrates, however, both that young people's reasons for voting or not voting are often complex and multifaceted and that they are engaging in a range of ways they see as more effective and satisfying than voting (Zukin et al., 2006; Levine, 2007; Dalton, 2008).

Chareka and Sears (2006) examined conceptions of voting among a small group of young people (aged 14-25) in Eastern Canada and found they lacked neither the basic information about the mechanics of voting nor more complex understandings of the place of voting in democratic governance. In fact, participants in the study "exhibited a fairly sophisticated understanding of voting and its place in the political system. They knew the role voting plays in democratic governance and had a fairly well-developed sense of its evolution as a democratic right" (p. 532). In spite of this most said they did not vote or did not intend to vote when they became eligible. Overall they believed voting was ineffective for three reasons:

there are no real differences between and among political parties; individual constituency members of parliament have no real power to shape policy; and politicians cannot be trusted. Leaving aside discussion of the relative accuracy or inaccuracy of these perceptions, it is clear that voter education programs that focus on providing information about the basic mechanics and purposes of voting will do little to either inform these young people or to alter the framework through which they understand voting as democratic participation.

Similarly, research in Australia demonstrates students' conceptions of voting as a means of civic engagement are quite complex. Saha (2007) found the sense that voting is important has a significant positive influence on young people's intentions to vote but the other key factor is their sense of preparedness for voting. The latter, he argues, has been neglected as a focus for research and policy development. Edwards' (2007, 92) work demonstrates that young Australians' "primary motivations for enrolling and voting were to comply with the law [Australia has compulsory voting] and avoid a fine." This is not a particularly satisfactory reason for participation, and she goes on to argue, "The fact that one of the goods of compulsory voting in Australia is the production of high turnouts, then, should not give us cause for complacency" (p. 93).

What research on prior knowledge tells us is that addressing students' cognitive frameworks of democratic participation generally or voting in particular is not as simple as telling them 'the right answer.' The prior conceptions themselves have to be brought to the surface and then connected in meaningful ways to evidence that brings them into question. Students have to encounter other voices that cause them to think about and rethink their conceptions. As Gardner (2006) argues, the strength of prior conceptions is such that significant rethinking of them will not occur in one or two sessions but only after strong and repeated challenges. This leads directly to consideration of the second lesson.

Lesson Two: We Should be Teaching for Understanding

The authors of a recent major review of the citizenship curriculum in England expressed concern that "teaching Citizenship with History could mean a return to the old curriculum of British constitutional history and civics" (Ajegbo, Kiwan & Sharma, 2007, 9). Of course, if students are going to pay attention to the British context of English citizenship they must learn about British constitutional history and civics. What the committee was really concerned about was not subject matter but pedagogical approach. They worried about a traditional approach that presented constitutional and legal structures as fixed, final and forever and students as sponges whose main function was to absorb that material and release it again when squeezed at exam time. Gardner (2006, 135 & 147) calls this "the correct answer compromise" where knowing is reduced to "a ritualistic memorization of meaningless facts and disembodied procedures."

This approach to social education generally and civic education in particular has been all too common. The most comprehensive study of history and civics education in Canada found a "bland consensus version of history" was being taught across the country (Hodgetts, 1968, 24). Teaching of this type focused almost exclusively on political and military matters, avoided controversy, did not make any connection to the present, and emphasized the memorization of, among other things, "nice, neat little acts of parliament" (p. 19). In her more recent examination of history education in Australia and Canada, Clark (2008, 114) found the same thing. Students from across both countries told her they thought national history was important to know but that the history education they experienced was "excessively content-driven and teacher-focused" almost never allowing for the consideration of multiple perspectives or focused on developing deep understanding.

The IEA study largely confirms this pattern of teaching in civics across the 29 countries involved. Teachers reported relying mostly on transmissive approaches to teaching with rote learning activities far more common than those that promote critical engagement with material. These approaches "frequently consist of encyclopaedic coverage of details of government structures or historical documents that may have little meaning to students and do not connect to their own identity as a citizen with responsibilities and rights" (Torney-Purta & Vermeer, 2004, 14).

In contrast to this Gardner (2006) calls for education focused on developing understanding of key concepts, ideas and processes with a view to being able to employ those in new situations in creative ways. For Gardner (2006, 134), understanding is "the capacity to take knowledge, skills, concepts, facts learned in one context, usually in the school context, and use that knowledge in a new context, in a place where you haven't been forewarned to make use of that knowledge." In terms of citizenship then, understanding would mean being able to act effectively in an informed manner in the civic sphere; the major goal of virtually every civics curriculum across the democratic world.

Research in cognition demonstrates not only that children, including quite young ones, can handle more conceptual complexity than they are given credit for, but also that they are interested in important ideas. Brophy and Alleman (2006, 433), for example, point out, "We and others have found that primary-grade students are interested to learn a much greater range of social studies content than many educators give them credit for." Unfortunately their review of curricula across the USA indicates "primary students in most American elementary schools are not systematically introduced to such content, nor to much, if any significant social education content at all" (p. 3). They argue for continuing the focus on cultural universals because they are connected to children's experience and to "powerful ideas" affecting the human condition. "If cultural universals are taught with appropriate focus on powerful ideas and their potential life applications, students should develop basic sets of connected understandings about how the social system works, how and why it got to be that way over time, how and why it varies across locations and cultures, and what all of this might mean for personal, social, and civic decision making" (p. 422). The work of my colleagues and I with children from Canada and Russia demonstrates that quite young children can develop complex understandings of civic ideas and processes (Hughes & Sears, 2007).

In her interviews with students across Australia Clark (2008, 77) found that they wanted to discuss important ideas, deal with alternative understanding of events and engage in the consideration of controversial questions. What she found, however, was that overwhelmingly students were experiencing "a fragmented, repetitive and incomplete picture of their national story" consisting largely of the rote learning of large numbers of facts. A consequence of this was students who were completely turned off studying history and largely convinced of its irrelevance. All the evidence demonstrates that much teaching in the area of civics is the same superficial, disconnected and repetitive examination of forms of government or civic practices. Research demonstrates that children are capable of much more and motivated when teaching seeks to stretch them with attention to big ideas and nuanced understandings. Good civics teaching will take students seriously by recognizing their capabilities and challenging them to develop more complex understandings and skills.

If civics education is going to be focused on helping students develop sophisticated conceptual and procedural understandings it will necessarily eschew the coverage of vast amounts of material in favor of focusing in depth on a more limited range of ideas and processes. As Gardner (2006, 148) argues,

> Certainly the greatest enemy of understanding is coverage – the compulsion to touch on everything in the textbook or the syllabus because it is there, rather than taking the time to present material from multiple perspectives, allowing students to approach the materials in ways that are initially congenial to them but that ultimately challenge them, and assessing understandings in as direct and flexible a manner as possible.

Similarly, Brophy and Alleman (2006, 430) call for a social studies curriculum for young children where "the content is organized into clusters structured around big ideas, so these big ideas are the focus of the information presented to the students and the questions addressed to them." In the Spirit of Democracy project colleagues from Russia and Canada designed an approach to teaching civics centred around the fundamental concepts that underlie democracy "such as the rule of law, freedom, tolerance, equality, justice, privacy and so on" (Hughes & Sears, 2007, 83). Using pedagogy rooted in situated learning and anchored instruction, students from grade three through high school have wrestled with questions of how these concepts have been worked out and manifested in democratic jurisdictions across time and contexts.

Concentration on the key concepts and processes of civic life does not imply that specific information is not important. The most basic test for understanding of any concept is whether or not the learner is able to correctly categorize something as an example or non-example. Take the very broad concept of democracy, for example. The fact that students can parrot a definition of the concept provided by the teacher or the textbook is not a reliable test of understanding at all. Students quite regularly mimic these types of definitions but are completely confounded when asked to apply them to real cases. Understanding of democracy is evident when students can reasonably judge whether, or the degree to which, particular systems are democratic. Making this kind of judgement will mean comparing the specific attributes of the system in question with those of the concept in the abstract as well as specific manifestations of those attributes in other democratic jurisdictions. It requires a complex and connected understanding of both theoretical knowledge and specific information. Research evidence demonstrates that students are far more likely to remember specific information learned in this sort of connected or "anchored" manner than they are to remember it when presented in a superficial and disconnected manner (Hughes & Sears, 2004; 2007).

Here again, civics educators would do well to learn from work in history education. Scholars in that field have developed a fair degree of international consensus around the key concepts and processes that make up what are termed "historical thinking" and "historical consciousness" (Seixas, 2004; Lévesqute, 2008). These have become the foundation for significant national curriculum initiatives in the UK, Australia, Canada and elsewhere and are literally transforming history education. A body of work in civics education which delineates the key concepts and processes students should know as well as setting out a range of levels of understandings of these would greatly strengthen our ability to influence policy and curriculum development in positive ways.

Teaching for understanding in civics requires well-educated teachers with both content and pedagogical expertise. Research in cognition demonstrates clearly that merely bringing students into contact with accurate information is not enough for them to acquire the kind of understanding described above that allows them to use the information in new and creative ways. Teaching for conceptual change and deep understanding requires on the part of the teacher quite sophisticated knowledge of the material to be learned, the learning process and the specific learners to be taught (Darling-Hammond & Bransford, 2005). A "strong body of research indicates that learning experiences that support understanding and effective action are different from those that simply support the ability to remember facts or perform rote sets of skills" (Hammerness et al., 2005, 370). Good teachers are absolutely necessary.

Civics curricula around the world reflect a broadly "constructivist" approach to teaching and learning and there is evidence from the IEA study and elsewhere that student achievement is positively related to open and democratic classroom environments and teaching focused on engagement (Hahn 1998; Torney-Purta et al., 2001). This is far more complex than what often passes for 'hands on' or 'active' learning. Barton and Levstik (2004, 185) make the point that all activity is not inquiry and argue, "Both academic research and our own classroom experiences suggest that teachers and students have enormous difficulty carrying out some of the key components of historical inquiry." Space does not allow for a detailed discussion of the features of constructivist or *"conceptual change teaching"* (Brophy & Allenman, 2006, 425) but it is explored in depth elsewhere (Hughes & Sears, 2004; 2007; Gardner, 2006; Mansilla & Gardner, 2008).

Unfortunately the teaching profession in North America and elsewhere is plagued with the phenomenon of "out of field teaching" (Ingersoll, 1999; 2001). In other words teachers being assigned to teach subjects or areas for which they have no academic background themselves. This is endemic in social education generally and civic education in particular. If the intent of education is the delivery of low-level information this is probably not significant but if the intent, as argued above, is to develop complex conceptual and procedural understandings it is quite significant. Teachers with little or no understanding of key ideas, concepts and procedures in a field can hardly be expected to teach them to students. It is time to put to rest for good the dangerous fiction that a good teacher can teach anything. Pedagogical expertise is a necessary but not sufficient condition for good teaching. Teachers also require proficiency with the concepts and processes related to the subject matter they are charged with teaching.

England is one of the few jurisdictions that have established substantive initiatives in both pre-service and in-service education for teachers of civics. Concurrent with the implementation of the national curriculum in citizenship in 2002 the country established places for educating citizenship specialists in undergraduate teacher education programs across the country. As well, funding was provided for a substantial, ongoing, coordinated program of in-service education through CitizEd, a consortium of teacher educators, teacher education institutions and other partners from across the country. A key implication of research in cognitive science is that teaching is a complex task requiring overlapping expertise in academic subject matter, human development and pedagogy. Both teacher education and placement have to be conducted with this in mind and at present that is happening almost nowhere.

Lesson Three: Context Matters

While I argue the lessons outlined above are generally true and apply across contexts, I also believe that generalization is often both overrated and over applied when it comes to educational research. Research on learning indicates clearly that broader social, cultural and political contexts matter both in terms of shaping the prior conceptions of learners as well as in facilitating or hindering particular kinds of learning. The key lesson for civic education is that 'one size will not fit all' and that aspects of policies and programs will have to be designed with particular contextual factors in mind.

The designers of the IEA Civic Education Study recognized the challenges inherent in attempting to create research instruments that would allow for cross-national comparisons of students from jurisdictions in North America, Europe, Asia and Latin America. Not only are specific civic institutions and practices very different across the range of the more than 20 countries involved, there are significant social and cultural differences as well and these play a role in shaping citizens' knowledge, attitudes and practices. Taking this into account the IEA for the first time approved a two-phase study the first of which would be qualitative case studies of the intended curriculum for 14 year-olds in participating jurisdictions. These case studies included attention not only to schools but also to civic ceremonies and practices in other arenas. This in-depth description of civic education was used to provide background for developing the tests and surveys used in the second round and to contextualize the data collected from those instruments. (Torney-Purta, Schwille & Amadeo, 1999).

A central finding from the second phase of the IEA work was that sociopolitical context was important in shaping how young people understand citizenship. As Torney-Purta and Vermeer (2004, 23) point out, "A variety of studies of elementary and middle school students, including the IEA Civic Education Study, shows that in democratic countries the average student is already a member of his or her political culture by age 14." This means that students have developed ways of understanding things like the proper role of government or what constitutes appropriate or effective civic engagement consistent with generally held views in their societies.

Hahn's (1998) research in four European countries and the USA also demonstrates the impact of socio-political context on student conceptions of citizenship. Hahn also conducted a two-phase study but she began with quantitative measures of variables such as political trust, knowledge of civic structures and processes, and attitudes toward civic engagement. She found distinct differences across the nations involved and her follow up qualitative work examining policy, curriculum, classroom practice and social context revealed interesting connections between differences in the variables tested in the first phase and the context examined in the second.

She found, for example, that students from Denmark had distinctly higher levels of trust in government and inclination to participate than did students in the Netherlands. On examining school practice she found the curriculum in Denmark emphasized discussing and taking action on public issues while that in the Netherlands had a more exam driven focus on particular historical facts and interpretations. Similarly, she found Danish society in general far more disposed to open and contentious public discussion and debate than Dutch society. Hahn does not claim that social context is a cause of the difference in scores, the limited nature of both phases of the research would prohibit that, but the results are in accord with those of the IEA research and other studies.

Some of the work in history education is also very relevant in this regard. There is considerable evidence that students in various contexts develop a strong sense of their national or community story. I have already discussed Barton and Levstik's (2004) findings that American students overwhelmingly tend to see their nation as a positive force for freedom both domestically and internationally. Work with students in Northern Ireland, however, reveals a cognitive frame that is far more negative. There they found students very pessimistic about the peace process holding the view that history made it clear long-term solutions to the divisions between the protestant and catholic communities were impossible. Barton and Levsitk argue that neither the overly sanguine and chauvinistic view of American students or the pessimistic one of students in Northern Ireland provide a good base for participating in pluralist democracy.

In the Canadian context Létourneau (2006, 71 & 72) found Francophone Québec students' had very well developed "mythistories" of the history of Québec and Canada. "Practically all students I tested, from Grade 11 to the university level, used a narrative that is, in a way, traditional. It refers to the timeless quest of Québecois, poor alienated people, for emancipation from their oppressors." This frame is, Létourneau contends, not consistent with the most recent work of historians. It seems obvious as well that such a framework would have considerable implications for the way young Québec citizens might understand appropriate civic participation.

Two implications for civic education of this work on context seem clear. First, in building the knowledge base of how children and young people understand the key ideas and processes of citizenship attention will have to be paid to both general and context specific factors. Second, policy and curriculum development will have to pay attention to these factors as well. Barton and Levstik (2004) and Létourneau (2006) argue that effective teaching in the societies they studied must be designed to specifically confront the particular cognitive frames that are dominant so as to foster rethinking and enhanced complexity in terms of student understandings.

There is a significant and growing body of research evidence that the structures of society, schooling and individual classrooms are as important in shaping civic knowledge and dispositions as the formal curriculum. The work of the IEA, Hahn and others demonstrates that wider socio-political context is an important factor and the more recent research conducted as part of the YES in Australia demonstrates that students obtain civic knowledge and dispositions in many places other than school and from many people other than teachers (Saha, Print & Edwards, 2007). Space does not allow for a full examination of how the overlapping contexts of classroom, school and society act as powerful civic educators so I will limit the discussion here to providing several examples of initiatives in the area of school and classroom structures.

The main features of school culture itself can serve to support or undermine the explicit goals of the curriculum and, in particular, any program of citizenship education. Research related to the development of the program of Education for Democratic Citizenship of the Council of Europe found that the generally authoritarian character of schools and classrooms can have a direct and powerful impact on school programs. The authors of the report concluded:

> The most powerful lessons that teachers and schools teach their pupils arise from the way they act and behave, not from what they tell them. Teachers and schools are individual and corporate role models. They are public and powerful manifestations of the values and beliefs that shape their thought and practice. And it is these actual practices that have the most powerful effect in forming the values and dispositions of the young people themselves (Harrison & Baumgartl, 2002, 33).

It is generally accepted as a tenet of good practice that the classroom and school ethos should support and nurture the learning outcomes being pursued as part of the formal program of instruction. Often this 'ethos' is viewed as reflecting the values that are embedded in the general practices of classroom life and are sometimes characterized as constituting the 'classroom climate.' In many jurisdictions where citizenship receives attention in the school program, there is at least some concern about this connection with the prevailing climate of learning and its impact upon the specific learning outcomes. Educators worry about a disconnect between these two elements that are so key in shaping learning. A focus of program development, then, should include an attempt to ensure that explicit instruction and classroom (and school) climate are mutually reinforcing.

Building on the *Civic Mission of the Schools* report from the Carnegie Foundation, the Education Commission of the States in the USA has provided a variety of resources to support schools in increasing the profile of citizenship education. Among these is the School Citizenship Education Climate Assessment (Homana, Barber & Torney-Purta, 2005). This resource reinforces the importance of the role of classroom and school climate in supporting citizenship learning and provides a mechanism for schools to self-monitor the connection of their learning climate with citizenship outcomes. The creation of the assessment was based on the view that "a positive classroom climate can enhance academic performance and cultivate the development of the knowledge, skills and dispositions necessary in a democratic society" (p. 5).

In England as well there has been considerable focus on developing consistency between the objectives of the national curriculum in citizenship and school structures and practices. The Department for Education and Skills (2004) has published guidance for substantially involving students in the governance of their schools through a policy document titled *Working Together: Giving Children and Young People a Say*.

As the work discussed above indicates, some overt attention is being paid to the role of school and classroom context in shaping citizenship education in Europe, England and the USA. The issue does not seem to be on the radar, however, in some other jurisdictions including Canada and Australia. Much more needs to be know about how these contexts impact on civic learning but they clearly do and any effective program of civic education will have to include attention to this area.

CONCLUSION

For several decades now concern about declining levels of civic participation particularly among young people has been growing. In democratic jurisdictions around the world there is consensus that this is a problem and that the way to address this problem is through enhanced programs of civic education. There is also consensus that generally constructivist approaches to teaching and learning constitute best practice in civic education (Hughes & Sears, 2008). A key premise underlying constructivist theory is that understanding and addressing the prior knowledge of learners is essential to effective teaching in any area. There is a considerable research base that demonstrates this in general and with regard to civic education in particular. I have argued in this chapter that the lessons for civic education from this body of work are: that prior knowledge matters and civic educators and practitioners need to focus on creating a substantial body of research on how children and young people understand key ideas and processes related to citizenship; that curricula and teaching ought to focus on developing understanding which means, taking students seriously by recognizing their ability to handle increased complexity, taking material seriously by focusing curricula on important and well delineated civic ideas and processes, and taking teaching seriously by recognizing the overlapping areas of expertise needed for effective practice and training and placing teachers appropriately; and that context matters so quality civic education will have both common and context specific features and attention will have to be paid to how social and educational structures enhance or inhibit civic education.

REFERENCES

Advisory Group on Citizenship. (1998). *Education for citizenship and the teaching of democracy in schools: Final report of the advisory group on citizenship*. London: Qualifications and Curriculum Authority.
Ajegbo, S. K., Kiwan, D., & Sharma, S. (2007). *Diversity and citizenship curriculum review*. London: Department for Education and Skills.
Arnot, M., & Dillabough, J.-A. (2000). *Challenging democracy: International perspectives on gender, education and citizenship*. London: Routledge/Falmer.
Arthur, J., Davies, I., & Hahn, C. (Eds.). (2008). *The sage handbook of education for citizenship and democracy*. London: Sage.
Barton, K. C., & Levstik, L. S. (2004). *Teaching history for the common good mahwah*. New Jersey: Lawrence Erlbaum Associates.
Brophy, J., & Alleman, J. (2006). *Children's thinking about cultural universals*. Mahwah NJ: Lawrence Erlbaum Associates.
Byrnes, J., & Torney-Purta, J. (1995). Naive theories and decision making as part of higher order thinking in social studies. *Theory and Research in Social Education, 23*(3), 260–277.
Chareka, O., & Sears, A. (2005). Discounting the political: Understanding civic participation as private practice. *Canadian and International Education, 34*(1), 50–58.
Chareka, O., & Sears, A. (2006). Civic duty: Young people's conceptions of voting as a means of political participation. *Canadian Journal of Education, 29*(2), 521–540.
Clark, A. (2008). *History's children: History wars in the classroom*. Sydney, New S Wales: University of New South Wales Press.
Dalton, R. J. (2008). *The good citizen: How a younger generation is reshaping American politics*. Washington: CQ Press.
Darling-Hammond, L., & Bransford, J. (Eds.). (2005). *Preparing teachers for a changing world: What teachers should learn and be able to do*. San Francisco: Jossey-Bass.
Edwards, K. (2007). Force us to be free! Motivations of Australian school students for enrolling and voting. In L. J. Saha, M. Print, & K. Edwards (Eds.), *Youth and political participation* (pp. 79–94). Rotterdam, The Netherlands: Sense Publishers.
Department for Education and Skills. (2004). *Working together: Giving children and young people a say*. London: DfES.
Faulks, K. (2006). Education for citizenship in England's secondary schools: A critques of current principle and practice. *Journal of Educational Policy, 21*(1), 59–74.
Gardner, H. (2006). *The development and education of the mind: The selected works of howard gardner*. London and New York: Routledge.
Gould, S. J. (1989). *Wonderful life: The burgess shale and the nature of history*. New York: W.W. Norton.
Hahn, C. L. (1998). *Becoming political: Comparative perspectives on citizenship education*. Albany, NY: State University of New York Press.
Hammerness, K., Darling-Hammond, L., Bransford, J., Berliner, D., Cochran-Smith, M., McDonald, M., et al. (2005). How teachers learn and develop. In L. Darling-Hammond & J. Bransford (Eds.), *Preparing teachers for a changing world: What teachers should learn and be able to do* (pp. 358–389). San Francisco: Jossey-Bass.
Hargreaves, A. (2003). *Teaching in the knowledge society: Education in the age of insecurity*. New York: Teachers College Press.

Harrison, C., & Baumgartl, B. (2002). *Stocktaking research on policies on education for democratic citizenship and management of diversity in south-east Europe.* Strasbourg: Council of Europe.
Hodgetts, A. B. (1968). *What culture? What heritage? A study of civic education in Canada.* Toronto, ON: OISE Press.
Homana, G., Henry Barber, C., & Torney-Purta, J. (2005). *School citizenship education climate assessment.* Retrieved November 2, 2005, from http://www.ecs.org/qna/docs/ climate_assessment_info.pdf
Hughes, A. S., & Sears, A. (1996). Macro and micro level aspects of a programme of citizenship education research. *Canadian and International Education, 25*(2), 17–30.
Hughes, A. S., & Sears, A. (2004). Situated learning and anchored instruction as vehicles for social education. In A. Sears & I. Wright (Eds.), *Challenges and prospects for Canadian social studies* (pp. 259–273). Vancouver, BC: Pacific Educational Press.
Hughes, A. S., & Sears, A. (2007). Teaching the contested and controversial nature of democratic ideas: Taking the crisis out of controversy. In H. Claire & C. Holden (Eds.), *The challenge of teaching controversial issues* (pp. 83–93). Stoke on Kent, UK: Trentham Books.
Hughes, A. S., & Sears, A. (2008). The struggle for citizenship education in Canada: The centre cannot hold. In J. Arthur, I. Davies, & C. Hahn (Eds.), *The sage handbook of education for citizenship and democracy* (pp. 124–138). London: Sage.
Hunt, T. C. (2002). *The impossible dream: Education and the search for panaceas.* New York: Peter Lang.
Ingersoll, R. M. (1999). The Problem of underqualified teachers in American secondary schools. *Educational Researcher, 28*(2), 26–37.
Ingersoll, R. M. (2001). The realities of out-of-field teaching. *Educational Leadership, 58*(8), 42–45.
Létourneau, J. (2006). Remembering our past: An examination of the historical memory of young Québécois. In R. W. Sandwell (Ed.), *To the past: History education, public memory, and citizenship in Canada* (pp. 71–87). Toronto, ON: University of Toronto Press.
Lévesque, S. (2008). *Thinking historically: Educating students for the twenty-first century.* Toronto, ON: University of Toronto Press.
Levine, P. (2007). *The future of democracy: Developing the next generations of American citizens.* Medford, MA: Tufts University Press.
Mansilla, V. B., & Gardner, H. (2008). Disciplining the mind. *Educational Leadership, 65*(5), 14–19.
Peck, C., Sears, A., & Donaldson, S. (2008). Unreached and unreachable? Curriculum standards and children's understanding of ethnic diversity in Canada. *Curriculum Inquiry, 38*(1), 63–92.
Print, M., & Saha, L. J. (2007). Youth, Democracy and politics: Issues in Australia. In L. J. Saha, M. Print, & K. Edwards (Eds.), *Youth and political participation* (pp. 1–14). Rotterdam, The Netherlands: Sense Publishers.
Qualifications and Curriculum Authority. (2007). *Citizenship: Program of study for key stage 3 and attainment target.* London: Qualifications and Curriculum Authority.
Saha, L. J. (2007). Are they prepared to vote? What Australian youth are saying. In L. J. Saha, M. Print, & K. Edwards (Eds.), *Youth and political participation* (pp. 51–64). Rotterdam, The Netherlands: Sense Publishers.
Saha, L. J., Print, M., & Edwards, K. (Eds.). (2007). *Youth and political participation.* Rotterdam, The Netherlands: Sense Publishers.
Sandwell, R. W. (2006). *To the past: History education, public memory, and citizenship in Canada.* Toronto, ON: University of Toronto Press.
Sears, A., & Hyslop-Margison, E. (2007). Crisis as a vehicle for educational reform: The case of citizenship education. *Journal of Educational Thought, 41*(1), 43–62.
Seixas, P. (Ed.). (2004). *Theorizing historical consciousness.* Toronto, ON: University of Toronto Press.
Stein, J. G. (2001). *The cult of efficiency.* Toronto, ON: House of Anansi Press.
Stearns, P., Seixas, P., & Wineburg, S. S. (Eds.). (2000). *Knowing, teaching, and learning history: National and international perspectives.* New York & London: New York University Press.
Torney-Purta, J., Lehmann, R., Oswald, H., & Schulz, W. (2001). *Citizenship and education in twenty-eight countries: Civic knowledge and engagement at age fourteen.* Amsterdam: IEA.
Torney-Purta, J., Schwille, J., & Amadeo, J. A. (1999). *Civic education across countries: Twenty-four case studies from the IEA civic education project.* Amsterdam: International Association for the Evaluation of Educational Achievement.
Torney-Purta, J., & Vermeer, S. (2004). *Developing citizenship competencies from kindergarten through grade 12: A background paper for policy makers and educators.* Denver, CO: Education Commission of the States.

Tyack, D. B., & Cuban, L. (1995). *Tinkering toward utopia: A century of public school reform.* Cambridge, MA: Harvard University Press.

Vromen, A. (2003a). 'People try to put us down . . .': Participatory citizenship of 'Generation X'. *Australian Journal of Political Science, 38*(1), 79–99.

Vromen, A. (2003b). Traversing time and gender: Australian young people's participation. *Journal of Youth Studies, 6*(3), 277–294.

Windschitl, M. (2002). Framing constructivism in practice as the negotiation of dilemmas: An analysis of the conceptual, pedagogical, cultural, and political challenges facing teachers. *Review of Educational Research, 72*(2), 131–175.

Wineburg, S. S. (2001). *Historical thinking and other unnatural acts: Charting the future of teaching the past.* Philadelphia: Temple University Press.

Zukin, C., Keeter, S., Andolina, M., Jenkins, K., & Carpini, M. X. D. (2006). *A new engagement? political participation, civic life, and the changing American citizen.* New York: Oxford University Press.

JOSEPH KAHNE AND SUSAN SPORTE

9. DEVELOPING CITIZENS

The Impact of Civic Learning Opportunities on Students' Commitment to Civic Participation*

Although the preparation of citizens is a stated goal of many schools' mission statements and a primary concern of many citizens, knowledge of whether and how schools actually fulfill the democratic aims of education remains quite limited (Galston, 2001; Rose & Gallup, 2000). Can high schools promote the kinds of civic commitments that would help to sustain a democratic society? In particular, can educators in classrooms help support the development of commitments to civic participation among low-income students and students of color? This study of public high school students in Chicago speaks directly to these questions.

Historically, the democratic aims of education have been a primary rationale for public schooling. This focus faded in recent decades – spurred, in part, by doubts raised in the 60's and 70's that what happened in high schools influenced student civic and political commitments (most notably, Langton & Jennings, 1968) and, more recently, by growing pressure to focus on reading and math in order to raise test scores. For example, a recently completed study by the Center on Education Policy (2006) found that 71% of districts reported cutting back time on other subjects to make more space for reading and math instruction. Social studies was the part of the curriculum that was most frequently cited as the place where these reductions occurred.

This research was generously supported with grants from the Spencer Foundation and the Chicago Community Trust. The authors, of course, bear full responsibility for any and all conclusions.

THE NEED FOR INCREASED AND MORE EQUITABLE LEVELS OF CIVIC PARTICIPATION

Some reformers, scholars, and foundation leaders are now looking for ways to reassert the democratic purposes of schooling (Gibson & Levine, 2003). Those promoting democratic priorities want schools to develop the skills and commitments students need in order to be concerned for the well being of others. They also want schools to teach students how government works and how they can work with others on solutions to community problems. This focus reflects concern for the health of American democracy. Numerous studies have found that levels of civic engagement in the United States are lower than desirable, particularly among youth (Galston, 2001; Macedo et al., 2005; Putnam, 2000). Indeed, as a panel of

M. Print and H. Milner (eds.), Civic Education and Youth Political Participation, 159–186.
© 2009 Sense Publishers. All rights reserved.

experts convened by the American Political Science Association recently found, "Citizens participate in public affairs less frequently, with less knowledge, and enthusiasm, in fewer venues, and less equitably than is healthy for a vibrant democratic polity" (Macedo et al., 2005, p. 1).

Although it currently receives less attention than data regarding low levels of civic and political participation, data regarding the inequitable nature of civic participation and influence is also troubling. Low-income and less-educated citizens, as well as recent immigrants and those less proficient in English, are often under represented in the political process, have far less voice, and the votes of elected officials align with those of higher income citizens to a far greater degree than with the rest of the population (APSA Task Force on Inequality and American Democracy, 2004; Stepick & Stepick, 2002). Verba, Schlozman, and Brady (1995) found, for example, that family income was a strong predictor of political voice. Bartels (2005) found that the policy preferences of constituents at the 75th percentile of the income distribution were almost three times as influential on the votes of U.S. Senators as the policy preferences of those at the 25th percentile. Indeed, the policy preferences of those in "the bottom third of the income distribution had no apparent statistical effect on their senators' roll call votes" (Bartels, p. 1).

Clearly, educational institutions are limited in their ability to offset the many ways social status and income can expand some individuals' political voice. However, studies indicate that the greater influence these individuals wield is not simply driven by their money or status, but by their greater participation at meetings, on boards, and in communication with officials (Verba, Schlozman, & Brady, 1995; Nie, Junn & Stehlik-Barry, 1996). If less advantaged citizens increased their engagement in the civic and political arena, their priorities would be more likely to get attention (Verba, 2003). Indeed, given the fundamental importance of ensuring all citizens equal voice in a democracy, it is important to deepen our understanding of whether providing particular kinds of learning opportunities to relatively low-income students in urban public schools can help promote higher and more equitable levels of civic and political engagement.

CAN SCHOOLS PROMOTE CIVIC OUTCOMES?

Recent studies that testify to schools' potential to advance civic and political development along with indications that schools are not doing all that they could to promote the democratic purposes of education have furthered interest in civic education. Specifically, Niemi and Junn's (1998) analysis of data from the National Assessment of Educational Progress revealed that some educational practices can increase students' civic and political knowledge. Michael Delli Carpini and Scott Keeter (1996) have shown that such knowledge improves the quantity and quality of civic participation. In addition, large scale studies such as the International Association for the Evaluation of Educational Achievement's (IEA) Civic Education Study of 14 year olds in 28 countries found that certain curricular features were associated with civic outcomes such as interest in politics the ability to apply knowledge accurately, and a range of civic and political commitments (Torney-Purta, 2002; Torney-Purta, Amadeo & Richardson, 2007). These findings have been reinforced by a number of well controlled studies of particular curricular initiatives (Kahne, Chi & Middaugh, 2006; McDevitt & Kiousis, 2004; Metz & Youniss, 2005). Findings are not universally positive, however. Some studies that control for prior commitments find significant effects only for "high quality" service learning, for example (Billig, Root & Jesse, 2005; Melchior, 1998).

The importance of these positive findings regarding the impact of curricular opportunities on students' civic commitments is reinforced by studies demonstrating that adolescents who express greater commitment to civic and political engagement are more civically and politically engaged as adults than adolescents who express less of a commitment to act (Ajzen, 2001; Fishbein, Ajzen & Hinkle, 1980; Oesterle, Johnson & Mortimer, 2004; Theiss-Morse, 1993).

A GAP IN CURRENT LARGE SCALE STUDIES OF CIVIC EDUCATION

Most studies that link classroom practices to civic commitments are relatively small scale in nature, focus on very specialized curricula, and therefore are not easily generalized. Large scale surveys of high school students demonstrate that students who report having particular experiences (debating issues in class, being taught civic skills, undertaking service learning) are more likely to also report being committed to and involved in various forms of civic and political engagement (Keeter, Zukin, Andolina & Jenkins, 2002; also see Gibson & Levine, 2003; Torney-Purta, 2002; Verba et al., 1995). However, the lack of random assignment to these opportunities, the use of retrospective accounts of educational experiences, and the lack of controls for prior civic commitments and for a range of potentially relevant academic, demographic, family, and community characteristics significantly limit the ability of these larger surveys to demonstrate causal relationships. Some longitudinal data sets such as the National Educational Longitudinal Survey (NELS) can be quite helpful in this regard (Hart, Donnelly, Youniss & Atkins, 2007), but these surveys do not ask about many of the classroom opportunities that civic educators believe are most important.

Finally, few empirical studies focus directly on the ways schools can and do influence the development of the civic and political commitments of low-income students and students of color. One study found that the gap in civic knowledge and expected participation between Latino adolescents and non-Latino students could be narrowed considerably by providing them with a more open classroom climate and more time devoted to political topics and discussion of democratic ideals (Torney-Purta, Barber & Wikenfeld, 2007). Similarly, Youniss and Yates' (1997) largely qualitative study of African American youth attending a Catholic school in Washington, DC demonstrates the ways that service learning experiences linked to meaningful classroom opportunities for reflection and analysis can spur the development of students' civic identity. These studies, while valuable, are subject to the same concerns as those noted above.

CONCEPTUAL FRAME: COMMITMENTS TO CIVIC PARTICIPATION AMONG ADOLESCENTS

Robust participation in the life of the community (following community issues, working on community problems, collective engagement with government agencies) is a fundamentally important component of life in a democratic society (Barber, 1984; Boyte & Kari, 1996; Dewey, 1916). Our emphasis on these community-based forms of participation rather than on more formal forms of political participation (working on campaigns, voting) also stems from indications that younger students are less likely to participate in formal political action and that it is important to include the broader civic and political aspects of adolescents' activities and beliefs (Flanagan & Gallay, 1995). Moreover, in most school settings, an emphasis on direct political engagement would be quite controversial. In addition, there is evidence that young people and perhaps young people of color in particular are more drawn to community-based forms of participation than to participation in traditional politics (Junn, 1999; Long, 2002; Sanchez-Jankowski, 2002).

Finally, it makes sense to study factors that may influence the development of commitments to civic participation during late adolescence because late adolescence is a critical period for development of sociopolitical orientations (e.g., Erikson, 1968). As Yates and Youniss (1998) explain, adolescence is a time when youth are thinking about and trying to anticipate their lives as adults. They are working to understand who they are and how they will relate to the broader society (also see, Atkins & Hart, 2003).

FACTORS INFLUENCING THE DEVELOPMENT OF YOUNG PEOPLE'S COMMITMENTS TO CIVIC PARTICIPATION

Below we highlight factors that research has shown to be the best predictors of the development of young people's commitments to civic participation.

Classroom Civic Learning Opportunities As noted earlier, scholars find strong associations between curricular approaches such as the provision of an open classroom climate, engagement in service learning, and the use of simulations on the one hand and students' civic commitments and capacities on the other (for example, Campbell, 2005; Hart et al., 2007; Torney-Purta, Lehmann, Oswald & Schulz, 2001; see Gibson & Levine, 2003 for a review).

In understanding why these opportunities may foster civic outcomes, our work has been heavily influenced by Youniss and Yates' (1997) conceptualization of factors that promote the development of a civic identity. They identify three kinds of opportunities that can spur such development: opportunities for Agency and Industry, for Social Relatedness, and for the development of Political-Moral Understandings. Their study of youth doing work in soup kitchens as part of a course shows how integrating community service and, by extension, other civic learning opportunities into the curriculum can provide opportunities for Agency (as students respond to social problems), Social Relatedness (as students join with others to respond to a societal need) and Political-Moral Understanding (as students reflect on and discuss the relationship between what is and what should be).

School-Based Supports for Students' Academic and Social Development We also examine whether students experience a strong sense of belonging to or membership in their school community, whether teachers provide caring and personalized support, whether peers are supportive of academic achievement, and whether parents encourage and support academic achievement. Currently, these attributes are most often viewed as a means of supporting scholastic goals such as academic performance, and dropout rates (Bryk & Schneider, 2002; Christenson & Thurlow, 2004; Wentzel, 1997; Zirkel, forthcoming; also see Juvonen, 2006 for a broad review). If these social and academic supports turn out to substantially support civic outcomes, then a special focus on civic learning opportunities may not be needed. Indeed, theorists like John Dewey (1900) and reformers such as Deborah Meier (1995, 2002) link experiencing a sense of belonging to a caring and supportive school community with the development of commitments and capacities for democratic ways of living. Systematic empirical studies have also found such contexts to promote pro-social behaviors such as helping, caring, and cooperating (Baumeister & Leary, 1995; Watson, Battistich & Solomon, 1997; Wentzel, 1997, 1998). Perhaps most directly, Flanagan, Cumsille, Sukhdeep, and Gallay (2007) find a positive relationship between school and community climates and civic commitments.

Extracurricular Activities High school students' participation in extracurricular experiences has been linked through high quality longitudinal studies to later civic and political engagement (McFarland & Thomas, 2006; Otto, 1976; Smith, 1999). Youth organizational membership is believed to socialize young people to value and pursue social ties while fostering exposure to organizational norms and relevant political and social skills that make maintenance of these ties more likely (Youniss & Yates, 1997).

Demographic Variables and Academic Capacities Educational attainment and socioeconomic status are strongly related to greater civic engagement (Nie et al., 1996; Verba et al., 1995). In addition, gender, ethnic identity, and race are related to both civic commitments and to forms of engagement (Burns, Schlozman & Verba, 2001; Marcelo, Lopez & Kirby, 2007a), though the nature of these relationships are not uniform for younger citizens (ages 15-25). In fact, the associations between race, ethnicity and gender vary depending on the particular civic outcome in question – girls, for example, are generally more likely to volunteer than boys, but less likely to be involved in electoral activities. White-American and African-American 18-24 year olds are substantially more likely to vote than Asian-Americans and Latinos, while Asian youth are the most likely to volunteer and Latinos (at least in recent surveys) are the most likely to be involved in protests (CIRCLE, 2007; Marcelo et al., 2007b). Although we do not necessarily expect uniform relationships between demographic characteristics and civic outcomes, we will consider and control for these factors.

Neighborhood and Family Civic Context Neighborhood and family civic contexts play a significant role in the development of civic orientations. Young people growing up in families and communities that are civically active and financially better off tend to end up more active themselves (Jennings, Stoker & Bowers, 2001; Nie et al., 1996; Niemi & Sobieszek, 1977). Discussion between parents and youth revolving around civic and political issues relates to a wide range of civic outcomes (Andolina, Jenkins, Zukin & Keeter, 2003; Torney-Purta et al., 2001). And a great deal of research has focused on the role social capital plays within communities in fostering norms and social networks that make democracy work more effectively (most notably, Putnam, 1993, 2000).

RESEARCH QUESTIONS

This study asks: What is the degree to which classroom based curricular experiences that directly target civic goals contribute to the development of commitments to civic participation among a population of largely low-income students of color? Since some may wonder if prior commitments lead students to pursue civically oriented learning opportunities, we also ask: Does the relationship between curricular experience and adolescent civic commitment persist if one controls for prior civic commitments? Finally, we ask: How do classroom based curricular opportunities compare with other factors (demographic characteristics, participation in extracurricular activities, features of students' neighborhoods and families, and qualities of students' school experience) when it comes to promoting students' commitments to civic participation?

METHOD

Sample Characteristics

Data for this study come from surveys given every two years by the Consortium on Chicago School Research as part of an agreement with the Chicago Public Schools and from CPS administrative records. The survey is part of an ongoing effort to study school contexts and practices and their relationship to varied educational policies and student outcomes. Although the survey includes some measures of classroom opportunities to develop commitments to civic participation, as well as a measure that assesses civic commitments, the prime focus of the survey is on school contexts and curricular practices that are believed to foster academic outcomes such as test scores and graduation rates.

We were mainly interested in survey and demographic data from 2005, although we also wanted to control for students' responses to selected questions in 2003. We selected students who responded to the 2005 survey as juniors and who also responded to the 2003 survey when most of them were freshmen. We only selected students who had values on our main variables of interest, which are described in the section below. Approximately 5% of our pool did not have achievement test scores. Initial analyses indicated that this variable was not linked to our outcome, so we imputed values for those students at their respective school means so as not to lose the information from all of the other data we had about them.

In addition to selecting students based on their available data, we also selected schools, based in part on whether or not they participated in the 2003 survey. Although all regular high schools are invited to participate in the survey, in each year approximately 35% of schools decline the invitation. Seventeen schools took the 2005 survey but not the 2003 survey. Each of these schools had fewer than nine students in our student pool. These juniors had attended a different school as freshmen. Because we were examining school level effects along with individual level effects, we did not want to include schools in our sample if the only students representing that school were students who had recently transferred in. This decision removed 73 students from our sample.

Our final analytic sample contained 4057 students representing 52 schools. Our sample has slightly higher test scores and a slightly different demographic mix than the rest of CPS. In particular, African American students are underrepresented. Since our goal is not to make statements about the precise level of civic learning opportunities or outcomes in Chicago, but rather about the ways varied factors shape civic commitments of students in urban contexts, the differences between our analytic sample and Chicago's juniors does not strike us as a significant concern. Details regarding our analytic sample and a comparison to all juniors in the Chicago Public Schools are provided in Table 1.

Table 1. Demographic comparison between analytic sample and all cps juniors

	N	African American	Latino	White	Asian	Female	Free lunch	PSAE reading
CPS	22,688	50%	34%	11%	5%	53%	78%	152
Analytic Sample	4,057	36%	42%	14%	8%	59%	79%	156

SURVEY MEASURES

Our indicators from the survey are of two types: single items and multiple item measures. Single items were expressed on a four-point scale, ranging in some cases from "strongly disagree" to "strongly agree" or in other cases from "never" to "often." Such individual items were treated as continuous after initial analyses indicated that they were linearly related to the outcome.

The multi-item measures were created using Rasch analysis (Wright & Masters, 1982). Rasch modeling puts all items on a hierarchical scale based on the likelihood that they were "endorsed" by respondents and puts all respondent scores on the same scale based on the likelihood that the respondent endorses each item in the suite of items (for an introductory discussion of Rasch modeling, see Bond & Fox, 2001).

This approach permits the creation of a latent variable such as "commitment to civic participation" that is conceptually and empirically cohesive. Items are assigned a "difficulty level;" persons are assigned a score indicating their position relative to all other respondents based on the probability of responding in a particular way on each item. After items are selected to meet a conceptual framework, the analysis helps uncover cases where the theory and the empirical data disagree. In that case, the decision to omit or include an item in the measure is based on consideration of the theoretical importance of the item and on the fit statistic. The measures described below that relate to civic commitments and civic learning opportunities were developed specifically for inclusion in the Consortium's 2003 and 2005 survey analyses. The other measures used in this analysis have been part of the Consortium's survey over time. In all cases we anchored the responses of our students in this larger sample, after checking to make sure their measure statistics did not differ significantly. Interested readers may contact the authors for exact details on how these measures were created.

Details of all indicators, including survey measures and items can be found in Appendix A. The list of items in each measure is provided, as well as its reliability. Furthermore, the mean and frequency distribution of each individual item used as a predictor is also provided

OUTCOME VARIABLE

In order to assess students' *Commitment to Civic Participation*, we employ a five item measure that was developed by Westheimer and Kahne (2004). This measure aims to provide an indication of relatively robust civic participation. That is, it asks whether students agree that in the next three years they are likely to "Work on a community project that involves a government agency," whether "Being actively involved in community issues is my responsibility," whether "I have good ideas for programs or projects to help solve problems in my community," whether "Being concerned about state and local issues is an important responsibility for everybody" and whether "In the next three years, I expect to be involved in improving my community." This measure has been used in multiple studies and its psychometric properties have been independently assessed (Flanagan, Syvertsen & Stout, 2007). We initially developed the Rasch measure for this analysis in 2003 on a sample of students in grades 8-10. It has an individual level reliability of .73. We anchored our current sample on these values so the measure has the same scoring over time.

PREDICTOR VARIABLES

We used survey responses to provide information related to classroom and school characteristics as well as information related to parent and family contexts. We used CPS administrative records to provide demographic and achievement values.

Classroom Civic Learning Opportunities First, we developed a measure of classroom based civic learning opportunities including: learning about problems in society, learning about current events, studying issues about which one cares, experiencing an open climate for classroom discussions of social and political topics, hearing from civic role models, learning about ways to improve the community, and working on service learning projects. This measure was based on earlier work by Kahne and Westheimer (2003) and drew on numerous other studies (e.g. Billig, 2000; Kahne et al., 2006; Niemi & Junn, 1998; Smith, 1999; Torney-Purta et al., 2001; Verba et al., 1995; see Gibson & Levine, 2003 for a recent review).

Most of these curricular opportunities formed a single measure of classroom civic learning opportunities. This measure has a reliability of .74. Our indicator of service learning experiences did not fit within the broader measure of civic learning opportunities, instead tapping into a slightly different construct. For this reason, in the analysis (models 3 and 4) we examine the significance of the overall measure and of the individual item asking students about their service learning projects.

School Supports for Students' Academic and Social Development In addition, because we wanted to see whether the provision of opportunities associated with promoting *academic* outcomes might also foster *civic* outcomes, we included a set of indicators related to whether the school and home context provided supports for students' academic and social development. Specifically, we assessed the impact of peer support for academic achievement, whether students developed a sense of belonging or attachment in relation to the school, teacher support, and parental press for academic achievement. All these measures have reliabilities between .80 and .85. See Appendix A for more details.

Extracurricular Activities The third type of school/educational variable was an indicator of extracurricular participation. Students were asked how often they participated in afterschool clubs, sponsored by the school or other organizations, and how often they participated in sports on teams, either in or out of school. We separated out the item that asked directly about sports because several studies have found that participation in sports, unlike other extracurricular activities, is often not related or is inversely related to civic participation (Verba et al., 1995).

Demographic and Individual Characteristics As controls for demographic and individual characteristics of the students, we included data on gender, racial and ethnic identification, and achievement test scores in reading, all of which come from district records. Our measure of achievement (PSAE Reading Score) is based on students' eleventh grade score on the Prairie State Achievement Exam (PSAE), administered about a month earlier than the survey.

In addition to the above indicators, we also were interested in measures of socioeconomic status. We considered three indicators: census-based information linking students to social and economic characteristics of their census block; self reports of level of mother's education; and an individual-level variable telling whether students qualify for free or reduced-price lunch. Because students' reports of their parents' education are often inaccurate (Adelman, 1999, p. 35) we chose not to use it. We decided to use the free and reduced-price lunch variable rather than the census block variable because the lunch variable was tied directly to the individual's family while the census block information was tied to the census block in which the student lived. As a check on this decision, we did the analyses separately using the census-based variables as well and found no substantive difference in our results.

Neighborhood and Family Civic Context Our measure of neighborhood social capital comes from the Consortium's core battery of items, and has been used since 1997. Consistent with James Coleman's (1988) perspective on the forms of social capital that would matter most for children, it assesses whether adults in the neighborhood are civically engaged and socially networked, and whether they monitor and support young people.

We also include a measure of the role parents and guardians play in shaping students' commitment to civic engagement. To assess the significance of family context, we included a relatively standard item that asked how often each young person discussed current events and politics with their parents or guardians, since the role of discussion between parents and students has been found, consistently, to be related to a range of civic outcomes (Andolina et al., 2003; McIntosh, Hart & Youniss, 2006; Torney-Purta et al., 2001).

Past Commitments Finally, there is reason to expect that a students' prior commitments to civic participation is related to the commitments reported in eleventh grade. Students with such prior commitments might be more likely to pursue civic opportunities noted above or to recall that they occurred. For this reason, we have included students' score on the commitment to civic participation measure (described above) from the prior administration of the survey which occurred two years earlier in the spring of 2003.

ANALYSIS

Student commitment to civic participation is shaped by a number of individual and group experiences as described above. In particular, those students taking the same classes or attending the same school experience the same general environment, which may also be independently related to the outcome of interest. Therefore, we used Hierarchical Linear Modeling, HLM, (Raudenbush & Bryk, 2002) to explore the significance of both individual and group characteristics. Ideally we would have nested students within classrooms, since we are interested in the relationship between the learning opportunities that occur in classrooms and students' commitments to civic participation. However, we were unable to do so for a variety of technical and theoretical reasons. First, students likely receive these opportunities in multiple courses/classrooms during a given year (e.g. English, social studies, health etc.). Without knowing which class or classes they were reporting on, we were not able to group students in any meaningful way at the classroom level. Second, even if we had limited the responses to a particular

DEVELOPING CITIZENS

subject, we would have had too few students in most classes to make meaningful cross-classroom comparisons.

Even though we were unable to group students in classrooms, we hypothesized that some schools might focus more on promoting civic development than others. Furthermore, because we assumed that students potentially may have experienced these opportunities in more than one class, it seemed important to see whether there was a school level effect on commitments to civic participation. We computed the intraclass correlations using the fully unconditional model and discovered that only 2.2% of the variation in students' commitments to civic participation was between schools.

Even with this low variation, we decided that the nesting structure still had advantages. First, we found schools did differ in their provision of civic learning opportunities. In fact, 9% of the variability in civic learning opportunities was between schools. In addition, as will be discussed below, using HLM allows us to adjust for individual level measurement error. And, as discussed below, even with this low between-school variability in civic commitments, we found statistically significant variability in the opportunities/commitments slope.

Because our outcome is itself a measure, it is subject to measurement error. We used three level HLM, where level 1 is a measurement model, level 2 is the individual student level, and level 3 is the school. The first level represents variation among the item scores within each student. Ordinarily, errors at level 1 in a hierarchical model have a constant variance, but in this case, each person-measure can have a different amount of measurement error. To correct for this heteroscedasticity, we multiplied each side of the equation by the inverse of each person's standard error. The level 2 outcome becomes each student's individual measure score adjusted for measurement error (Raudenbush & Bryk, 2002).

Following are the equation of the models we used. For a complete listing of the variables, see Table 2 and Appendix A.

Level 1:

$$\frac{\text{Civic Commitment}_{jk}}{s_{jk}} = \pi_{jk} \frac{1}{s_{jk}} + e_{jk},$$ where $e_{jk} \sim N(0,1)$, s_{jk} is the standard error estimated from the Rasch analysis for student j in school k and π_{jk} is the student's "true score."

Level 2:

$$\pi_{jk} = \beta_{0k} + \sum_{p=1}^{6} \beta_{pk} (\text{Student Demographic and Academic Characteristics}) +$$

$$\sum_{p=7}^{8} \beta_{pk} (\text{Neighborhood and Family Context}) + \beta_{9k} (\text{Service Learning}) +$$

β_{10k} (Classroom Civic Learning Opportunities) + $\sum_{p=11}^{14}$ β_{pk} (School Support for Academic and Social Development) + $\sum_{p=15}^{16}$ β_{pk} (Afterschool Activities) + β_{17k} (Prior Commitments) + r_{jk}

Level 3:

$\beta_{0k} = \gamma_{00} + \gamma_{01}$ (School Mean Civic Learning Opportunities)$_k$ + γ_{02} (School Mean Academic Achievement)$_k$ + u_{0k}
$\beta_{pk} = \gamma_{p0,}$ for p = 1 to 17 (models 1 and 2)
$\beta_{pk} = \gamma_{p0,}$ for p = 1 to 9, 11 to 17; $\beta_{10k} = \gamma_{10,0} + u_{10k}$ (models 3 and 4);

At the school level we also tried models including the racial composition of the school and the aggregate social status and poverty level of its students based on their census block addresses. Neither the racial composition nor the socio-economic variables ever reached the level of statistical significance, so we removed them from the school level equations.

In most of our analytic models all individual-level variables were standardized and grand-mean centered. Furthermore, based on the assumption that the relationship between, say, being female and having commitments to civic participation, was the same across all schools in our sample, all level 2 variables were fixed. However, in the models where we included our measure of classroom civic learning opportunities, we group mean-centered that variable at level 2 and included each school's mean value at level 3. This allowed us to directly estimate the difference in mean civic commitment for schools who differed by one unit in civic learning opportunities by reading the coefficient at level 3. We allowed the coefficient of classroom civic learning opportunities at level 2 to vary across schools, assuming that some schools might be better able to implement these curricular practices than other schools. The analysis indicated that there was significant variation between schools in the relationship between civic learning opportunities and students' commitment to civic participation (p = .02).

RESULTS

As discussed above, our study aims to identify the factors that may support the development of commitments to civic participation. We present these findings using four models. Model 1 includes only individual demographic characteristics. Model 2 adds two indicators of family and neighborhood context that are not demographic in nature: an indicator assessing parental discussion of politics and civic issues with youth and an indicator of social capital in the neighborhood. Model 3 adds indicators of educational contexts and practices (those that explicitly target civic development and those that are thought to promote more standard academic outcomes) and afterschool activities. Model 4 includes all the variables in Model 3 and adds a measure of commitments to civic participation taken two years earlier in 2003. This measure is identical to the measure used in 2005 and acts as a control for prior commitments. We also ran a model using each item in our measure of classroom civic learning opportunities as a separate indicator to make sure that no individual item was driving the result. We found that each individual item was significantly related to the outcome, and the size of each separate coefficient was about the same. We do not report on that model here.

We provide the results in Table 2. Because of the different grouping strategies, the intercept has a slightly different interpretation depending on the model. In Models 1 and 2, the intercept is the civic commitment score for a student who is average for the sample on all predictors. For Models 3 and 4, the intercept is the civic commitment for a student who is average for his/her school in civic learning opportunities and average for the system in all other respects. We give the standardized coefficients for each model. For Model 4 we also provide effect sizes. To calculate effect sizes we divide the standardized coefficient by the standard deviation of the outcome, computed by taking the square root of the sum of all variances in the unconditional model.

To interpret the meaning of a score on a Rasch measure such as a student's commitment to civic participation, one needs to look at the expected responses to each item for a person with that measure score. Since this is not transparent from Table 2, we provide a brief explanation. In this particular sample, a student scoring at the mean of commitments to civic participation would score at the intercept of each model. Such a student would agree with the four items that are easiest to endorse: "Being concerned about state and local issues is an important responsibility for everybody," "In the next 3 years I expect to be involved in improving my community," "I have good ideas for programs or projects that would help solve problems in my community," and "In the next 3 years I expect to work on at least one community project that involves government agency." This student would disagree with, "Being actively involved in community issues is my responsibility." Students with civic commitments one half standard deviation below the mean (at about the 30th percentile in the distribution) would agree with the two easiest items to endorse, and would disagree with the three hardest items. Students with civic commitments one half standard deviation above the mean (at about the 70th percentile in the distribution) would agree with all five items.

Student Demographic and Academic Characteristics

As shown in Model 1 (see Table 2), eleventh graders' demographic characteristics do not appear to be strongly related to their level of civic commitment. In fact, when only student demographics and academic characteristics were included in the model, they explained only 1% of the total variance. In addition, the only indicator that achieved statistical significance was average achievement at the school level, showing that, on average, students attending schools with higher average achievement develop higher commitments to civic participation. However, this relationship disappeared once other variables were included in the model. In Model 2, white students were associated with less of a civic commitment than African Americans, the omitted category in our analysis, although this difference disappeared when other variables were added in subsequent models. Our measure of student socioeconomic status, whether a student was eligible for free or reduced lunch, reached marginal significance in our final model. Its effect size was quite small.

Neighborhood and Family Context

Our measures of neighborhood and family context were strongly related to students' commitments to civic participation. As predicted, high school juniors' reports of neighborhood social capital were positively related to their overall level of commitment to civic participation. Specifically, high school juniors who report that their community is one in which adults both care about youth and work to make the community better are more likely to report high levels of commitments to civic participation. This relationship (though diminished in magnitude) remains even after controlling for different school experiences (Model 3) and after additionally controlling for their level of commitments to civic participation as 9th graders (Model 4).

We found that having parents who discussed current events and politics with their children was positively associated with students' level of commitments to civic participation. Again, this positive relationship remained after controlling for school experiences (Model 3) and prior commitments (Model 4).

School Supports for Academic and Social Development

We found that several of these supports did promote desired commitments to civic participation, though the magnitude of these effects was generally modest. Specifically, when students experienced their peers as supportive of academic achievement by, for example, helping each other prepare for tests or do homework or, more generally, by sharing a commitment to doing well in school, they were also slightly more likely to express commitments to civic participation. And when students expressed more of a sense of belonging to the school, they reported higher levels of commitments to civic participation. Perceived teacher support was not associated with commitments to civic participation when controlling for the other variables. One exception to this pattern occurred with parental press for academic achievement. We found a small but statistically significant and *negative* relationship between student reports that their parents attended to and supported their focus on academic achievement and their reported levels of commitment to civic participation.

Afterschool Activities

Participation in afterschool extracurricular activities other than sports was related to increased commitments to civic participation. The effect sizes of these opportunities are relatively modest compared to some classroom opportunities that more explicitly target civic and political issues. Participation on either in-school or out-of-school sports teams was not related to increased civic commitments before or after controlling for prior civic commitments.

CLASSROOM CIVIC LEARNING OPPORTUNITIES

The impact of civic learning opportunities and of experiencing service learning was both sizable and substantially larger than any other measure in our study including students' prior commitments to civic participation.

Explaining Variation at the School and Individual Level

As Table 2 shows, as we add predictors, our models explain increasing amounts of the variation in students' commitments to civic participation. Our final model explains 63% of this variation. While only 9% of the variation in classroom civic learning opportunities was at the school level, the schools' level of civic learning opportunities was a marginally significant predictor of students' commitments to civic participation in Models 3 and 4.

Discussion

One of the most important results of this study is that what happens in classrooms can have a significant impact on students' commitments to civic participation. In addition, because the students in this sample are primarily low-income students of color, this study highlights activities that may help offset some of the striking inequalities in political voice that currently characterize our democracy. These results are particularly powerful given that previous civic commitments were controlled in the analyses. In what follows, we discuss these and other findings from the study.

First, we have found that experiences that focus directly on civic and political issues and ways to act (e.g. undertaking service learning projects, following current events, discussing problems in the community and ways to respond, providing students with a classroom in which open dialog around controversial issues is common and where students study topics that matter to them, as well as exposure to civic role models) are a highly efficacious means of fostering commitments to civic participation. In fact, the effect size of both service learning opportunities (.26) and the overall measure of classroom civic learning opportunities (.41) are larger than any other factor in this study. These findings are consistent with recent research by Torney-Purta et al., (2007) and with other studies that have examined the association between varied classroom practices and commitments to civic participation (Gibson & Levine, 2003). Indeed, the primary contribution of this study is demonstrating that these associations are quite sizable even when controlling for prior civic commitments and a range of other neighborhood, school, and family characteristics – something other large scale studies of multiple civic learning opportunities have not done.

The efficacy of these particular civic learning opportunities might be viewed by some as in conflict with findings from early longitudinal studies (most prominently Langton & Jennings, 1968 – also see Cook, 1985 for review) that called into question the ability of schools to influence students' levels of civic participation. These earlier studies found that taking civic education or government courses did not spur desired outcomes. However, since such courses likely vary widely in the degree to which they provide the kind of civic learning opportunities we examine, we do not view these findings as contradictory. Indeed, they speak to the need for policymakers and educators to focus on ensuring that students receive these efficacious practices rather than simply requiring students to enroll in particular courses.

Second, since this study focused on predominantly low-income students and students of color, it is important to highlight that these curricular approaches appear to provide significant benefits for students from groups that generally have less political voice than others (APSA Task Force, 2004; Verba et al., 1995). Indeed, analysis from this sample indicates that classroom civic learning opportunities can more than offset the impact of neighborhood or home contexts that are relatively inattentive to civic and political issues when it comes to the development of commitments to civic participation. Consider for example, a student who was average with respect to demographics, aspects of schooling related to academic achievement, afterschool participation in extracurricular activities, and civic learning opportunities, but one standard deviation below average when it comes to neighborhood social capital and conversations with parents. This student would be at the 40th percentile in terms of his or her commitment to civic participation. If, on the other hand, this student experienced a level of civic learning opportunities that was one standard deviation above the system average, then, despite the lack of focus on these issues in the students' neighborhood and home, this same student would be at the 70th percentile in commitment to civic participation.

Thus, schools appear able to help lessen the participatory inequality that exists in our civic and political life. Indeed, this finding takes on added importance in light of recent studies finding that the provision of these school-based civic learning opportunities is unequal. For example, a study by Kahne and Middaugh (2008) that draws on a nationally representative survey of high school students and a survey of high school students in California indicates that students of color, those whose academic performance is less strong than others, as well as those who are part of classrooms with relatively more low-income students all receive far fewer classroom based civic learning opportunities. Though we do not know the degree to which equalizing the access of all students to these opportunities might ultimately help resolve some of the civic and political inequalities noted at the outset of this paper, this study of youth in Chicago indicates that such an effort might well help.

Third, while we saw strong evidence that providing explicitly civic learning opportunities was efficacious, we did not see strong evidence that experiencing more general academic and social supports in school fostered civic outcomes. Indeed, focusing on teacher, student, and peer relationships associated with academics and social development appears insufficient as a means of fostering commitments to civic and political engagement. Our study finds, at best, only small effects for some of these measures. We suspect these limited effects are due to the academic focus of these relationships and supports. Specifically, as discussed in our conceptual framework, recent research (Hart, 2005; Kahne & Westheimer, 2003; Youniss & Yates, 1997) indicates that classroom opportunities with an explicitly civic dimension can develop students' sense of civic agency, social relatedness, and political and moral understandings–key building blocks of a civic identity. In line with this model, since academic and social supports have a less direct relationship to civic and political dimensions of students' identities, they would not be expected to have as great an impact on students' civic commitments.

These findings have significant implications for policy. In particular, it appears that mainstream school reform agendas will be insufficient when it comes to civic development. Practices that directly target civic outcomes will be necessary in order for schools to exert a sizable impact on students' commitments to civic participation. Indeed, it is interesting to note that coming from a family where students said their parents emphasized academic achievement by doing such things as encouraging them to work hard, talking with them about their school work, or talking with them about their performance in school, is inversely related to students' commitments to civic participation. While we are not clear why this relationship exists, it would be interesting to examine whether and under what circumstances parental emphasis on academic success may crowd out attention to civics.

Fourth, in addition to the sizable impact of school-based civic learning opportunities, we found that students were more likely to express higher levels of commitment to civic participation when they saw examples of neighbors dealing with community problems, when they felt adults looked after children, and when they had a general sense that their neighborhood supported young people. It appears that when youth feel attended to by their community's adults it supports their civic commitments – a finding consistent with other recent work by Flanagan et al. (2007a). In addition, and consistent with research noted earlier (Andolina et al., 2003; McIntosh et al., 2006; Torney-Purta et al., 2001), having parents who discussed current events with them contributed to students' commitment to civic participation. In short, it appears that when students witnessed concern for the community and current events in their home, school, or neighborhood, they were more likely to be committed to civic participation. Moreover, that the experience of civic and civil communities may foster commitments to civic participation among youth provides an additional argument for community development and renewal strategies that aim to engage the public in efforts to improve their neighborhoods and communities (Fung, 2004). These findings also appear consistent with the theory laid out in our conceptual framework. When young people experience their neighborhood as one that monitors and responds to their needs and when they engage in discussions with their parents about current events, it seems reasonable to expect that their sense of agency, of social relatedness, and their sense of political and moral understanding would grow.

Finally, the potential value of extracurricular activities as a means of developing commitments to civic participation has long been noted (McFarland & Thomas, 2006; Otto, 1976; Scott & Willits, 1998; Smith, 1999). Our findings are consistent with these studies in indicating benefits from participation in extracurricular opportunities other than sports. At the same time, participation in extracurricular opportunities is voluntary and, when compared with classroom civic learning opportunities, our data suggest that their impact is more modest. We should note, however, that the relatively smaller size of this effect may be due to a lack of differentiation with respect to the emphasis place on civic issues in varied extracurricular activities. Just as explicit attention to civic issues strengthens a school's impact on commitments to civic participation, we suspect that extracurricular activities focused directly on civic issues and actions would be more consequential when it comes to civic outcomes. McFarland and Thomas' (2006) present study indicates that this is the case.

There are several limitations to the present study. Though the large sample size and ability to control for prior civic commitments are strengths of this data set, other qualities of the data present limitations. For example, as discussed earlier, the fact that all youth in our sample are from the Chicago public schools limits our ability to examine the ways demographic diversity may matter and thus to generalize our findings beyond large urban environments. In addition, due to space constraints on the survey, three of our measures consist of only one item (our measure of parent civic discussion with youth, of service learning experiences, and of extracurricular sports participation). Relying on a single item is never desirable and likely presents the most significant problem when it comes to our measure of parent civic discussion. Parental contributions likely take other forms as well. Similarly, while this study indicates that participation in extracurricular sports is differently related to civic outcomes than participation in other extracurricular activities, more detailed work focusing on particular opportunities would help us understand why this is the case. In addition, since so many civic learning opportunities are delivered in classrooms, it is a limitation that we cannot undertake a classroom level analysis as part of our HLM. This limitation stems both from the fact that students receive civic learning opportunities in a variety of subjects (e.g. English, social studies, science) and because of technical limits of the data base. Finally, while research indicates that self-reports of commitments to civic participation are solid predictors of future behaviors (Fishbein et al., 1980; Oesterle et al., 2004; Theiss-Morse, 1993), clearly, our reliance on self-report methodology leads to questions of accuracy. These self-reports do not enable identification of the actual forms of civic participation that stem from increased commitments. A follow-up study of participants in this study focusing on their behaviors would be enormously valuable.

CONCLUSION

In their discussion of high school civic education, Langton and Jennings (1968) write that "there must be a radical restructuring of these courses in order for them to have any appreciable pay-off" (p. 867). More recently, Galston (2001) argued that "researchers cannot afford to overlook the impact of formal civic education and related school-based experiences. (p. 232)" The findings of this study show that providing a set of desired classroom civic learning opportunities to youth in urban public schools can very meaningfully support the development of students' commitments to civic participation.

* This chapter has been published as an article in the American Educational Research Journal, 2008, 45, 3, 738-766. It is reproduced here with the permission of the authors and the AERJ.

REFERENCES

Ajzen, I. (2001). Nature and operation of attitudes. *Annual Review of Psychology, 52,* 27–58.
Adelman, C. (1999). *Answers in the tool box: Academic intensity, attendance patterns, and bachelor's degree attainment.* Washington, DC: U.S. Department of Education.
Andolina, M. W., Jenkins, K., Zukin, C., & Keeter, S. (2003). Habits from home, lessons from school: Influences on youth civic development. *PS: Political Science and Politics, 36*(2), 275–280.
APSA Task Force on Inequality and American Democracy. (2004). American democracy in an age of rising inequality. *Perspectives on Politics, 2*(4), 651–689.
Atkins, R., & Hart, D. (2003). Neighborhoods, adults, and the development of civic identity in urban youth. *Applied Developmental Science, 7*(3), 156–164.
Barber, B. (1984). *Strong democracy: Participatory politics for a new age.* Berkeley, CA: University of California Press.
Bartels, L. M. (Revised August, 2005). *Economic inequality and political representation.* Retrieved from the Web on 11/30/05. http://www.princeton.edu/~bartels/economic.pdf
Baumeister, R. F., & Leary, M. R. (1995). The need to belong: Desire for interpersonal attachments as a fundamental human motivation. *Psychological Bulletin, 117*(3), 487–499.
Billig, S. H. (2000). Research on K-12 school-based service-learning: The evidence builds. *Phi Delta Kappan, 81,* 658–664.
Billig, S., Root, S., & Jesse, D. (2005). *The impact of participation in service learning on high school students' civic engagement* (CIRCLE Working Paper 33). Washington, DC: Center for Information and Research on Civic Learning and Engagement.
Bond, T. G., & Fox, C. M. (2001). *Applying the Rasch model: Fundamental measurement in the human sciences.* Mahwah, NJ: Lawrence Erlbaum Associates.
Boyte, H. C., & Kari, N. N. (1996). *Building America: The democratic promise of public work.* Philadelphia: Temple University Press.
Bryk, A., & Schneider, B. (2002). *Trust in schools: A core resource for improvement.* New York: Russell Sage Foundation.
Burns, N., Schlozman, K. L., & Verba, S. (2001). *The private roots of public action: Gender, equality, and political participation.* Cambridge, MA: Harvard University Press.
Campbell, D. E. (2005). *Voice in the classroom: How open classroom environment facilitates adolescents' civic development* (CIRCLE Working Paper 28). Washington, DC: Center for Information and Research on Civic Learning and Engagement.
Center on Education Policy. (2006). *From the capital to the classroom: Year four of the No Child Left Behind Act.* Washington, DC: Center on Education Policy.
Christenson, S. L., & Thurlow, M. L. (2004). School dropouts: Prevention considerations, interventions, and challenges. *Current Directions in Psychological Science, 13,* 36–39.
CIRCLE (2007). Trends by race, ethnicity, and gender: Fact sheet. Retrieved from the web on August 20, 2007 at http://www.civicyouth.org/quick/trends.htm
Coleman, J. S. (1988). Social capital in the creation of human capital. *American Journal of Sociology, 94,* 95–120.
Cook, T. (1985). The bear market in political socialization and the costs of misunderstood psychological theories. *The American Political Science Review, 79*(4), 1079–1093.

Delli Carpini, M. X., & Keeter, S. K. (1996). *What Americans know about politics and why it matters.* New Haven, CT: Yale University Press.
Dewey, J. (1900). *The school and society and the child and the curriculum.* Chicago: University of Chicago Press.
Dewey, J. (1916). *Democracy and education.* New York: Free Press.
Erikson, E. H. (1968). *Identity: Youth and crisis.* New York: W.W. Norton & Co.
Fishbein, M., Ajzen, I., & Hinkle, R. (1980). Predicting and understanding voting in American elections: Effects of external variables. In I. Ajzen & M. Fishbein (Eds.), *Understanding and predicting behavior* (Chap. 13). Englewood Cliffs, NJ: Prentice Hall.
Flanagan, C. A., Cumsille, P., Sukhdeep, G., & Gallay, L. S. (2007). School and community climates and civic commitments: Patterns for ethnic minority and majority students. *Journal of Educational Psychology, 99*(2), 421–431.
Flanagan, C. A., & Gallay, L. S. (1995). Reframing the meaning of "political" in research with Adolescents. In M. Hepburn (Ed.), *Perspectives in Political Science: New Directions in Political Socialization Research* (pp. 34–41). New York: Oxford University Press.
Flanagan, C. A., Syverstsen, A. K., & Stout, M. D. (2007). *Civic measurement models: Tapping adolescents' civic engagement.* Washington, DC: Center for Information and Research on Civic Learning and Engagement.
Fung, A. (2004). *Empowered participation: Reinventing urban democracy.* Princeton, NJ: Princeton University Press.
Galston, W. (2001). Political knowledge, political engagement and civic education. *Annual Review of Political Science, 4,* 217–234.
Gibson, C., & Levine, P. (2003). *The civic mission of schools.* New York and Washington, DC: The Carnegie Corporation of New York and the Center for Information and Research on Civic Learning.
Hart, D. (2005). The development of moral identity. In G. Carlo & C. P. Edwards (Eds.), *Nebraska Symposium on motivation: Vol. 51. Moral motivation through the lifespan* (pp.165–196). Lincoln, NE: University of Nebraska Press.
Hart, D., Donnelly, T. M, Youniss, J., & Atkins, R. (2007). High school community service as a predictor of adult voting and volunteering. *American Educational Research Journal, 44*(1), 197–219.
Jennings, M. K., Stoker, L., & Bowers, J. (2001). *Politics across the generations: Family transmission reexamined.* (Working Paper 2001-15). Berkeley, CA: Institute of Governmental Studies.
Junn, J. (1999). Participation in liberal democracy: The political assimilation of immigrants. *The American Behavioral Scientist, 42*(9), 1417–1438.
Juvonen, J. (2006). Sense of belonging, social bonds, and school functioning. In P. A. Alexander & P. H. Winne (Eds.), *Handbook of Educational Psychology* (pp 655–674). Mahwah, NJ: Lawrence Erlbaum Associates.
Kahne, J., Chi, B., & Middaugh, E. (2006). Building social capital for civic and political engagement: The potential of high school government courses. *Canadian Journal of Education, 29*(2), 387–409.
Kahne, J., & Middaugh, E. (2008). Democracy for some: The civic opportunity gap in high school Working paper available from http://www.civicsurvey.org/Democratic_Education_Reports_%26_Publications_.html
Kahne, J., & Westheimer, J. (2003). Teaching democracy: What schools need to do. *Phi Delta Kappan, 85*(1), 34–40, 557–566.
Keeter, S., Zukin, C., Andolina, M., & Jenkins, K. (2002). *The civic and political health of the nation: A generational portrait.* Retrieved November 30, 2005, from http://pollcats.net/downloads/civichealth.pdf
Langton, K., & Jennings, M. K. (1968). Political socialization and the high school civic curriculum in the United States. *American Political Science Review, 62,* 862–867.
Long, S. (2002). *The new student politics: The Wingspread statement on student engagement.* Providence, RI: The Campus Compact.
Macedo, S., Alex-Assensoh, Y., Berry, J. M., Brintnall, M., Campbell, D. E., & Fraga, L. R., et al. (2005). *Democracy at risk: How political choices undermine citizen participation, and what we can do about it.* Washington, DC: Brookings Institution.
Marcelo, K. B., Lopez, M. H., & Kirby, E. H. (2007a). *Civic engagement among minority youth.* Washington, DC: Center for Information and Research on Civic Learning and Engagement.
Marcelo, K. B., Lopez, M. H., & Kirby, E. H. (2007b). *Civic engagement among young men and women.* Washington, DC: Center for Information and Research on Civic Learning and Engagement.

McDevitt, M., & Kiousis, S. (2004). *Education for deliberative democracy: The long-term influence of kids voting USA*. (CIRCLE Working Paper #22). Washington, DC: Center for Information and Research on Civic Learning and Engagement.

McFarland, D. A., & Thomas, R. J. (2006). Bowling young: How youth voluntary associations influence adult political participation. *American Sociological Review, 71*, 401–425.

McIntosh, H., Hart, D., & Youniss, J. (2006). *The influence of family political discussion on youth civic development: Which parent qualities matter.* Unpublished manuscript.

Meier, D. (1995). *The power of their ideas: Lessons for America from a small school in Harlem.* Boston: Beacon Press.

Meier, D. (2002). *In schools we trust: Creating communities of learning in an era of testing and standardization.* Boston: Beacon Press.

Melchior, A. (1998). *Final report: National evaluation of Learn and Serve America and community-based programs.* Waltham, MA: Center for Human Resources at Brandeis University.

Metz, E. C., & Youniss, J. (2005). Longitudinal gains in civic development through school-based required service. *Political Psychology, 26*(3), 413–438.

Nie, N. H., Junn, J., &. Stehlik-Barry, K. (1996). *Education and democratic citizenship in America.* Chicago: University of Chicago Press.

Niemi, R., & Junn, J. (1998). *Civic education.* New Haven, CT: Yale University Press.

Niemi, R., & Sobieszek, B. (1977). Political socialization. *Annual Review of Sociology, 3*, 209–233.

Oesterle, S., Johnson, M. K., & Mortimer, J. T. (2004). Volunteerism during the transition to adulthood: A life course perspective. *Social Forces, 82*(3), 1123–1149.

Otto, L. B. (1976). Social integration and the status attainment process. *American Journal of Sociology, 81*, 1360–1383.

Putnam, R. (1993). *Making democracy work: Civic traditions in modern Italy.* Princeton, NJ: Princeton University Press.

Putnam, R. (2000). *Bowling alone: The collapse and revival of American community.* New York: Simon & Shuster.

Raudenbush, S. W., & Bryk, A. S. (2002). *Hierarchical linear models: Applications and data analysis methods* (2nd ed.). Thousand Oaks, CA: Sage Publications.

Rose, L. C., & Gallup, A. M. (2000). The thirty-second annual *Phi Delta Kappan* poll of the public's attitudes toward the public school. *Phi Delta Kappan, 82*(1), 41–57.

Sanchez-Jankowski, M. (2002). Minority youth and civic engagement: The impact of group relations. *Applied Developmental Science, 6*(4), 237–245.

Scott, D., & Willits, F. K. (1998). Adolescent and adult leisure patterns: A reassessment. *Journal of Leisure Research, 30*(3), 319–330.

Smith, E. S. (1999). The effects of investment in the social capital of youth on political and civic behavior in young adulthood: A longitudinal analysis. *Political Psychology, 20*, 553–580.

Stepick, A., & Stepick, C. D. (2002). Becoming American, constructing ethnicity: Immigrant youth and civic engagement. *Applied Developmental Science, 6*(4), 246–257.

Theiss-Morse, E. (1993). Conceptualizations of good citizenship and political participation. *Political Behavior, 15*(4), 355–380.

Torney- Purta, J. (2002). The school's role in developing civic engagement: A study of adolescents in twenty-eight countries. *Applied Developmental Science, 6*(4), 203–212.

Torney-Purta, J., Amadeo, J., & Richardson, W. K. (2007). Civic service among youth in Chile, Denmark, England, and the United States: A psychological perspective. In M. Sherraden & A. McBride (Eds.), *Civic service worldwide: Impacts and inquiries.* Armonk, NY: M.E. Sharpe.

Torney-Purta, J., Barber, C. H., & Wilkenfeld, B. (2007). Latino adolescents' civic development in the United States: Research results from the IEA Civic Education Study. *Journal of Youth and Adolescence, 36*, 111–125.

Torney-Purta, J., Lehmann, R., Oswald, H., & Schulz, W. (2001). *Citizenship and education in twenty-eight countries: Civic knowledge and engagement at age fourteen.* Amsterdam: International Association for the Evaluation of Educational Achievement (IEA).

Verba, S. (2003). Would the dream of political equality turn out to be a nightmare? *Perspectives on Politics, 1*(4), 663–680.

Verba, S., & Nie, N. (1972). *Participation in America.* New York: Harper and Row.

Verba, S., Schlozman, K. L., & Brady, H. E. (1995). *Voice and equality: Civic voluntarism in American politics.* Cambridge, MA: Harvard University Press.

Watson, M., Battistich, V., & Solomon, D. (1997). Enhancing students' social and ethical development in school: An intervention program and its effects. *International Journal of Educational Research, 27*, 571–586.

Wentzel, K. R. (1997). Student motivation in middle school: The role of perceived pedagogical caring. *Journal of Educational Psychology, 89*(3), 411–419.

Wentzel, K. R. (1998). Social support and adjustment in middle school: The role of parents, teachers, and peers. *Journal of Educational Psychology, 90*(2), 202–209.

Westheimer, J., & Kahne, J. (2004). What kind of citizen? The politics of educating for democracy. *American Educational Research Journal, 41*(2), 237–269.

Wright, B. D., & Masters, G. N. (1982). *Rating scale analysis: Rasch measurement*. Chicago: Mesa Press.

Yates, M., & Youniss, J. (1998). Community service and political identity development in adolescence. *Journal of Social Issues, 54*(3), 495–512.

Youniss, J., & Yates, J. (1997). *Community service and social responsibility in youth*. Chicago: University of Chicago Press.

Zirkel, S. (forthcoming). Creating more effective multiethnic schools. *Review of Educational Research*.

APPENDIX A: INDICATORS USED IN THIS ANALYSIS

Table A1. Outcome Variable from Survey

Indicator	Type	Response categories	List of items
Commitment to Civic Participation Prior Commitment to Civic Participation	Measure Rel=.73	Strongly disagree, Disagree, Agree, Strongly agree	*How much do you agree with the following:* Being actively involved in community issues is my responsibility. In the next 3 years, I expect to work on at least one community project that involves a government agency I have good ideas for programs or projects to help solve problems in my community In the next 3 years I expect to be involved in improving my community Being concerned about state and local issues is an important responsibility for everybody

Table A2. Predictor Variables from Administrative Records. Demographics and academic achievement

Indicator	Type	Percent if dichomous Mean (standard deviation) if continuous
Female	Dichotomous	59%
Latino/a	Dichotomous	42%
Asian	Dichotomous	8%
White	Dichotomous	14%
Free/reduced lunch	Dichotomous	79%
Prairie State Achievement Exam Reading Score	Continuous	156 (15.55)

Table A3. Predictor Variables from Survey

	Type	Response categories	List of items if measure: Frequencies if single item
Parent/Neighborhood			
Neighborhood Social Capital	Measure Rel=.73	Strongly Disagree, Disagree, Agree, Strongly Agree (SD,D, A,SA)	*How much do agree with the following statements about the community in which you live?* If there is a problem in the community, neighbors get together to deal with it People in this neighborhood can be trusted You can count on adults in this neighborhood to see that children are safe & don't get into trouble The equipment and buildings in the neighborhood park or playground are well kept There are adults in this neighborhood children can look up to Adults in this neighborhood know who the local children are No one in this neighborhood cares much about what happens Here (reverse coded)
Parent Civic Conversation	Single item	SD,D, A,SA (1-4)	This year my parent/guardians have discussed current events/politics with me Mean: 2.69 Category frequencies: 1: 19% 2: 22% 3: 31% 4: 28%
School Context			
Teacher Support	Measure Rel=.80	SD,D, A,SA (1-4)	*In my school this year, there is at least ONE teacher who:* Knows who my friends are Would be willing to help me with a personal problem Really cares about how I am doing in school I could talk to if I was having problems in a class I could ask to write me a recommendation for a job, program, or college

(Continued)

Peer Support for Academic Achievement	Measure Rel=.84	SD,D, A,SA (1-4)	*How much do you agree with the following:* My friends and I help each other prepare for tests My friends think it is important to attend every class My friends and I help each other with homework assignments My friends try hard in school My friends and I talk about what we did in class My friends think it is important to do well in school
Sense of Belonging	Measure Rel=.81	SD,D, A,SA (1-4)	*How much do you agree with the following:* People at this school are like family to me I participate in a lot of activities at this school People care if I'm not at school There are people at this school I can talk to about personal matters I fit in with the students in this school There are people at this school who will help me if I need it
Parental Press for Academic Achievement	Measure Rel = (.80)	Never, Rarely, Sometimes, Frequently	*This year my parents/guardians have:* Talked to me about my homework assignments Talked to me about what I'm studying in class Talked to me about how I'm doing in my classes Encouraged me to work hard in school Encourage me to continue my education after high school
Participate in afterschool activities sponsored by school*	Single item	Never, once in a while, once a week, almost every day. (1-4)	This year how often have you participated in school clubs or afterschool activities (student council, drama ethnic/cultural clubs, newspaper, After School Matters)? Mean: 2.15 Category frequencies: 1: 39% 2: 23% 3: 22% 4:16%

(Continued)

Participate in activities sponsored by non-school organizations*	Single item	Never, once in a while, once a week, almost every day. (1-4)	This year how often have you participated in activities organized by groups OUTSIDE of school (classes or programs at Boys/Girls Club, park program, church group) Mean: 1.88 Category frequencies: 1: 50% 2: 21% 3: 20% 4: 9%
Participate in sports	Single item	Never, once in a while, once a week, almost every day. (1-4)	This year how often have you participated in sports teams, either in school or out of school (while in season) Mean: 2.18 Category frequencies: 1: 45% 2: 17% 3: 12% 4: 25%
Civics related			
Classroom Civic Learning Opportunities	Measure Rel=.74	Strongly disagree, Disagree, Agree, Strongly agree never, rarely, sometimes, often	*In at least one of my classes this year:* I am required to keep up with politics or government, either by reading a newspaper, watching tv or going to the internet I learned about things in society that need to be changed I met people who work to make society better I learned about ways to improve my community *How often do teachers:* Focus on issues I care about Encourage students to make up their own minds about political and social topics Encourage students to discuss political and social topics on which people have different opinions
Service Learning	Item	Strongly disagree, Disagree, Agree, Strongly agree	In at least one of my classes this year I worked on a service learning project to improve my community Mean: 2.54 Category frequencies: 1: 8% 2: 37% 3: 46% 4: 8%

*these two items were arithmetically combined into a single item

Table 2. Hierarchical Linear Models Predicting Eleventh Graders' Commitment to Civic Participation

Predictors	Model 1: Demographic and Academic Characteristics	Model 2: Adds Neighborhood and Family Context	Model 3: Adds curricular and extracurricular opportunities	Model 4: Adds Prior Commitments to Civic Participation
Intercept	5.00***	5.02**	5.02***	5.02***
School Level				
Mean Civic Learning Opportunities			.06~	.06~
Mean Academic Achievement	.11*	.03	.01	.01
Individual Level				
Demographic And Academic Characteristics				
PSAE Reading Score	-.01	.02	-.02	-.01
Gender (Female = 1)	.01	.01	-.02	-.03
Latino	-.07	-.02	.00	.00
Asian	-.02	.00	-.02	-.03 ~ (.02)
White	-.04	-.07*	-.04	-.04
Free/Reduced Lunch	-.07	-.04	-.07	-.09 ~ (-.06)
Neighborhood and Family Context				
Parents discuss current events and politics		.40***	.19***	.17***(.12)
Neighborhood Social Capital		.53***	.23***	.20***(.14)
Educational Contexts and Practices				
Service Learning Experiences			.36***	.36***(.26)

Classroom Civic Learning Opportunities			.62***	.57***(.41)
Peer Support for Academic Achievement			.09***	.08***(.06)
Sense of Belonging			.07~	.07* (.05)
Teacher Support			-.03	-.03
Parent Press for Academic Achievement			-.08**	-.08** (-.06)
Afterschool Activities				
School and other clubs			.16***	.14* (.10)
Sports			.02	.02
Prior Civic Commitments				
Prior Commitments to Civic Participation (from 2003)				.27***(.19)
% Variance Explained	1%	27%	59%	63%

~ = p < .10   * = p < .05   ** = p < .01   *** = p < .001

All Coefficients Standardized. Numbers in parentheses are effect sizes.

HENRY MILNER

10. DOES CIVIC EDUCATION BOOST TURNOUT?

A Natural Experiment

INTRODUCTION

It is well established that more politically informed citizens vote and participate in politics more. It is also well established that the democratic world in the past 30 years has seen a secular decline in the sense of civic duty to so participate. In the absence of such a duty, the political knowledge dimension becomes increasingly salient. Having informed citizens is a value in itself; it also becomes crucial as a means of stemming the decline in, if not boosting, political participation.

Moreover, there is no shortage of data to reveal that declining political participation and a diminishing sense of a civic duty to vote are in good part generational phenomena. Young people arriving at the age of citizenship are in the process of developing habits that will affect choices they will make throughout their lives. Yet sociological and technological changes have made those reaching adulthood in the past 15 years less subject to the traditional socializing influences of family and community. Young adults have arrived at maturity in the world of the Internet and of digitalized information, one in which the shared social and informational network of the geographical (and political) community is increasingly replaced by an individualized virtual community, Hence a greater political-socialization burden is placed on the school, the only wide-ranging institution physically linking young people to the geographical community, even as it filters knowledge – including political knowledge – from increasingly electronic sources.

The set of activities and initiatives involved in carrying out this role are normally termed citizenship education, while the specific courses and related activities in the schools carrying out this mission – where they exist – are usually termed civic education or civics. Since the early 1990s there has been a resurgence in school-delivered civic education programs stemmed by compelling investigative reports notably in the United Kingdom, the United States and Australia. In light of this new policy environment, many jurisdictions, including a number of Canadian provinces, have implemented a variety of new civic education related measures through a reformed school curriculum (Lewis: this volume; Llewellyn et al., 2007).

Not enough is known, however, of the effects of such initiatives on political participation. Even the effects of civic education on political knowledge are not undisputed. Some remain sceptical (e.g. McDevitt & Chaffee 2000); most, however, find that civic education can increase political knowledge (Niemi & Junn,

1998) and, especially, close knowledge gaps between advantaged and disadvantaged groups, particularly for African-American students (see e.g. Finkel and Howard 2005; Lay 2006). And while there is a connection between learning about politics in school and expressing an intention to vote as an adult, there is a dearth of evidence that this intention is actually realized in the form of increased turnout (see e.g. Phillips 2004). There is, of course, a wide literature showing a correlation between civic education and attitudes of tolerance toward others, respect for diversity, and the like. While it is difficult, when using such dependent variables, including intention to vote, to control for the perceived social desirability of the response; overall, it is clear that civic education has beneficial effects irrespective of its influence on turnout. Nevertheless, as turnout declines and the "democratic deficit" grows, it is reasonable to expect civic education to address it.

TURNOUT DECLINE IN CANADA

By the late 1990s Canadian observers of political participation were coming to the realization that not only was the general decline hitting their country especially hard, but that the generational dimension was especially salient in Canada. More than most comparable countries, Canada underwent a precipitous decline in voter turnout starting at the end of the 1980s (see Figure 1). As we can see, in 1988 the turnout of registered voters was 75.3%, a number close to the average for the previous 30 years, dropping dramatically to 64.1 in 2000 and 60.9% in the 2004 federal election. Though it rose in the 2006 election to 64.7 percent, in 2008 (which is not included in Figure 1), it continued its descent to 59.1.

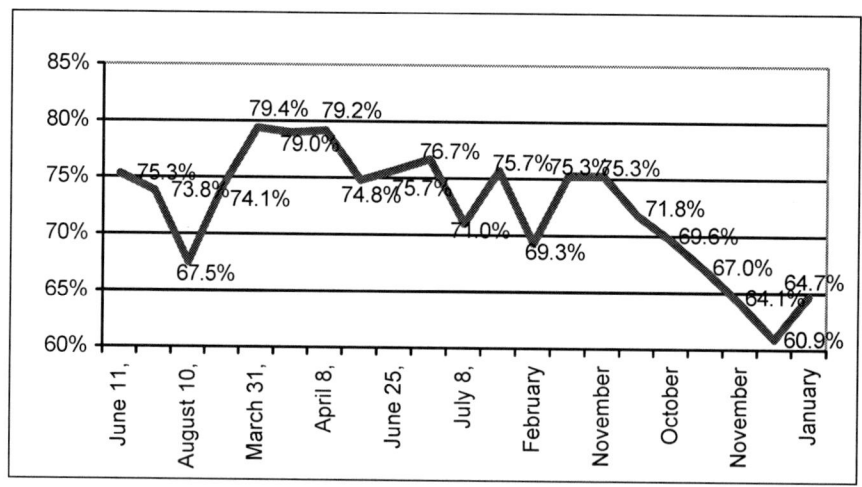

Figure 1. Turnout rate in Canadian federal elections (1945–2006)*

*Official turnout in Canada is based on the number of electors on the final lists of electors.
** Date of the referendum on the Charlottetown Accord proposing constitutional changes.
Source: Elections Canada.

As in Europe (Goerres 2008), the decline corresponded to a decline in other forms of political participation, resulting in what Cross and Young (2004), who estimate the average age of party members to be 59, describe as "the greying of political parties." A 2000 survey found that only 2 percent of Canadians in the youngest age group had ever been a member of a political party, a figure climbing to a high of 33 percent among those over 57 years of age (O'Neill, 2001).[1]

Unlike in the United Kingdom, official voting results in Canada do not divulge whether particular voters actually turned up, hence the voting turnout rate for cohorts has been estimated from opinion surveys, which tend to inflate numbers. Still the trend was unmistakeable: analysis of reported turnout data revealed that the fact that young Canadians traditionally vote less than older ones[2] did not explain the decline among recent generations. Instead, it became apparent that the key lay in generational patterns of turnout. Canadian Election Study (CES) data suggested that the 14 percentage point drop in turnout between the 1993 and 2000 elections was almost entirely due to the behaviour of those born since the seventies, i.e. first eligible to vote in the 1990s or subsequent elections (Gidengil et al. 2004).

ELECTIONS CANADA'S RESPONSE

Out of concern for the plummeting youth turnout rate indicated in these survey results, Canadian federal and provincial public policy makers began to pay attention. Elections Canada, the independent body which administers federal elections, developed a number of programs encouraging young people to vote, having made reaching young people a priority,[3] beginning with efforts to get those turning 18 onto the National Register of Electors. The main initiatives included simulations, contests, and special events, and games such as crossword puzzles containing democratic words such as 'Vote', 'Assembly' and 'Elections', and a Trivia game on the Internet that involved players answering questions about Parliament and elections. One contest asked students to create public service announcements telling their peers why democracy is important and why it is important to vote. Another contest, in partnership with four student associations[4] during the 2004 election was to produce posters to be displayed on campuses across Canada. And most recently, those who sent in the best videos participated in a televised debate among Canadians 18 to 25 about their qualifications and aptitude to be "The Next Great Prime Minister".[5]

A number of initiatives were based on collaboration with civil society organizations. Elections Canada supported the running and publicizing of federal election simulations in the schools. It also contributed to a youth voter education kit as part of Youth Vote 2004 and 2006, an education and media initiative launched by a civil-society organization, the Dominion Institute. Along with the latter and other public and private donors it supported a series of surveys carried out by Innovative Research, on issues related to youth political participation, as well as 63 all-candidates debates organized at high schools and universities. Elections Canada also funded musical events organized by "Rush the Vote,"[6] at which performers encouraged voting and democratic involvement in Ottawa,

Toronto and Edmonton, and worked in partnership with another civil-society organization, the Historica Foundation, to develop a new *YouthLinks* education module on citizenship and voting, entitled "Voices".[7]

In order to test the effectiveness of such interventions, Elections Canada instituted a new methodology for measuring turnout using a very large sample of electors identified by age.[8] Based on the application of the method to the election results in 2004 and 2006, it estimated (Table 1) that overall turnout, which increased by 4.4 percentage points in 2006, rose somewhat more for youth aged 18 to 24 (6.8 percent). Most interesting, and indeed unexpected, was the gap between first-time voters and the remaining under 25s, who had been eligible to vote in the previous election, the former group's turnout was only 2.7 percentage points higher, while the latter's climbed a hefty 9.9 points over the same age group in 2004.

Table 1. *Estimated participation rate by age group (2004 and 2006 Canadian general elections)*

	Cohort	Participation (number of voters/number of electors in the population, %)		Difference
		2006	2004	
Canada	First-time voters	42.2	39.6	2.6
	Previously eligible	44.2	34.3	9.9*
	18–24	43.8	37.0	6.8*
	25–34	49.8	44.0	5.7*
	35–44	61.6	54.5	7.1*
	45–54	70.0	66.0	4.0
	55–64	75.4	72.9	2.4
	65–74	77.5	75.5	2.0
	75+	61.6	63.9	-2.3
	All	62.8	58.5	4.4*

* Significant at a 95% confidence level.
Source: Elections Canada. (The bottom line estimated national average of 62.8 percent is below the official turnout rate of 64.7 percent – it should be noted – to take account of the fact one can register to vote at the polls: being thus based on potential voters rather than eligible electors.)

In any case, the dismal 2008 overall turnout numbers suggest that the positive effects of these various efforts to boost youth turnout were, at least partially, temporary. Though we do not yet have an age breakdown for 2008, it would be surprising indeed if young citizens did not contribute their share to the 5 percent drop from 2006.

A NATURAL EXPERIMENT ABOUT CIVIC EDUCATION

The anomaly in the 2006 figures in Table 1, which shows significantly increased turnout not among the first-time voters, but rather those under 25 who had been eligible to vote in the previous election in 2004, is, I suspect, due to a 2006 methodological innovation brought in to make sure the votes of the young were taken into account, that may have had the effect of over-representing university students in this age group. Unlike the 2004 general election, which was held in late June, when the students were at home, the 2006 general election took place on January 23, at the start of a university semester. Because of the students being able to choose whether to vote at their university or family home, elections Canada chose to take this geographic concentration into account. Consequently, electoral districts with at least one large campus were included in the sample. This meant that electoral districts in which universities were located were overrepresented by the sampling technique. It is reasonable to expect that the turnout discrepancy between university students and those the same age no longer in school increases as we go from 18 to 20 year-olds right up to 24 year-olds, since the educational level distance between them increases with each year.

Thus, the boost in the youth vote in 2006 contributes less, and that of other age groups contributes more, to the overall 4.4 percent increase than indicated in Table 1. Moreover, however, since there is no reason to expect such overrepresentation to be inconsistent across the country, it should not affect our experiment, which contrasts youth turnout in Ontario, where more than one third of Canadians reside, with that in the rest of the country.

Using these figures, Ontario provides an ideal setting for an experiment to test the possible effects of civic education on youth turnout. In recent years, most provincial education systems have seen changes in the approach to civic education, with more emphasis on volunteerism and community values. But only one province, Ontario, with one of the lowest levels of reported federal election youth turnout (Milan 2005), instituted a designated civics course for all high-school students. Ontario took the initiative in 1999 when, as part of an updated high-school curriculum, the government introduced a compulsory civics education course. The 55 hour course, entitled "Profile for Civics," is given over six-weeks in grade 10.[9]

Thus, among the 18-24 year olds eligible to vote in both 2004 and 2006, there were young Ontarians who had taken this course, and ones who did not, identifiable by their date of birth. Moreover, since no comparable change took place elsewhere in Canada in this period, the level of turnout in 2004 and 2006 of those of age to have taken the course and those too old can be compared with the same age groups in the other provinces, the latter serving as a control group, creating a natural experiment. The results of that experiment for each election are presented in Tables 2 and 3 below. The cut-off ages for the 2004 and 2006 elections are such as to provide two categories (first for Canada as a whole, then for Ontario, and then for rest of the country): those at an age to have normally reached grade 10 before the compulsory civics course was introduced in Ontario (bottom row), and those who did so earlier (top row: the upper cut-off age for this latter category was chosen to have a roughly equal sample of the two groups). The numbers are thus greater in 2006 since more students that had taken the course were now at voting age.

If there is a positive relationship between civic education and voting, it is not found in Table 1. Indeed, the numbers point in the opposite direction. In 2004, the subgroup of Ontarians at an age to have taken the course turned out at the same level (38.2 percent) as those older who did not (38.0); while there was an improvement for the corresponding age groups in the rest of Canada, from 34.5 to 37.1 percent. Such a small difference may be dismissed as merely statistical, except that it grew significantly in 2006: those young Ontarians of an age to have taken the course voted much less (41.8 percent) than those who did not (46.8), while this time there was no difference between the corresponding age groups in the rest of Canada (40.2 and 40.0 percent). Given the confidence limits (in parentheses) for the data,[10] it is still possible that the difference is only in the statistics and not among the population. We can say, however, that if there is a relationship, it is a perverse one.[11]

Table 2. Turnout in the 2006 general election

Age group		Canada turnout	Ontario turnout	Rest of Canada
Born between January 1, 1985 and January 23, 1988	18-20.1	40.8 (±2.6)	41.8 (±4.3)	40.2 (±3.4)
Born between January 1, 1981 and December 31, 1984	20.1-25.1	42.5 (±4.2)	46.8 (±8.9)	40.0 (±4.2)

Table 3. Turnout in the 2004 general election

Age group		Canada turnout	Ontario turnout	Rest of Canada
Born between January 1, 1985 and December 31, 1986	18-19.5	37.5 (±3.4)	38.2 (±7.9)	37.1 (±2.5.)
Born between January 1, 1983 and December 31, 1984	19.5-21.5	36.1 (±3.1)	38.8 (±6.8)	34.5 (±2.9)

The failure of compulsory civic education to in any way boost turnout, a key goal of introducing the course is puzzling as well as disappointing. To begin to try to solve the puzzle, we first need to look at the possible effects of the second thrust of the new curricular requirements. Along with the civic education course, the 1999 Ontario regulations required that students complete 40 hours of volunteer (sic) community service before graduation from high school.[12] While such activity is encouraged in other provinces, I am not aware of it being compulsory outside Ontario, though this is common in American states.

Henderson et al. (2007) surveyed Ontario university students about taking part in volunteering, community service, and other forms of civic and political engagement. Using a quasi-experimental design, they surveyed 1768 first year Ontario university students who had completed high school in 2003. Because the government, at the same time, shortened the high school curriculum from 5 to 4 years, the 2003 high school graduating class contained two cohorts, only one of which was required to complete a mandated community service requirement (as well as take civic education). The authors were thus able to compare two groups of students with very similar backgrounds, but which differed in whether or not they had been required to perform the community service to obtain their high school diploma. To their surprise, they found "no differences in current attitudes and reported civic engagement that might plausibly be attributed to participation in the mandatory service program" (p. 849). They were surprised further that the civics course that the same cohort was obliged to complete had an apparently negative effect on reported interest in politics and political media exposure. The authors' only explanation was that the age groups are "on opposite sides of a critical political responsibility cusp (18 years) in our society", (an average age difference of a year and a half between the two sample groups), an explanation partially confirmed by the fact that when they controlled for age, the effect on political media exposure "fades to statistical non-significance (p. 857)."

However, unless this age effect is more salient in Ontario than elsewhere in Canada, the puzzle remains unresolved. Henderson et al. (2007) found greater political interest among subjects who described themselves as having engaged in service than those who did not, a relationship quite opposite to that when the engagement resulted from being in the cohort required to perform service in high school and political media exposure, leading them to suggest, based on the literature, that the explanation may lie in the mandatory nature of the volunteering.

To understand the possible effect of the mandatory nature of the requirement, and, particularly, of the civics course, we need to distinguish perception from reality. Something that is mandatory but, to your knowledge, has always been so, is very different from something imposed on you and not your peers. This is exactly what distinguished the two groups in the experiment on the effects of the community service requirement – and is also the case with regard to the civics course requirement. Ontario teen-agers entering grade 10 in 2000 found themselves unexpectedly saddled with two obligations that their older peers and siblings had managed to avoid, a civics course and 40 hours' volunteering.[13] Moreover, there is good reason to suggest that the school environment was generally less than welcoming to the new requirements. The provincial government introduced the new curriculum (which was revised only a few years into its existence) with little fanfare and support. It is fair to say that, overall, there was little concerted effort on the part of education administrations at the provincial, board and school levels to successfully implement the new program. Hence, not only did the students feel unfairly burdened with this unwelcome imposition, but this sense of unwelcomeness tended to be reinforced by the school environment.

One reflection of the low priority of the course for many school boards (notably the large boards of Toronto and Ottawa) was their refusal to even allow the civics teachers to be interviewed for a research study (Lewis: this volume). Though thus unrepresentative, the results of the interviews in that study do shed some light on these findings.[14] The teachers generally complained that the course was too short; and expressed dissatisfaction with the curriculum and the listed textbooks. They consistently noted that the students came to the course unacquainted with current events and lacking any desire to participate politically. The students thus, naturally enough, found Canadian political institutions – i.e. the largest unit in the curriculum – boring. This impression was confirmed by another study which asked a self selected – and hence more likely to be positive about civic education – group of Ontario high school students if they enjoyed learning about politics in school. A clear majority responded negatively (Goodyear-Grant & Anderson 2008).

Moreover, Lewis found clear inconsistency even within the same schools in the content of the courses, especially over the importance given to institutions. Such flexibility can be constructive, but only in the hands of trained and experienced teachers. Anecdotal evidence suggests that this was seldom the case: school principals tended to treat civics as a timetable "dumping ground", and to assign them to teachers who were inexperienced and even untrained (in social studies or history). In sum, there is good reason not to be surprised by our results; it would be surprising, rather, if the course had boosted political participation. If it is understandable, given the depoliticized environment of young Ontarians, why the government should have taken this sort of action, it is also understandable why it may have backfired.

CONCLUSION

We are reminded, thus, that context matters, whether in the content of a civics course, or in participation in community service. From the point of view of informed political participation, a civic education program that places great emphasis on service learning, even if optimal in the context of American institutional arrangements, may not be so effective elsewhere. Canada may very well be an example of just such a poor fit. As O'Neill notes:

> Models of citizenship are surprisingly devoid of government and politics. The role of discussion and debate, of political parties, of protest and demonstration, and of political ideologies do not appear to form a central component of citizenship….They do little to reinforce the difficulty of attempting to reach decisions within the reality of competing interests, values and demands. Citizenship ought to include simple elements such as joining a party, attending debates, contacting officials and reading the newspaper. But it ought also to include running for office…. Citizenship ought to include an understanding that while politics might be 'messy,' its avoidance is impossible (O'Neil this volume: 18).

Applying what we have learned in this chapter to Ontario's decision to emulate American practices, a trend that other Canadian provinces appear to following as well,[15] raises this paper's question in a very practical way. Rather than combining a compulsory civics course with a requirement of community volunteering, more effort should be given to developing a civics curriculum that incorporates the political/electoral dimension in and outside class. The conclusion is not to eschew civics courses, but to adopt a more European than American approach. While approaches to civic education can vary depending on the context, as a general rule, they should seek to incorporate rather than exclude the political dimension (see Milner 2009).

NOTES

[1] Stolle and Cruz (2005: 85-5) summarize the data on party membership in Canada, showing that the 18-30 year old are significantly underrepresented among party members in both the old and newer parties.

[2] Reported voter turnout in federal elections since 1968 suggest that the propensity to vote typically increases by about 15 points between ages 20 and 50 (Gidengil et al. 2003).

[3] The Chief Electoral Officer (*Electoral Insight* – July 2003) put it this way. "We also developed a series of outreach initiatives for young people.... Community relations officers for youth identified neighbourhoods with high concentrations of students ... assisted in locating polls in places easily accessible to youth, and informed the community and youth leaders about registration and voting."

[4] The Canadian Federation of Students, the Fédération étudiante universitaire du Québec, the New Brunswick Student Alliance, and the Canadian Alliance of Student Associations. A total of 3,200 posters were sent to these associations for distribution to their 119 member associations.

[5] This took place in an "American Idol" type of format with former prime ministers as judges.

[6] This is an organization that aims to increase youth voter turnout and political awareness through "edutainment, affiliated with the American program", "Rock the Vote."

[7] *YouthLinks* is a free on-line education program that links high school students in Canada and abroad and operates in some 400 high schools across Canada. A new module, "Voices", was launched in late fall 2004 designed to provide a practical teaching tool on elections and the democratic process.

[8] In Canada the law does not permit recording who in fact turns out. But the methodology used by Elections Canada permitted a close estimate. It used a sample of electors previously registered who voted at the polls on election day plus almost 3 million actual electors, comprised of those who registered at the polls and voted on election day drawn from actual recorded votes in 50 constituencies, those who voted at advance polls, and those who voted by special ballot (SVR), i.e. away from their polls.

[9] The course is broken down into three units, respectively 15, 25 and 15 hours: Democracy - Issues and Ideas; The Canadian Context; and Global Perspectives. The curriculum guidelines stress the historical and institutional approach, with emphasis on knowledge of government procedures, as well as teaching Canadian civic virtues, especially tolerance of diversity, and commitment to the democratic process.

[10] The confidence limits provided by Elections Canada based on the sampling methodology used means that, at the 95 percent confidence level, the 46.8 figure for 2006 for the older (non-civic education) Ontario population, the group whose turnout is higher than expected, can in principle have been anywhere from 37.9 to 55.7, so conceivably no different or even lower than the 41.8 percent of the ones who received civic education.

[11] An American study similarly found practically no positive effects on later voting from exposure to various forms of civics related courses in high school (Lopez 2003).

[12] I know of know quantitative studies of how these 40 hours have actually been used, but anecdotal evidence suggests that most students followed the path of least resistance in meeting these requirements, i.e. little changing their behavior, but dressing it up in language that allowed them to claim having met the requirements

[13] They were also saddled with the additional difficulties entailed in adjusting to the shortening of the high school curriculum a year in which the last year of high school included a "double cohort", something experienced in no other province. Could this also have had a negative effect on turnout once eligible to vote?

[14] In addition, among those where such permission was granted, a certain self-selectivity of teachers with a particular interest in the subject was inevitable.

[15] A review of provincial civics documents reports signs that Canada is following the US along this path (see Westheimer et al., 2007).

REFERENCES

Cross, W., & Young, L. (2004). The contours of political party membership in Canada. *Party Politics, 10*(4), 427–444.
Finkel, S. E., & Howard R. E. (2005). Civic education in post-apartheid South Africa: Alternative paths to the development of political knowledge and democratic values. *Political Psychology: Journal of the International Society of Political Psychology, 26*(3).
Gidengil, E., André, B., Neil, N., & Richard, N. (2004). *Citizens.* Vancouver, BC: UBC Press.
Goerres, A. (2008). *Are parties "Old School"? An analysis of age group differences in party membership across Europe.* Presented at the annual conference of EPOP, Manchester, United Kingdom.
Goodyear-G., & Anderson. (2008). *Adolescents' attitudes toward political participation: assessing recent evidence from Ontario.* Presented at the Civic Education and Political Participation workshop, Université de Montréal, Montréal, Québec.
Henderson, A., Steven, D. B., Mark, P., & Kimberly E. –H. (2007). Mandated community service in high school and subsequent civic engagement: The case of the "Double Cohort" in Ontario, Canada. *Journal of Youth and Adolescence, 36*(7), 849–860.
Lay, J. C. (2006). Learning about politics in low-income communities: Poverty and political knowledge. *American Politics Research, 34*(3), 319–340.
Llewellyn, K. R. Llewellyn, S. C., Joel, W., Luz Alison, M. G., & Karen S. *The state and potential of civic learning in Canada.* CPRN Research Report. June 2007.
Lopez, M. H. (2003). *Civic and social studies course taking and civic engagement.* Paper presented at the International Conference on Civic Education Research, New Orleans, Louisiana.
McDevitt, M., & Steven, C. (2000). Closing gaps in political communication and knowledge: Effects of a school intervention. *Communication Research, 27*, 259–292.
Milan, A. (2005). Willing to participate: Political engagement of young adults. *Canadian Social Trends (Winter).*
Milner, H. (2002). *Civic literacy: How informed citizens make democracy work.* Hanover, NH: University Press of New England.
Milner, H (2009) *Political Dropouts or Engaged Citizens: Democracy and the Internet Generation.* Hanover, NH: University Press of New England.
Niemi, R. G., & Jane, J. (1998). *Civic education: What makes students learn.* New Haven, CT: Yale University Press.
Phillips, J. A. (2004). *The relationship between secondary education and civic development.* CIRCLE (Center for Information and Research on Civic Learning and Engagement) 14.
Stolle, D., & Cesi, C. (2005). Youth civic engagement in Canada: Implications for public policy. In *Social capital in action: Thematic policy studies.* Ottawa, ON: Policy Research Initiative.
Westheimer, J., Cook, S. Llewellyn, K., & Girón, A. M. (2007). *The state and potential of civic learning in Canada.* Democratic Dialogue Occasional Paper Series. Ottawa, ON: DemocraticDialogue.com.
Westheimer, J., & Joseph K. (2004). What kind of citizen? The politics of educating for democracy. *American Educational Research Journal 41*(2).

CIVIC EDUCATION BIOS

ELLEN CLAES is currently preparing her PhD at the Catholic University of Leuven. Her research focuses on the effects of citizenship education on the social capital of 16 to 18 year olds. She has also recently received a grant from the DFAIT Canadian Studies Faculty Research Program to conduct interviews about the recent developments of citizenship education policy in Canada and Belgium.

MARC HOOGHE is Professor of Political Science at the Catholic University of Leuven, Parkstraat 45, B-3000 Leuven, Belgium; e-mail: marc.hooghe@soc.kuleuven.be. He has published mainly on social capital, social cohesion and political socialization. He is also Principal Investigator of the Belgian Youth Survey 2006-2008 (BYS 2006-08), which focuses on the development of civic attitudes and behaviour among Belgian youth, aged 16 to 18. The BYS is integrated into the Comparative Youth Survey (with Canada and Romania).

JOSEPH E. KAHNE is the Abbie Valley Professor of Education and Dean of the School of Education, Mills College, 5000 MacArthur Blvd., Oakland, CA 94618; e-mail: jkahne@mills.edu. His work emphasizes the democratic aims of education and urban school reform. He is currently studying the impact of classroom-based civic learning opportunities and digital media participation during high school in relation to civic engagement as youth become adults. See www.civicsurvey.org for details.

ANDREAS LADNER is Professor of Political Institutions and Swiss Public Administration at the Swiss Graduate School of Public Administration (IDHEAP) in Lausanne, Route de la Maladière 21, CH-1022 Chavannes-près-Renens, Switzerland; e-mail: andreas.ladner@idheap.unil.ch. His research focuses on political parties, municipalities, institutional change, and e-democracy. He has been a board member of the National Centre of Competence in Research (NCCR) "Challenges to Democracy in the 21st Century" research program of the Swiss National Science Foundation since 2005, as well as head of the "Transfer Module", and the project leader of two projects (IP15 "Civic Education" and IP16 "smart-voting") within the NCCR.

J.P. LEWIS is writing his doctoral dissertation at Carleton University, Ottawa, Canada on the pedagogical narrative of citizenship education in Canada, jlewis3@connect.carleton.ca. He has presented papers at CPSA and APPSA annual meetings on the topic of citizenship education and will be soon resubmitting an article to the Canadian Journal of Education on the topic of civic and character education.

CIVIC EDUCATION BIOS

HENRY MILNER, Universite de Montreal (email - henry.milner@umontreal.ca), is also Visiting Professor at Umeå University in Sweden. In 2004-2005 he held the Chair in Canadian Studies at the Sorbonne, and in 2005-2006, he was Canada-US Fulbright Chair, at SUNY (Plattsburgh). He has been a visiting professor or researcher at universities in Finland, Australia and New Zealand and at the Institute for Research in Public Policy (IRPP). He is coordinator of the Civic Education Database Project based at IDEA (civiced.idea.int) in Stockholm, and on the International Advisory Committee of Democracy: A Citizen Perspective, Interdisciplinary Centre of Excellence, Abo Academy University, Finland. He is also co-publisher of Inroads, the Canadian journal of opinion and policy.

BRENDA O'NEILL is Associate Professor of Political Science at the University of Calgary, Department of Political Science, Room 716, 2500 University Drive, NW Calgary, Alberta, Canada; e-mail: bloneill@ucalgary.ca. Her current research interests include women's feminist and religious beliefs and their role in shaping public opinion, gender and political party leadership in Canada, and the changing nature of political and civic engagement. She is principal investigator of a SSHRC funded research project entitled "The Political Behaviour and Attitudes of Women in Québec."

CHI NGUYEN holds an MSc from the London School of Economics. Her research areas include civic literacy, public participation and political engagement. As a former Canadian Parliamentary intern Chi took an active interest in promoting politics among young women and launched a national campaign to encourage young women to vote. Chi has worked with Professor Henry Milner as the Research Associate to the IDEA International Database and is currently the Director of Participation Process at MASS LBP, a public consultation firm.

MURRAY PRINT teaches in the Faculty of Education, University of Sydney, Australia; e-mail: m.print@edfac.usyd.edu.au as well as co-chair of the Sydney Democracy Forum, University of Sydney. He is an international authority on civics, citizenship and political education, and has been recognized for his research through numerous invitations to be a visiting professor or a visiting scholar including most recently at the Centre for Political Research, University of Leuven, Belgium (2007), University of Oldenburg, Germany (2008) and Kansai University, Japan.

ALAN SEARS is Professor of Social Studies Education at the University of New Brunswick, P.O. Box 4400, Fredericton, NB, Canada E3B 5A3; e-mail: asears@unb.ca.
He has written widely about social studies education in general and civic or citizenship education in particular; he has been principal investigator of national studies of citizenship education curricula in Canada for the Senate of Canada, the Department of Canadian Heritage, and the International Association for the Evaluation of Educational Achievement. Most recently Dr. Sears has worked on

two SSHRC funded projects (one as principal investigator) designed to map how young people understand key ideas related to democratic citizenship.

SUSAN E. SPORTE is the Associate Director for Evaluation and Data Resources at the Consortium on Chicago School Research, University of Chicago, 1313 East 60th St., Chicago, IL 60637; e-mail: *ssporte@ccsr.uchicago.edu*. Her work focuses on high school reform in general and on the relationship between small schools and student academic and non-academic outcomes.

VINCENT TOURNIER is Assistant Professor of Political Science at the University of Grenoble, 1030, ave. Centrale – Domaine Universitaire, 38400 Saint-Martin-d'Heres, Grenoble, France; e-mail: tournier@cidsp.upmf-grenoble.fr. Since completing his doctorate in 1998 on the role of the family in the forming of political opinions, he has continued to focus his research on the political socialisation of young people. He is currently studying the effects of individualism on civic and political opinion.